INDUSTRIES AND MARKETS IN CENTRAL AND EASTERN EUROPE

Industries and Markets in Central and Eastern Europe

Edited by

BRUNO S. SERGI
University of Messina, Italy,

WILLIAM T. BAGATELAS
City University Bratislava, Slovakia, Vysoká Škola Manažmentu
Central European University Budapest, Hungary
University of New York Prague, Czech Republic
The New Anglo-American College Prague, Czech Republic

JANA KUBICOVÁ
University of Economics Bratislava, Slovakia

Routledge
Taylor & Francis Group
LONDON AND NEW YORK

First published 2007 by Ashgate Publishing

Reissued 2018 by Routledge
2 Park Square, Milton Park, Abingdon, Oxon OX14 4RN
711 Third Avenue, New York, NY 10017, USA

Routledge is an imprint of the Taylor & Francis Group, an informa business

A Library of Congress record exists under LC control number: 2006025019

ISBN 13: 978-0-815-38972-9 (hbk)
ISBN 13: 978-1-351-15568-7 (ebk)

Contents

List of Contributors

William T. Bagatelas City University Bratislava, the Slovak Republic, Central European University, Hungary, and The New Anglo-American College in Prague, Czech Republic.

Mikhail Balaev Department of Sociology, University of Oregon, USA.

Aristidis Bitzenis South-East European Research Center, City Liberal Studies, Affiliated Institution of the University of Sheffield, Greece.

Pavel Ciaian Katholieke Universiteit Leuven, Belgium.

Jan Drahokoupil Department of Sociology, Central European University, Budapest, Hungary.

Per Högselius Lund University and Royal Institute of Technology, Sweden.

Dovilė Juršytė ISM University of Management and Economics, Vilnius, Lithuania.

Lutz Kaufmann WHU – Otto Beisheim School of Management, Herbert Quandt Endowed Chair for International Management, Vallendar, Germany.

Jana Kubicová Faculty of National Economy, University of Economics Bratislava, the Slovak Republic.

John Marangos Department of Economics, Colorado State University, USA.

Dirk Panhans WHU – Otto Beisheim School of Management, Herbert Quandt Endowed Chair for International Management, Vallendar, Germany.

Ján Pokrivčák
Slovak Agricultural University in Nitra, the Slovak Republic, and Katholieke Universiteit Leuven, Centre for Agricultural and Food Economics, Belgium.

Gediminas Ramanauskas ISM University of Management and Economics, Vilnius, Lithuania.

Bruno S. Sergi Faculty of Political Science, University of Messina, Italy, a Visiting Fellow with the University of Greenwich Business School in London, and a Fellow with the Contemporary Europe Research Centre at the University of Melbourne, Australia.

Caleb Southworth Department of Sociology, University of Oregon, USA.

Evgeny Vinokurov Institute for World Economy and International Relations, Russian Academy of Sciences, Moscow, Russia.

Foreword
Challenges of Globalization: The Case of Croatia

Dr. Zeljko Rohatinski
Governor of the Croatian National Bank

The collapse of the former Yugoslavia, war destruction, transition problems and an extremely high level of business risk, caused a sharp decline in economic activity in Croatia at the start of the 1990s. Compared with their levels in 1989, GDP in 1993 was lower by 40 percent and industrial production by 50 percent. Employment in the state sector declined by 20 percent, which could not be absorbed by the private sector, so unemployment was doubled. Nearly two-thirds of the fall in economic activity in Croatia actually took place before its independence in 1991, but the remainder took place in the following years after the intensity of war related destruction was being reduced, and when economic policy was confronting consequences of the actual situation at that time, especially high inflation.

After a rise in consumer prices at an average monthly rate of 11 percent in 1991, inflation increased to 22 percent monthly the next year and reached 29 percent in 1993. It was partly 'war inflation' influenced by a decrease of production and aggregate supply, but as it was not super-imposed on a previously stable situation, but instead on a pro-inflationary structure of national economy, it had a hypertrofic feature and multiplying consequences. In such conditions, the redistributive role of high inflation reached, relatively soon, the threshold of economic and social endurance concerning the depressed position of direct inflationary 'losers', who sought to be protected by indexation of their incomes from further inflationary taxation, and, if possible, recover a part of earlier losses. With the acceleration and long duration of high inflation, this process was intensified and had less and less connection with inflationary redistribution of current incomes for various destinations of final consumption (particularly of government expenditures), because in the given structure of the national economy, the inflation itself generated and stimulated it. Combined with consequent inflationary expectations, it was pushing inflation away from its beginning forms in the more influential sectors of the economy, and in this way, inflation became an automatic reproductive phenomenon, tending to hyper-levels.

That is why government finally decided to undertake radical measures for anti-inflation policy. This policy produced its primary effects almost immediately. This was done by applying shock therapy focused on the breakdown of self-reproducing mechanisms concerning inflationary expectations, by appropriate use of market imbalances that had previously been reinforced by the hyperinflation itself. The opening of the foreign exchange market, introducing internal convertibility of the national currency, and fixing the upper limit for exchange rate fluctuations exercised the greatest influence in achieving this. These actions allowed for the real money balance (earlier drastically reduced by inflation and substitution through the transfer of foreign exchange) to induce a substantial increase of supply on the foreign exchange market, and to stop exchange rate indexation as the main indicator of inflationary expectations.

In that way, with the end of the war, the successful curbing of high inflation took place, along with intensification of transition processes and liberalization of the economic system, the Croatian economy started its gradual recovery. Since than, GDP has been growing at an annual growth rate of 4.3 percent, reaching in 2005 its pre-war level. At the same time, inflation has remained low and in the last five years, the average annual inflation rate has been below 2.5 percent. Although GDP growth, has been primarily based on increased productivity, it has also contributed to halting further unemployment growth, and the unemployment rate has finally started to decline after it reached 17 percent in 2000.

The central bank has maintained stability of the exchange rate, not only to keep inflation low but also to preserve overall stability of the entire highly euro-oriented financial system. With 80 percent of savings deposits denominated in foreign currency, foreign currency deposits account for 60 percent of total liquid assets (M4). On the other hand, around 90 percent of loans in the national currency are exchange rate indexed. This unfavorable characteristic of the Croatian financial system emphasizes the problem that based on domestic consumption and infrastructural investment, economic growth lacks balance. The liberalization of foreign trade led to increased imports, while the level of domestic savings in GDP terms was 7 percent lower than the level of investments.

Thus, GDP growth (2001–2005), was accompanied by a twin deficit. There is a consolidated general government deficit on a level of 5 percent of GDP, and a current account deficit of 6 percent of GDP. It has been a particular result of an expansive fiscal policy under conditions where government expenditures have already reached 50 percent of GDP. A part of these deficits were financed by foreign portfolio investment, but the main part was financed by external borrowing, which resulted in fast foreign debt growth; from 60 percent of GDP in 2000, to 82 percent of GDP in 2005. In addition to government and corporate foreign borrowing, commercial banks have also borrowed heavily abroad. Their share in Croatia's total foreign debt increased from 18 percent to 35 percent. Owned by foreign banks, these banks borrow from their parent banks and convert the obtained foreign currency into the national currency, which is than converted into exchange rate indexed domestic loans.

As a result, of the privatization of the major domestic banks at the end of the 1990s, foreign banks now control 91 percent of the loan market in Croatia. Their average annual loan growth is 20 percent. As interest rates offered are still much higher than those in the European Union these banks' return on equity is over 15 percent. This encourages them to increase further their credit potential by foreign borrowing. In such circumstances, the central bank has operated in accordance with the principles of a currency board. But large foreign borrowing creates pressures on the national currency to appreciate in real terms, which reflects negatively on the global competitiveness of domestic producers.

Croatia thus faces similar problems, as other transition countries. Financial system liberalization, coupled with large inflows of foreign capital, has a dual effect. On the one hand, it promotes domestic economic activity and faster GDP growth while on the other hand it adds to imbalance and increased risks of a financial crisis. As central bank international reserves are sufficient to cover almost 6 months worth of goods and services imports, and the total domestic holdings is maintained by these reserves, the country's external liquidity is not at risk, and Croatia is thus able to regularly service its financial obligations abroad. But, with a foreign debt to GDP ratio of 82 percent, a foreign debt to goods and services exports ratio of 167 percent, and foreign debt to gross international reserves of central bank ratio of 345 percent, the financial system can be perceived as increasingly vulnerable in terms of the exchange rate and interest rate risk. Therefore, the central bank issued in 2003 restrictive measures to slow down credit growth on the domestic market, and also in 2004 and 2005, measures on capital controls to destimulate external borrowing of the banks and slow down growth of their external debt.

However, the reasons for growing debt cannot be sought solely in the field of domestic demand. As Alexandre Lamfalussy, former General Manager of BIS, pointed out:

> ... debt accumulation could not have taken place without the demand for funds meeting the supply, or vice versa. There could not have been 'overborrowing' without 'overlending'. But, which of the two – supply or demand – was the driving force behind the process of debt accumulation, varied from case to case ... Who can say that apparently demand-led 'overborrowing' was not initiated, or at least encouraged, by the lenders? After all, roadshows by potential issuers of debt have often been organized or facilitated by financial intermediaries – mainly Western investment banks – which have a stake in finding opportunities for lenders to lend and investors to invest. Moreover, there have been numerous instances when the leading role of supply appears in the price indicators: eroding risk premiums or upward pressure on the exchange rate of capital-importing countries. (A. Lamfalussy, *Financial Crises in Emerging Markets*, pp. 57–58, Yale University Press, 2000).

These are all activities that take place in the process of globalization where, encouraged by the IMF and World Bank, the developing countries liberalized their financial systems and opened them to foreign capital. Of the total capital inflow, 70 percent can be attributed to foreign capital in the form of bank loans, and only 30 percent to investments in equity and bonds. The benefits for the debtor derived from this process are indisputable: from the entry of capital, new technology and new organization into the real sector, to the improving of the financial sector's efficacy as well as general strengthening of market discipline. However, it is also indisputable that the obvious benefits the global mobility of capital brings to its creditors are the main driving force and the main rationale behind the concept of 'free market'. Particularly in the field of financial markets liberalization, where funds accumulated by large international banks, are channeled, directly or indirectly, to international companies rather than to small and medium local firms.

Between the two groups of benefits, or from a debtor's point of view, between the benefit and the price that has to be paid, there is an element of risk, essentially asymmetric for creditors and debtors. This is a risk to macroeconomic stability associated with capital inflows, and particularly with capital outflows and operating risks associated with capital management. These risks may generate, and have generated, financial crises in transition countries. Recent studies (Calvo) indicate that countries with the following characteristics are particularly exposed to such risks:

1. economies closed to international trade in terms of their small share of exports compared with domestic imports absorption;
2. significant level of foreign and public debt;
3. high financial system 'dollarization' and high currency assets and liabilities mismatch.

In other words, such economies:

- are very vulnerable to changes in the global environment that may require sudden and big changes in the balance of payments and the exchange rate;
- big exchange rate changes may turn a sustainable fiscal position into an unsustainable position and put the country's solvency at risk; and
- an economy's vulnerability is relatively independent of the exchange rate regime.

At first sight, it seems Croatia does not follow this pattern. But, it is only on first glance. Namely:

1. with average share of goods and services exports in GDP of 48 percent, the Croatian economy is naturally not closed. However, such exports are insufficient relative to the import needs and preferences, so that there is a permanent deficit in international trade of 10 percent of GDP;
2. with the share of total public debt around 50 percent of GDP, Croatia does not have a particularly unfavorable fiscal position. There is a large foreign currency risk, however, given the fact that external debt of the public sector is 34 percent of GDP, and the largest portion of internal debt is foreign currency indexed, while government revenues are realized with the national currency;

3. although the share of foreign currency deposits in the structure of total deposits has a downward trend, they still represent a dominant element in the overall monetary aggregate structure.

As a result, the liberalized financial system of the Republic of Croatia is very sensitive to potential shocks, both external and internal, so that maintenance of its stability represents the primary objective of economic policy.

The main factor in financial system liberalization was the sale of all major banks to foreign owners, and as a result foreign banks indirectly started to take control of the other segments of the financial system as pension and investment funds, leasing companies, insurance companies etc., and not only this. Their influence becomes very strong in the area of the goods and services market as well. Such liberalization occurred in the period of stagnation of economic activity, and a fall in return on capital in the EU in which conditions even the small Croatian market started to attract foreign capital. In order to manage such a market, it has been important to gain control over the banking sector, which is the main reason for the largest internationalization of this sector relative to all other sectors of the Croatian economy.

In connection with a low level of domestic savings, banks started to borrow from abroad, where over 60 percent of growth in the borrowed funds relates to a growth in short term credits and deposits. At the same time, banks strongly stimulated loan demand by reducing interest rates, by making general requirements for loan approval more lenient, as well as by intense advertising. The result has been an increase of imports and rise of the trade deficit, without sufficient support to exports. This was followed by monetary policy creating restrictive measures adopted by the central bank. These measures could have been insufficient for a significant reduction in trade and the current account deficit, financed by direct borrowing of government and corporations abroad. The possibilities of using the exchange rate regime to reduce the current account deficit are also limited, because in conditions of almost full indexation of financial liabilities to the nominal exchange rate, a stronger real exchange rate depreciation would effect income reduction in real terms, including a reduction in overall demand on the domestic market, more quickly and intensely than it would effect an improvement in the current account.

These are primary challenges the Croatian economy has been facing in conditions of liberalization and globalization, which demand a new strategic approach. In this context, exports of goods and services are an issue of utmost importance for the development of the Croatian economy. It requires the enhancing of competitiveness not only of domestic producers, but also of the national economy as a whole.

On the other hand, high payments of principal and interest on external debt, reaching average annual levels of about 15 percent of GDP, limiting possibilities to substantially reduce the size of the current account deficit in the short-term, indicate Croatia will continue to rely on relatively large amounts of external financing, about 27 percent of GDP per annum in the following years. In order to insure these funds and to avoid the worsening of its rating grade in financial markets, as well as outlook for economic growth and inflation in the stated period, Croatia has to undertake significant efforts to decrease the twin deficit.

Parallel with these efforts, Croatia has started EU membership negotiations with the European Commission. In addition to the complex reforms of the total system, the focus of negotiations will be towards policies relevant for observing the Maastricht and Copenhagen criteria. Goals and methods of economic policy, which are determined by the need to mitigate the current economic problems in Croatia, correspond closely to the goals and methods of the policy that will aim to observe EU membership criteria. Both frameworks thus form a unique policy aimed at simultaneous fulfillment of designated goals. Its main goal is to increase competitiveness of the Croatian economy and to enhance its ability to withstand EU market pressures. In particular, this requires first,

1. A stable macroeconomic environment and continued fiscal consolidation supported by privatizations and judiciary reform;
2. Restructuring and increased exposure of infrastructural sectors and enterprises in government ownership to market competition; a decrease in subsidies and increase in transparency;
3. Simplified procedures for entry and exit from the market, support for the development of SMEs and increased labor market mobility; and
4. Development of financial markets and the non-banking financial sector.

The attainment of such a complex goal requires more intense activities in the field concerning reform of individual segments of the economic system, as well as radical changes in the sphere of economic policy. The basic characteristics of these reforms and changes are defined in two documents that have significant influence on the shaping of the overall economic and social situation in Croatia.

The first one is a document of the EU Commission, 'Opinion on the application of Croatia for membership of the European Union' (April 2004), which in particular surveys the present condition and proposes the economic system reforms for the purpose of meeting the Copenhagen criteria. The second one is the 'Memorandum on Economic and Financial Policies' prepared by the Government of the Republic of Croatia during the conclusion of the precautionary Stand-By Arrangement with the IMF, where economic policy for the 2004–2006 period was defined.

According to this, economic policy in the forthcoming years has to limit external vulnerability arising from the high current account deficit and the heavy external debt burden, and prepare Croatia for EU accession. To achieve these objectives, the program of the Croatian government relies on fiscal adjustment to stabilize the external debt-to-GDP ratio, and structural reforms to reduce the role of the state in the economy and promote private sector activity. These goals are complementary: the long-term competitiveness and growth of the economy and, in particular, accession to the EU require a stable macroeconomic environment and a low fiscal deficit. The basic approach to achieving these goals is:

1. The immediate objective of macroeconomic policies is to reduce external vulnerability. Fiscal policy is the main instrument to achieve this objective. The external imbalance can only be addressed by a lasting reduction in the domestic savings-investment gap. Given its focus on exchange rate stability, monetary policy can only play a supporting role; the burden for narrowing the savings-investment gap falls on fiscal policy. The fiscal effort will encompass not only the central government but also extra-budgetary funds, agencies and the broader public sector.
2. Achieving the main short-term objective of the program will be facilitated by the return of the pace of economic growth to a more sustainable level. The unwinding of the credit boom and the restoration of fiscal discipline are expected to maintain real GDP growth at 4.5 percent and keep the current account deficit around 3 percent of GDP. Inflation will remain at the range of 2–3 percent per year. Given this economic outlook, the policies have to result in decreasing the external debt-to-GDP ratio at around 70 percent until 2011. If developments during the program period indicate a significant deviation from these macroeconomic objectives, in particular a sizeable increase in the external debt-to-GDP ratio net of official and commercial bank reserves, macroeconomic policies will be adjusted, in particular fiscal policy, to achieve these targets.
3. The main objective of fiscal policy is to restore transparency and order in our public finances, and begin the process of medium-term consolidation. Government aims at a general government deficit of below 3 percent of GDP) in 2007. To achieve this major adjustment, the government will rely on a combination of expenditure and revenue measures. At the same time, budget financing will be shifted to domestic sources. This would reduce the government's exposure to exchange rate risk, boost the development of the domestic capital market, and may help absorb excess liquidity in the private sector.
4. Monetary policy has a secondary but nonetheless important role in reducing external vulnerability. Given the openness of the economy, strong trade links with the euro area, large capital flows, and limited hedging opportunities for kuna holders, the central bank intends to pursue its price stability mandate by continuing to maintain the exchange rate of the kuna broadly stable against the euro. Coupled with the high degree of integration of Croatian banks and corporates with the international capital market, this limits the ability of the central bank to affect the level of economic activity, the current account deficit, and foreign debt. In the event that massive private capital inflows threaten to undermine macroeconomic stability, the central bank will introduce additional price-based controls on capital movements.
5. Structural reforms are a key part of the program in order both to supplement macroeconomic policies and to prepare the Croatian economy for EU accession. Most of these measures require consistent implementation over time and will only bear fruit in the medium and long term. They are an important part of the

> Croatian economy because they will raise the long-term potential growth rate and prepare the country for competing within the EU. Moreover, some of these measures will facilitate the achievement of our short-term macroeconomic objectives. These reforms include enhanced transparency and efficiency in public expenditure and debt management; preparation of a medium-term fiscal policy framework; ensuring the long-term sustainability of the pension system; improving the privatization process, the business environment, and financial sector supervision, etc.

The date of Croatia's entrance to the EU and the efficiency of integration into a common European market, as well as the general modalities that determine the functioning of its economy in today's globalized world will, depends upon achieving this goal. Even in this case, Croatia will not become an EU member until 2009.

It is beyond dispute that opportunities, which this globalized world offers a small country, while experiencing the limitations with respect to market, capital and technology, are numerous. However, apart from potential benefits, this world also brings increased risks, ranging from general risks such as asymmetric transfer of economic cycles to partial risks that arise from conflict of interest or differences in the economic power of individual entities operating in the globalized economic area. Foreign portfolio investment for example, is exclusively motivated by its intention to destroy competition that exists in individual market segments. This generates extra profit by monopolizing the local markets without developing their production capacities; squeezing out the local competition by implementing dumping policy; exhausting the national wealth, and transferring 'dirty' and labor-intensive industries, thereby building the local and national production structures, which makes the country unable to benefit from general economic progress, etc. These are only some of the usual examples showing the scope and intensity of these risks.

On the other hand, however, the decision not to join into the primary globalization process, if possible at all, would mean the isolation and subsequent marginalization of the national economy, accompanied by growing differences between economic, technological and civilization related values. The Croatian economy has no other alternative but to take an active role in the globalization processes. The maximization of benefits and minimization of risks associated with globalization of the national economic area will thus become the main determinants of economic policy overall, and the overall policy of the country.

Preface

This book is a natural consequence of our previous research and activity concerning economics and politics as they apply to a proper and more realistic understanding of the economic and political transformation in Central and Eastern Europe. No doubt, this crucial region has become one of the foremost topics of discussion in diplomatic and academic circles over the previous 15 years. With the help of excellent and outstanding researchers and experts who have agreed to pursue this research with us, we now officially offer their research and related output, which, along with our considerable efforts, have allowed us to reach another crucial goal relevant to the continuing growth in literature concerning these important fields of study. Specifically, this means we are offering a more precise analysis, regarding evolution of the industry sector and markets in this region. For those of us involved, it has been a taxing yet wonderful experience staying in contact with all contributors for around a year, exchanging opinions and assessments, readings, sources, suggestions, etc. These activities and efforts have been, and are, devoted to enhancing our growing confidence concerning what will be expressed and explored in these very relevant chapters.

The outcomes presented here will have great practical interest and usefulness for readers of all kinds, as well as enlightening further degrees of research and spurring on-going debate among students and scholars. In fact, our primary endeavor is to address a specific topic of great importance, that is, trade and business change in Central and Eastern Europe, and their impact upon politics, which is generating interest in very diverse audiences. With this latest book in our continuing research activity, we will broaden this scope to new levels, thus welcoming new segments of readers.

This book's primary goal is to offer a final account concerning economic, business and political transformation in Central and Eastern Europe, with particular focus concerning dynamics and implications of radical and non-radical change, and how this region under consideration might affect the global setting regarding a variety of issues. Transformation in Central and Eastern Europe has had intended and unintended consequences upon the population, concerning their actual impact upon evolving business, economic and political events. With respect to our point of reference, the following inquiry into the evolution of economics-business-political performance in Central and Eastern Europe, the reading of these chapters should inspire new areas of research through extended and detailed evaluation concerning the consequences of business and economics and their relation to political transformation in this crucial part of Europe. Such a result from our work should be feasible as well as offer very interesting results. As always, we trust these chapters are of great interest to you, and your comments, feedback, and evaluation to the editors and/or authors would and will be, very much appreciated.

Bruno S. Sergi
William T. Bagatelas
Jana Kubicová

Acknowledgements

Special thanks go to our senior editor, Brendan George, for his very valuable and helpful guidance emanating from the very beginning of our book proposal. To Brendan, we owe much, and have learned a great deal. To our readers, we appreciate your appreciation of this solidly grounded work, which will truly impact the evolving debate as to what actually happened and why during and throughout the all-important transition period in Eastern and Central Europe.

Immense gratitude must be offered and expressed to Dymphna Evans, the Publishing Director for Social Sciences and Reference at Ashgate, as well as for senior desk editor, Sarah Horsley, without whose professional assistance the scope and content of our work would not have been achievable. Gratitude of equal importance belongs to Claire Annals, the proof reader for our massive project, whose outstanding effort made our task so very much easier. Margaret Younger and Donna Hamer must receive special mention as well. We thank all of you immensely and with heartfelt gratitude.

Introduction

Bruno S. Sergi, William T. Bagatelas, and Jana Kubicová

The introduction to this book has two main purposes. First, the information it introduces as contained throughout these chapters, should inspire new research emerging from careful, thorough and consistent reading of these arguments, which emanate and evolve due to our commitment to answering still lingering questions many have regarding what really is happening at all levels of the transformation process. Second, the introduction carefully diagrams for the reader and describes, using measured doses of each chapter, those parts by the author or co-authors, which offer readers an ethical reason to pursue the chapters in their entirety. A new approach to development is what supports the overall argumentation and documentation behind each of the unique and primarily business oriented approaches to understanding and, above all, appreciating the transition process from beginning to end.

In fact, transition economics is inextricably linked to business and economics, as both impact and influence each other at all times throughout any development process, whether transition related or not. One cannot simply assume that a development process ever contains the perfect balance between needs and interests (people and politics), as it is humanly impossible to create a perfect development blueprint both meeting needs of the populations and their ruling and governing politicians, while claiming scientific and quantitative validity. Any attempt by any group of reformers at any stage of a transition development process to make such a claim, must immediately invite deep suspicion and skepticism on the part of any and all readers. Thus, the uniquenesas of the effort regarding this book and the following chapters is that the reader is in the hands of true experts in many varied fields from many varied countries and related regions, thereby offering readers true expertise in several difficult, technical and traditionally confusing areas of transition realities. The ability of these experts to fuse economic, technical and other realities concerning their impact on development and the political process separates this book and its methodology from all others. These experts are thoroughly unique in that their direct knowledge of the on-going, ever-evolving transition-development process was not tainted by direct experience with politics and political decision making, while at the same time each of their chapters is able to accurately and carefully appreciate and discuss the parallel political forces directly affecting the transition-development process. With that, let the reader begin a thoroughly new, extremely credible and very, very interesting journey into the newest realms of trade and industry realities.

The first chapter is written by Aristidis Bitzenis. The author analyses globalization, being a term used to express the tendency of the world economy to integrate, not only in respect to markets, finance, technology, and cross-country trade and investment, but also in regard to harmonization of laws and regulations regarding every day activity (political, economic, social, cultural and ideological). The core of the concept of globalization is that the world displays a strong tendency to become one entity. Globalization in its economic form, envisages an interdependent world economic system dominated by global corporations not identified with any individual country. Apart from economic activity, globalization also encompasses other aspects of life. Foreign direct investment can play a key role in improving the capacity of these countries to respond to opportunities offered by global economic integration. Foreign investors and know-out can become key aims of any development strategy, and an increased growth rate. The globalization concept implies that a growing share of foreign direct investment is worldwide in scope, with transition countries in particular attracting increasing percentages of investment inflow. There are many countries, that opened their economies to trade and foreign businesspersons, however, the share of foreign direct investment is not the same in all interested countries. The limited extent of liberalization reforms, along with ineffective transition programs; the increasingly competitive worldwide investment environment, which offers various alternative opportunities to multinational enterprises, together with changing opportunities countries have to offer through passage of time, led us to conclude that globalization and transition reforms can help countries in order to attract investment from abroad, and become market economies.

According to Dirk Panhans and Lutz Kaufmann (chapter 2), established frameworks do not allow for easy measurement of the proliferation of the various international expansion strategies with readily available data. Therefore, a new framework must be created and tested within the scope of a larger research project. As one part of this project, this chapter provides insights concerning expansion strategies foreign companies employ towards European Union countries. As a first step, an exploratory analysis addresses the question of what strategies are predominantly employed in the new European Union countries, along with where respective foreign companies originate from, and what industries are especially affected by those strategies. Their analysis indicates the new European Union countries are, on average, still mostly regarded as export markets. Yet, especially Estonia, Hungary and Slovenia partially function as globally integrated platforms. In a second step, they test the determinants of the strategies as predicted by the framework. Overall, analysis by Panhans and Kaufmann suggests that for these countries, hidden trade barriers have a stronger impact on strategic choice than straightforward import duties. In addition, the location of globally integrated platforms depends more on local technological know how than on wage levels.

Mikhail Balaev and Caleb Southworth study the collapse of the Soviet Union in 1991 (chapter 3). Many analysts argued that Russia attempted to maintain some semblance of its former imperial power through political intervention, military threats, international aid and, especially, through trade relationships with its former autonomous republics. There are numerous examples of Russia's attempts to influence domestic and international politics concerning the new independent countries. In 1993, Moscow introduced special tariffs in order to force Moldova to join the Commonwealth of Independent States; throughout the 1990s, Russia was periodically cutting or threatening to cut energy supplies to Ukraine (revealing are recent events occurred during December 2005 and January 2006 between Russia and Ukraine concerning the cost of natural gas and the deal between Gazprom and Naftogaz, the two countries' state-run natural gas companies), demanding at first that Ukraine join the Commonwealth of Independent States and then the Common Economic Space between Russia, Belarus and Kazakhstan, which Ukraine eventually joined in 2004; in 1997, former Russian president, Boris Yeltsin, forfeited the energy debt owed from Belarus in exchange for creating a formal union between the two countries. The formal dissolution of the USSR resulted in official formation of 15 independent states with different political systems ranging from highly authoritarian to reasonably democratic. Some of these states have legal guarantees concerning independence of the media and personal freedom of expression. Researchers have hypothesized that such ties with Russia, along with Soviet-era economic and political relationships, could explain the sort of political regime that developed in the post-Soviet period. A majority of other social science researchers also tend to depict Russia as the central player in the post-communist world, using the arguments concerning economic dependence of the post-communist countries on Russia. The research question for this chapter concerns the relationship between trade ties to Russia and the possible development of democratic political regimes in the 14 former Soviet republics. Specifically, Balaev and Southworth analyse the trade ties of 14 post-Soviet countries to Russia for the period from 1995 to 2003. Then these are compared to freedom indicators, being press freedom and measures of individual rights. Finally, we draw conclusions about the relationship between post-Soviet countries and the Russian Federation, and the extent of democratic development in these former Soviet states. To presage main finding, unlike many analysts of Russian geopolitics, the chapter finds that systematic examination of the data on trade relationships between Russia and its former republics shows little impact on political outcomes.

The fourth chapter written by Evgeny Vinokurov starts with analysis of the negotiation process leading to adoption of the Concept of the Common Economic Space between the European Union and Russia. Focusing on the Russian side, it delineates the phases and main activities of the negotiations. The chapter comes to the conclusion that the negotiating process on the Russian side was essentially top-down in nature, with the dominant role played by government bureaucracies and little participation of the business community and public. The overall impact of the economic assessments and studies was limited in scope as well. Evgeny Vinokurov proceeds with analysis concerning choice of a model for the Common Economic Space. It argues that this concept represents an original model in itself, combining elements of the European Economic Area and Swiss models; that is, it unites both horizontal and sectoral approaches. It is questionable whether the model envisaged is capable of providing a satisfactory solution to the policy challenge.

Per Högselius describes the dynamics of innovation in Central and Eastern Europe in chapter 5. The generation and exploitation of new technologies, processes and products, i.e. innovations, is today widely regarded as the principal driving force in all long-term, socio-economic development. Future development of today's countries, also in the post-communist world, will likely be determined by their capability to generate and exploit various types of innovations. The purpose of Högselius' chapter gives an overview of the most important characteristics of post-communist dynamics of innovation in Central and Eastern Europe, and provides a basis for understanding forces that shape these dynamics. He offers analyses concerning developments underlying these overall patterns by outlining the historical heritage of post-socialist countries in terms of innovative capabilities they possessed in communist times. This forms a suitable point of departure for assessing the post-socialist development. Particular questions taken up in the remaining sections address issues such as transformation of socialist research and development from the late 1980s onwards, along with the challenge of exploiting inherited competencies from the communist era; the restructuring of innovation networks, the build-up of linkages to foreign, thus more advanced systems of innovation, and the prospects for building post-communist styles of innovation, which either strive for harmonization with western styles, or seek to build innovative strength by developing differing styles.

John Marangos (chapter 6) works on the collapse of centrally administered economies having given rise to economies based on market relations. The introduction of market relations transformed the decision-making process from a vertical one, between central authorities and enterprises, to a horizontal process, between enterprises. This automatically resulted in substantially reducing the relative value of vertical relationships. The term marketization had the effect of making enterprises interact with each other and with consumers through purchases and sales at equilibrium prices. Consequently, the hegemony of market process among economists as a means of stimulating growth implied a transformation in all dimensions of the economic system. While most economists agree on the introduction of market relations in Central and Eastern Europe, the market as such is not a homogeneous entity. As experience shows, different market economies have developed market relations in a different manner. Consequently, the question arises as to what kind of market economy has emerged in different regions. To this end, the aim of Marangos' chapter is to consider alternative international trade policies and the role of foreign aid, resulting from alternative models of transition. Alternative models of transition are the result of different methods of economic analysis, different political structures and different speeds of implementing the transition policies. As a result, several models of transition are considered in the chapter and as such, these models result in alternative international trade policies and differing roles associated with the provision of foreign aid. The chapter is restricted to international trade policies and the role of foreign aid in alternative models of transition. An analysis of recommended international trade policies by alternative models of transition takes place, together with the role of foreign aid in assisting the transition process.

Pavel Ciaian and Ján Pokrivčák probe into agriculture developments in post-communist societies (chapter 7). In socialist economies, agriculture was an integral part of the socialist centrally planned economy. The state regulated all agricultural production the same way it regulated industrial production. Resources used in agricultural production, including land, were also in reality owned by the state, though legally most land was owned privately. Their data show that state support of agriculture, as measured by the Producer Support Estimate calculated by the OECD, was high. In many countries, agricultural support exceeded the European Union protection level, and in Russia and Estonia, it also exceeded the protection level of the most protectionist countries like Japan. Poland was an exception to the rule.

The eighth chapter by Dovilė Juršytė and Gediminas Ramanauskas analyses who the stakeholders are according to the managers within Lithuanian companies, and how the latter perceive their relationship with different stakeholder groups. Importantly, it is also an attempt to investigate what management does and how they interact with various stakeholder groups. The method chosen to achieve the objective is that of qualitative analysis regarding interview transcripts, reinforced by quantitative investigation of additional company related data. The results show that managers of the firms identify shareholders, employees, customers, suppliers, community, governmental institutions, the natural environment and the media as stakeholders of the company, and recognize that development of the relationship with different stakeholder groups is an inseparable part of successful operations of the company. Nevertheless, it is important to single out that stakeholders are categorized within the respective role-based stakeholder groups in terms of power and salience and, as a result, are given unequal priorities. Moreover, it has to be noted by Juršytė and Ramanauskas that even though the attitudes of managers towards different stakeholder groups, from both private and public sectors, are quite similar, their decisive influence and beliefs as regards stakeholder management are largely determined by ownership type of the company. Also quite recent market reforms such as the introduction of the market economy and transition from public to private ownership, had considerable influence in the formation of stakeholder relationships, therefore, some negative aspects such as management inefficiency or lack of implemented standards for stakeholder management, particularly when referring to public companies, might still be observed. Overall, Dovilė Juršytė and Gediminas Ramanauskas's study reveals that positive signs with respect to stakeholder relationship development and management can be seen within Lithuanian companies however further improvements need to be achieved for full implementation of stakeholder policy, particularly while discussing public companies.

The concluding chapter of the book (chapter 9) is written by Jan Drahokoupil. The chapter concerns the emergence of the 'regional tiger under Tatras', as the financial press refers to radical neo-liberal reforms in Slovakia. The post-socialist states have embarked upon developmental strategies based on supply-side management and foreign-direct-investment attraction. The practice of capitalist governance was inculcated in the complex process of re-contextualization, within which the inflows of such practices were not a matter of simple replications or homogenization, but processes whose outcomes depended upon local history, its environment, and upon the strategies pursued by both local and external agents. This chapter provides a regulationist, state-theoretical account of the transformation of state projects, intervention, and strategy in relation to their effects on the production and reproduction of capitalism in Eastern-Central Europe. Thus, it is concerned with the role of the state in the mutual constitution of economic and extra-economic realities. The underlying concern of Drahokoupil's inquiry is how the reproduction of capital accumulation, which includes the reproduction of labor-power as a fictitious commodity, can be achieved. Given the fact that the these states have experienced the transformation from state socialism to capitalism only recently, Drahokoupil focuses not only on reproduction but also on the very production of capitalist relations and forms. Thus, first, the author investigates a state project that enabled generic forms of capital relation to institutionalize. Second, Drahokoupil describes particular state forms that have co-constituted specific economic dynamics in the Visegrad Four states, i.e. Czech Republic, Slovak Republic, Slovenia and Hungary. Thus, the chapter describes emergence and transformations of dominant state projects, and accumulation strategies with respect to their functional adequacy in relation to the dynamic of capitalist accumulation. Overall, Jan Drahokoupil's chapter is a generalized characterization of a descriptive nature, while the description is theoretically rich in and of itself, as it helps the reader to comprehend the overall economic dynamics that the state co-constitutes.

Chapter 1

New Industry Policy in the Post-communist Countries: Globalization, Regionalization, FDI and Multinationals

Aristidis Bitzenis

Introduction

Globalization is a term used to express the tendency of the world economy to integrate, not only in respect to markets, finance, technology, and cross-countries' trade and investments, but also in regard to the harmonization of laws and regulations of every day activity (political, economic, social, cultural, and ideological). The core of the concept of globalization is that the world displays a strong tendency to become one entity.

Globalization in its economic form, envisages an interdependent world economic system dominated by global corporations not identified with any individual country. Apart from economic activity, globalization also encompasses other aspects of life. FDI can play a key role in improving the capacity of the host country to respond to the opportunities offered by global economic integration a goal increasingly recognized as one of the key aims of any development strategy.

Globalization is mainly used to describe the increase in international trade and financial flows that have taken place since 1960, but more so in the post-1980 period. The term is used extensively in the international bibliography. However, it is regarded as highly debatable. The growing interest in the concept of globalization increases the probability that the term will be used in contradictory ways. To a certain extent, these views eventually tend to derail globalization from its true meaning and intent. Thereby doubts about globalization become more profound. Economic globalization is based on liberalization of international trade, goods and services and the free market. The growth of the services sectors, especially the ones dealing with knowledge and information, and the rapid growth of a new generation of technology are some of the indicators of transformation concerning the global perspective of business operations. Development in technology leads to a boom in foreign investment and to a degree of openness. Globalization should not be understood entirely as an economic concept, or simply as development of a world system, or even as development of large-scale global institutions, but also as representing increasing influence upon all of us from a greater and greater distance.

The huge and quick circulation/distribution of information, mainly through the Internet and facilitation of communication among people from different corners of the earth through satellites of the mass media, through e-mail, fax and telephone are some examples of the globalization concept. This international communication network allows the transmission of political and cultural ideology, fashion-trends, and ideas worldwide. Apart from the easier interaction of the intangible components of life, the reduction of distances through the reduction of time needed to get quickly from one place to another due to the revolution in transportation, allows facilitation for movements of tangible elements like people or commodities.

Enterprise activity is no longer constrained by national boundaries. Both capital and labor should migrate to whatever points on the globe yields the highest returns. There is labor mobility from markets with a lack of employment opportunities to markets with shortages of labor, especially throughout the European Union. More and more people are studying abroad, either by physical presence or even by distance through the use of Internet facilities. The mobility of capital is almost unrestricted, since in the 1980s and 1990s many countries significantly reduced or even abandoned international capital controls. The international facilitation of economic and financial transactions (the stock market, for example) through electronic means, and the computerized information networks reduced transaction costs and the time needed to the minimum. Compared to the international mobility of capital, labor mobility has remained rather steady. This is a reflection of many factors such as the immigration laws, which are still restrictive in many countries and of other factors that may, in the future, be eliminated because the process of such globalization is rapidly accelerating. Migration does not only affect the economic environment of the country, but also the cultural environment, since the culture of the immigrants continues to develop, affected by the new culture, and in turn affects the culture of the new country. The developments in transportation and communication technology were actually the catalyst for the boom in international transactions, both physical and financial.

The past two decades have been characterized by the rapid integration of the financial markets. The Bretton Woods system rested on the foundation of closed capital accounts and fixed exchange rates. Thus, financial globalization was not even on the policy agenda at that time and the world lived with a system of separate national financial markets. However, with the breakdown of the Bretton Woods system in the 1970s, there was a drastic change. The world monetary system underwent three revolutions all at once: deregulation, internationalization, and innovation. The financial liberalization made possible the improved and faster knowledge of the foreign markets, the development of financial transactions and the emergence of new financial instruments, especially derivatives.

UNCTAD (1996, p. 43) documented that globalization is defined by the progressive removal of barriers to merchandise trade throughout the period since the Second World War, by the deregulation of financial markets in the 1980s, by the productive processes which were controlled by the MNEs and have become more dispersed geographically, and by the technological revolution, which has greatly reduced the costs of information processing and international communications. Prior to the First World War, only global capital mobility received general support from the developed market economy countries. Moreover, since the late 1980s, a global trend towards financial liberalization took simple steps such as the unification of exchange rates and the removal of controls over the allocation of credit in the domestic market, to full-blown liberalization of the financial sector that included the opening up of capital accounts.

The examples of the stock market crises manifest the globalization of information, economic activity and capital/stock markets. Due to globalization and the quick distribution of information, the world markets shift downwards or upwards, simultaneously. It is apparent that the 'financial panic' effect (domino effect), usually generated by speculators is very much globalized. Most of the time, this 'cause and effect relationship' is also a 'psychological artifact' or a self-fulfilling prophecy. The spasmodic reactions of the shareholders may lead the local market into a crisis, created by panic rather than any specific external factor. This happened in 1999 with the Greek Athens Stock Exchange, in which Greek investors reacted to the war in a neighboring country as if Greece was participating in the war. Although the results of this war were not expected to affect the Greek economy significantly, the reaction of the Greek investors brought a crisis to the local stock market. This also took place in the worldwide stock market crisis, firstly initiated in the Dow Jones General index (due to the terrorism event of 9/11 in New York city, USA), which caused simultaneously a crisis in all the worldwide stock market exchanges (the decrease in the stock market exchanges lasted a week and then those stock market exchanges recovered).

Is Globalization a New Phenomenon? Similarities and Uniqueness of the Latest Phase of Globalization

Globalization involves steady declines in the importance of national political boundaries and geographical distance, and increasingly complex interdependencies among countries. Globalization can be frightening, stimulating, overwhelming, destructive or creative. Globalization has its own set of economic rules, its own dominant culture, and its own defining technologies. It forces the integration of people, trade-liberalization, FDI and financial policies, technologies, markets and economies.

Globalization is not a new phenomenon, but it is just a new episode, something that is much more pervasive, deeper, and different from previous episodes. For example, in 1914, at the end of a previous phase of globalization, west European foreign investment was more globally oriented before the First World War than in the 1990s (UN/ECE 2000, pp. 7–8). Thus, in the current globalization phase, the world is more integrated than ever, since more countries participate in the globalized system and more countries open their borders and receive FDI flows. However, the distribution of FDI is unequal as a small number of countries receive the majority of FDI and trade flows. A mapping of FDI inflows indicates the extent to which host countries integrate into the globalized world economy, and the distribution of benefits of FDI.

According to the World Investment Report (UNCTAD 2001, pp. 4–5), through comparison of the world's FDI maps, we can conclude that in the year 2000 more than 50 countries (24 of which are developing countries) have an inward stock of more than $10 billion, compared with only 17 countries 15 years ago (7 of them developing countries). However, FDI is unevenly distributed. The world's top 30 host countries account for 90–95 percent of the total world FDI inflows/stocks. The top 30 home countries account for around 99 percent of outward FDI flows and stocks. They are mainly industrialized countries. In developing countries and especially in developed countries, globalization has resulted in the increase of foreign direct investment as the share of cross-border capital flows, increases. In this way, the role of MNEs becomes more significant. However, the share of FDI is not the same in all countries and the FDI inflows in less-developing or poor countries show little growth or no growth at all.

The UN/ECE (2000, pp. 7–8) argued that:

> What is clear from the data is that far from becoming more global, west European trade has become more and more concentrated on the European region itself… the extensive trade liberalization which occurred in eastern Europe and the Baltic states after the revolutions of 1989 has led to a rapid re-orientation of trade away from the former CMEA towards western Europe … Thus the general evolution of European trade has not been towards a more global distribution of relationships, but instead towards a more intense integration with close neighboring countries. Interdependence among the economies of the region has strengthened but with the rest of the world it has weakened.
>
> In 1914, at the end of a previous phase of globalization, west European foreign investment was more globally oriented before the First World War than in the 1990s.

Also, Tanzi (2004, p. 525) noticed that in the period from around 1870 to the beginning of the First World War, economies were relatively open, goods and capital had moved in great quantities and freely across countries, and large numbers of individuals had migrated to far away places with the prospect of gaining better opportunities. People, goods and services, financial capital, enterprises, technology, ideas, culture and values now move more easily across national frontiers than at any time since the beginning of the First World War. Between 1870 and 1914, the international trade in goods and services was as free as it is today. Although the range of financial instruments that traded internationally was of course much more limited in those days, mobility of people, including international migration, was less restricted during the Gold Standard days[1] than it is today. Moreover, Kleinkencht and

1 The period from 1880 to 1914 is known as the classical gold standard. During that time the majority of countries adhered (in varying degrees) to gold.

Wengel (1998, p. 638) mentioned that in 1973 exports and imports as a percentage of GNP in most countries were lower than in 1913. They added that this was due to the fact that international trade had suffered from two world wars and from protectionism induced by the economic slowdown after 1929.

The pervasiveness of the current form of globalization has much to do with the liberalization of trade, the expansion of FDI and the emergence of massive cross-border financial flows. As a result, competition in global markets is on a rise due to the combined effect of two underlying factors: policy decisions to reduce national barriers to international economic transactions and the impact of new technology. The growth of the services sectors, as already stated, especially those services dealing with knowledge and information, and the rapid growth of a new generation of technology are the most important factors directly connected and supportive of the latest globalization phase. These features, absent in the previous phase, make globalization an established, unstoppable and irreversible process. Tanzi (2004, p. 526) mentioned that the current phase of globalization is much more pervasive, deeper and different from previous episodes due to new technologies, the facility and rapidity of the distribution of the information, trade liberalization, reduction of transportation cost of goods, capital and people, and finally due to the 'abolishment' of the countries' isolation and the loss of their independence. The economies that lag in adopting new technologies cannot participate in the globalization process and their transition to a market economy is hindered. As a result, they lag in economic development and in better living standards. On the other hand, countries with a high level of economic development are either free-open economies or earlier adopters of the transition reforms because economic developments have created healthier conditions for the onset of globalization.

Impact of Globalization

As mentioned above, some researchers accept that globalization is an established process, is unstoppable and irreversible, but although they share the view that it is likely to be beneficial they are not so certain that this will in fact be the case in the future and they are more sensitive to the risks created by social disruption and increased anxiety. The academic community is divided regarding the question of the existence of globalization as a phenomenon. Many researchers contend that it is a trend toward integration of the world economy by means of trade and FDI. However, there are others who deny its existence. A third group comprises scholars who argue that globalization is a phenomenon that does exist, cannot be stopped, is long lasting, beneficial, brings about greater prosperity, equality, increases living standards, increases the domain of democratic institutions and strengthens the basis for peace as well. On the other hand, others believe that globalization is a phenomenon which may cause social disruptions and increased tension among countries, increases insecurity among large sections of the population and thereby increases inequalities within and among countries. Furthermore, globalization leads to a steady deterioration in the environment.

Nevertheless, in Friedman and Ramonet (1999), Friedman (p. 111) views globalization as a reality and argues that it is a phenomenon, not solely a new economic trend but an integration of markets, finance and new technologies which minimize the geographical and cultural distances among people. Furthermore, he understands that this phenomenon has its own dominant culture and this is why integration tends to be homogenizing. This sort of event had continually taken place throughout history. The Romanization of Western Europe and the Mediterranean world, the Islamization of Central Asia, the Middle East, North Africa, and Spain by the Arabs, and even the Russian/Soviet Union impact (Russification) on Eastern and Central Europe and parts of Eurasia, are some examples.

Contrary to this approach, Rugman and Hodgetts (2001) argues that globalization as well as global strategies are a mere myth, since business dealings carried out by large multinational corporations take place in regional blocks. Government regulations, differences among cultures, technological advances, have all divided the world into the following three blocks: EU, ASEAN, and NAFTA. Further on, they argue that managers of large corporations are the driving force of the globalization process, which is actually regional and takes place inside the triad blocks. They analysed the strategies of specific well-known multinationals such as McDonalds, Coca Cola and Euro Disney in order to prove that these MNEs adjusted their global strategy to fit into the local one. In this way, these companies accept the tastes of the local population and offer services closely related to the local population preferences. Moreover, Moore and Rugman (2003, p. 2) for example, argued that the US companies are regional companies and not very global at all. They also mentioned that:

> ... if you examine the data on the US's 25 largest multinationals, it becomes clear that they are what we would call home-region based. Of the US 25 largest MNEs, 22 have more than 50 percent of their sales in their home region of North America. None of these US MNEs are 'global'. For example, Wal-Mart has 94.1 percent of its sales in the North American Free Trade Area; GM has 81 percent, and so on. Indeed, the average intra-regional sales figures for all the 185 US MNEs, is 77.3 percent. With well over two-thirds of their sales in North America, these are home-triad based MNEs.

Tanzi (2004, p. 526) argued that countries that have a less educated population and strong traditions, and have more ethnically diverse populations are likely to have difficulties benefiting from globalization, and so they need more time to make the changes required by globalization. According to Tanzi, the opposite is true for well educated and more ethically homogeneous populations that are not excessively bound by strong traditions. However, Tanzi added that when globalization makes the whole country richer, it may still generate a great deal of discontent if the increase in income is not evenly distributed (Tanzi, 2004, p. 529).

Many researchers view globalization as a commitment and desire for a better future. In a sense, it will convey optimism and offer infinite possibilities for growth, renewal, and revitalization for every member of world society. Globalization was created to describe what many felt to be a new and central reality of the times. It involves steady declines in the importance of the national political boundaries and geographic distance, while it creates increasingly complex interdependencies among countries.

Thus, a major debate is going on regarding the question of benefits and the cost of globalization. On the one hand, proponents of the globalization process who have accepted the globalization process as a reality, maintain this is a beneficial phenomenon. On the other hand, the opponents who do acknowledge the globalization process minimize its advantages and emphasize its disadvantages only. Opponents of globalization contend that globalization only brings about more poverty as well as inequality among the people worldwide. The gap between the more developed wealthy countries and poor countries deepens. Furthermore, globalization puts under risk the independence of countries, the employment rate, etc. Opponents also support the idea that global integration, FDI flows, and competition are part of an unfair game. This statement, however, is opposed by its supporters, who argue that despite globalization, all the negative phenomena will still exist. Since globalization makes all these processes much easier, in the long run, economic growth and employment are and will be on the highest level. However, sometimes, multinational corporations (MNCs) have much more power and money than specific developing countries, although it can be said that their activities in free and open markets can be the best contributors and indicators of the economic progress in these markets. This is a reason that governments ask for FDI inflows and thus, investments from multinationals, offering at the same time significant incentives in order to attract FDI inflows.

To this end, Farrell et al. (2004) ascertained that many governments restricted the activities of MNEs in order to protect the local industry. In this way, they maximized the spillover for their economy, such as local-content requirements and joint venture requirements. Farrell et al. (2004) and the McKinsey Global Institute (MGI), based on research, concluded that both incentives and regulations, in order to attract FDI, simply do not work. They recommended that the most important issues in the case of developing countries and transition economies are to forget the incentives and regulations and to concentrate on stabilization of their economy and promotion of competitive markets.

Overall, Farrell et al. concludes that in order to promote competitive markets, the economies must reduce restrictions on foreign investment, lower import tariffs, streamline the requirements for starting new businesses, and encourage new market entrants. Moreover, Farrell et al adds that the developing and transition economies should promote fair competition and crack down on companies in the informal economy, which do not pay taxes. Furthermore, Farrell et al. point out, that countries should improve their infrastructure in order to attract further FDI inflows. Finally, they argue their research shows clearly that globalization has broadly improved global standards of living. At the same time, Farrell et al. calculated the impact of FDI on local industries in Brazil, India, China, and Mexico. They found in 14 industry studies that FDI unambiguously helped the receiving economy in its productivity, its output, employment, living standards, prices of products, etc.

It is true that there are cases in which globalization tends to increase insecurity among large sections of the population and to increase inequalities within and among countries. It also leads to a steady deterioration in the environment and in the general quality of living standards. Globalization is also sometimes responsible for increasing poverty, and even, in some cases, for impeding growth. Some countries have largely managed to take full advantage of globalization, receiving the benefits, while others have taken more of the costs. For example, Stiglitz (2003) mentioned that East Asia provides the strongest example in favor of the positive effect of globalization on growth, and on the other hand, the global financial crises and their aftermath brought home the dark side of globalization.

Furthermore, the anti-globalists assume that globalization pressures stemming from the major financial institutions such as the IMF, World Bank, and the WTO create greater dependency between them and the other developing countries, not seen since the era of colonialism. Stiglitz (2003, p. 509) added that it is not true that liberalization measures are undertaken voluntarily. He concluded that politicians and governments in power believe that they gained more from the liberalization measures than they would suffer from the consequences of not undertaking them.

Moreover, Apodaca (2002, p. 892) mentioned that supporters of economic globalization argue that FDI is a catalyst for economic development because of the transfer of technology, know-how, and access to export markets. Actually, technology, know-how, management and liquidity-related advantages could now be exploited to prevail over the inherent disadvantages of FDI (Pitelis, 1996, p. 193). Furthermore, FDI benefits economic growth and capital accumulation. It encourages the transfer of technology, and it increases human capital. Apodaca's study (2002) is restricted to the region of East and Southeast Asia (for 11 counties, from 1990 to 1996), but the evidence provided is very important. Apodaca (2002, p. 904) found that FDI is the only globalization variable that promotes every aspect of human and economic development in Asia. Apodaca's findings were that in the case of East and Southeast Asia, the state continues to be a positive factor for the social, economic, and political needs and requirements of the people in this region, because the state secures human rights and protects its citizens from the adverse effects of globalization. In addition, FDI was beneficial both for the state and for poor countries in this region. Lastly, he suggests that if western governments want to encourage development abroad, they should pursue trade and FDI rather than financial aid.

Globalization from a Statistical Point of View

Summarizing both the supporters' and the opponents' arguments for and against the globalization process, we can argue that globalization cannot be classified as bad or good. It is its evaluation that matters most, because challenges and threats are subject to continuous changes. Even with the use of statistics, globalization cannot be classified as a bad or good procedure because these statistics are either misleading, inappropriate, or can be read from different dimensions. For example, people that are against globalization argue that the three richest men in the world own more wealth than 600 million people in the world's 48 poorest nations. Of the 100 largest economies in the world, 51 are transnational or multinational corporations. General Motors is bigger than Indonesia. Microsoft Corporation enjoys annual profits of $12.5 billion, while $9 billion would give every child on the planet a basic education. In 1998, the richest country in the world possessed 115 times more *per capita* income than the poorest. Twenty percent of the richest countries of the world had a *per capita* income 13 times more than that of the 20 percent poorest.

The GDP of developing countries as a group grew faster that that of developed and high income countries. Almost a quarter of the world's inhabitants live in poverty (1.2 billion out of 6 billion people live on less that 1$ a day). The richest fifth of the world's population owns 80 percent of the world resources, while the poorest fifth owns barely 0.5 percent. Even in the EU, there are 16 million unemployed people and 50 million living in poverty. The combined wealth of the 358 richest people in the world (billionaires) equals more than the annual revenue of 45 percent of the poorest in the world or 2.6 billion people (Ramonet, in Friedman and Ramonet 1999). World income inequalities have been rising during the last two or three decades, and this trend is sharpest when incomes are measured by market-exchange rate incomes and not by PPP-adjusted incomes (Wade, 2004).

On the other hand, people in favor of globalization argue that the poorest countries, including 50 percent of the world's population, had a share of world income between 10 and 20 percent in 1965 as well as in 1997, but that this share was higher in 1997 due to globalization. Over the past 20 years, the number of people living on less than $1 a day has fallen by 200 million, after rising steadily for 200 years (James Wolfensohn, president of the World Bank). The proportion of people worldwide living in absolute poverty has dropped steadily in recent decades, from 29 percent in 1990 to a record low of 23 percent in 1998. The best evidence available shows ... the current wave of globalization, which started around 1980, has actually promoted economic equality which provided reduced poverty. Evidence suggests that the 1980s and 1990s were decades of declining global inequality which provided reductions in the proportion of the world's population in extreme poverty. As mentioned above, the GDP of developing countries as a group grew faster than that of developed and high income countries. However, the absolute gap between a country with an average income of 1000$, growing at 6 percent and a country with an average income $30000, growing at 1 percent, continues to widen until after the 40th year (Wade, 2004).

Thus, there is a different way of expressing the same statistical data in order to measure the impact of globalization, such as the case in which we compared the top and bottom 10 percent decile of the world's population, in which we found that world inequality, has increased. However, if we compare the top and bottom third, the reverse will be true. Moreover, there is a lack of reliable price comparisons, even when using the purchasing power parity exchange rates among countries. This is because there is a change in the way the international poverty line was calculated throughout the years (thus biased comparisons). Furthermore, there are significant income inequalities not only among different countries but also inside a country, a fact which has not been examined by the World Bank, which conducted these surveys. Some countries such as China and India (with 38 percent of the world's population) have not participated in surveys conducted by the World Bank regarding income inequalities. Therefore, the findings for these countries were based on a few surveys, specifically for a few cities and regions in China and India, a fact that supports misleading conclusions regarding the impact of globalization on the world (Wade, 2004).

Finally, the World Bank distinguishes countries as globalized, newly globalizing and even globalizers, those that have significantly increased the trade/GDP ratio in the time period 1977–1997, and at the same time have had faster economic growth, no increase in inequality and a reduction in poverty. On the other hand, non-globalizing countries or less globalized ones, are those with a limited change in the trade/GDP ratio. According to Wade, this is also biased because in this way, countries with high but not rising levels of trade over GDP ratio are excluded from the 'more globalized' category. Moreover, he argued it is possible that some poor countries are dependent on trade only due to the few natural resources available, and low skill endowment of their population. However, Wade added that certainly many countries have benefited from their more intensive engagement in international trade (trade/GDP) and investment (FDI/GDP) over the past decades, due to their more intensive external integration (trade liberalization, abolishment of trade barriers/protective barriers, etc.).

In evaluating the impact of globalization, the basic criterion is to look at what has happened to the rates of economic growth (GDP, and GDP per capita in PPP), both globally and across countries. On the one hand, the expanding global markets for goods and services provided new outlets for their exports. On the other hand, the emergence of a global production system and liberalized investment rules generated new opportunities for their MNEs, increasing their global reach and market power. Moreover, the growth of global financial markets provided expanded opportunities for investments with higher returns in emerging markets. A minority of developing countries reaped significant benefits that have been highly successful in increasing their exports and in attracting large inflows of FDI.

Globalization, FDI, Regionalization, and Regional Initiatives

Fortanier and Maher (2001, p. 113) stressed that increased liberalization, lowering of trade barriers, investments and financial reform support, privatization and regulatory reforms are factors that contributed to considerable growth of international investments over previous decades. Furthermore, regulatory reforms and harmonization of European legislation merge with a liberalized internal market. This leads to intensified intra European investments and trade patterns. In addition, NAFTA, Asia

(ASEAN4), Africa (SADC6), Australia and New Zealand (ANZCERTA) applied regional integration systems in order to liberalize trade as well as investment paths. Currently, bilateral investment treaties are an important factor for promotion and protection of investment flows, which legally provide security for the investors. Many bilateral investment agreements were signed, aimed at protectionism and incremental levels of FDI flow in 1990; hence many governments tried to facilitate FDI flows. In 1997, there were 1330 bilateral investment agreements in 162 countries. The most important fact is that these numbers are going up every year.

In the 1980s and 1990s, many countries from Central and Eastern Europe had entered into bilateral regional agreements, most of them among themselves as well as with developed and developing countries. Brewer and Young (1997) argued that there is an increased use of incentives by national and sub-national governments in the ever more competitive worldwide environment, created from pressures regarding globalization and new forms of regionalism. A broader use of incentives is the exploitation of the international investment multilateral agreements (regional initiatives) by foreign investors. These agreements produce welfare gains, influence legal frameworks, boost economic growth, increase the number of potential consumers, increase opportunities for market growth and provide stability, peace, unity and prosperity. Multinational enterprises (MNEs) try to enter markets, which have established not only bilateral regional agreements, but also multilateral agreements (e.g., CEFTA, SECI, BSEC, CEI, SEECP, etc.). Moreover, Floyd (2001) wondered if there exists, a situation of globalization in the strictest sense or according to recent developments in the business environment, where we see instead more regionalization or Europeanization.

Finally, Floyd concluded that if we used an interdisciplinary approach, we could deduce that this is not globalization, but in fact regionalization or Europeanization. Also, in the 1980s, many bilateral regional agreements were signed among developing countries such as China, Chile, Algeria and the Republic of Korea. Latin America and the Caribbean have only recently commenced implementing these agreements (UNCTAD, 1997). Bilateral and regional agreements were signed in order to improve investment conditions, which at the same time improve the relationship between triad members (UNCTAD, 2003).

It can be argued there is a regional concentration of FDI, as can be seen from the examples of Greek MNEs that became dominant entrepreneurs in the Balkan region, with Austrians in Slovenia and Croatia, the Nordic countries (Sweden, Norway, and Finland) in the Baltic region (Estonia, Lithuania and Latvia), Germany, France, and the UK in the ex-Visegrad countries (Poland, Hungary, the Czech Republic, and Slovakia), Spain in Latin America, the UK, France, Germany and Netherlands in advanced economies such as Belgiam, the USA in Canada and Mexico, Japan in China, and in the whole of SE Asia, etc. (Bitzenis, 2004; Bitzenis 2005). Moreover, Rugman and Hodgetts (2001) argues that large MNEs take place in regional blocks, EU, ASEAN, and NAFTA, and that MNEs are shifting from a global strategy to a local one (think global and act local). Moreover, Rugman (2003) concluded that even the 20 most 'international' MNEs (those with the highest ratio of foreign-to-

total sales), are mainly home-TRIAD based on their activities, as such strategic management of MNEs needs to be regionally focused, not global.

Thus, there is a regional concentration of FDI in transition economies. For example, FDI inflows in Estonia come from neighboring Nordic countries such as Sweden (40 percent of total accumulated FDI inflows in the country), and Finland (26 percent of total accumulated FDI inflows in the country), while strong economies with important multinationals from France, Germany, the UK and Italy have less than 3 percent each in the entire transition period in Estonia. At the same time, Denmark, with 17 percent of the total stock FDI inflows in Lithuania, is the top foreign investor followed by Sweden with 16 percent. Moreover, Austria is the leading foreign investor in Slovenia due to its geographical proximity with that nation. Finally, although there is an accumulation of FDI stock in the whole CEE region, on the other hand, up to the year 2003, the CEE region received only 3.1 percent of total world FDI inward flowing stock. However, according to UNCTAD (2004), in the year 2002, the ratio regarding the stock of FDI inflows relative to CEE GDP was 24.8 percent. This ratio decreased to 23.7 percent in 2003. Actually, this significant ratio for the CEE region was only 0.2 percent in 1985, and only 1.3 percent in 1990. At the same time, this ratio (FDI stock of inflows/GDP) in the year 2003 was equal to 32.8 percent for the EU, 20.7 percent for the developed countries, and 22.9 percent for the whole world (it was 9.3 percent in 1990, and 8.3 percent in 1985) (Bitzenis and Marangos, 2005).

Globalization and Alternative Terms

Globalization today is perhaps most usually connected with the rise and power of global markets, economies, and multinationals. There are powerful minorities (superpower multinationals) on the global scale seeking to take full advantage of market economies. However, there are many people all over the world who consider globalization an exclusive privilege for the elite, or the dominant superpower, the United States of America. Thus, 'Westernization' may be an alternative term for globalization. What is perceived as globalization may be interpreted as being under the scope of the rising influence of western civilization, culture and economic style upon the rest of the world. The domination of the on-going concept, stating that western ways of life and economic activity are the most developed and most appropriate, combined with the tendency of less developed and developing countries to look up to the western model, disguises the overwhelming persistence by western countries to maintain and promote their culture, at the expense of the rest of the world through globalization. The rapid development of technology, especially in communication related technology, usually produced and mainly consumed in western countries has underlined domination of the term westernization.

Still, parts or much of the entire globe do not accept Western or American civilization as the optimal way of life, and if the countries in question could efficiently avoid economic dependence on Western countries, they would attempt to prevent globalization from impacting them. The conflicts arise mostly with political issues, which are perceived differently by the various civilizations in terms of culture, ideas, morals, and even the perception of science, rather than economic issues, which are more or less perceived in the same way by most countries. It can be said that globalization is one thing and American hegemony another, but it is obvious the US is promoting globalization further and further in ways that serve its interests primarily. An advantage for the US is use of the English language in most international transactions and in international computer communication, and the use of the dollar as the key currency for international transactions. The domination of the US is more economic, military, political and cultural. Moreover, in the last few years, there is also domination by the European Union, especially after creation of the Economic and Monetary Union (EMU) and introduction of the Euro. However, the EU as a trade bloc does not appear to be more integrated with the world economy, as might be suggested by globalization. Less than 10 percent of the EU's GDP tends to be exported to non-EU countries. So, there is a clear trend of 'Europeanization' concerning export and import relations over the previous 35 years, as the EU seems to be a very closed economy (Kleinknecht and Wengel. 1998, p. 641).

Globalization, Neo-liberalism, and the Role of Multinationals

Neoliberalism is a term used to describe the contemporary forms of worldwide economic restructuring as a result of globalization. Neoliberalism is the process of liberalizing national economies to allow the entry of multinational enterprises (MNEs), and to adopt the advice of the World Bank, WTO and IMF. In the opinion of Wade (2004, p. 567), the neoliberal arguments say that distribution of income among the world's people has become more equal over the past two decades, and the number of people living in extreme poverty has fallen, for the first time in more than a century and a half (this is true only when inequalities are measured using the 'population-weighted countries' per capita PPP adjusted incomes', then taking a measure of average inequalities, and finally combined inequalities among and within countries). Neoliberalism claims these progressive trends are due in large part to the rising amount of economic integration among countries, which has made for rising efficiency of resource use worldwide, as countries and regions specialize in line with their comparative advantage.

In order to achieve their goals, MNEs from different countries often enter into so-called cross-border agreements as a complement to traditional FDI activities. Analysis showed that the number of these agreements has permanently been on the rise (UNCTAD, 1997). Most cross-border agreements were concluded within the TRIAD members. Rugman (2003) mentioned that a powerful indicator of triad/regional economic activity is the concentration of the world's largest MNEs in the TRIAD. In 2000, of the world's largest 500 MNEs, 430 were in TRIAD. The US accounts for 185 of the companies; the European Union (EU) has 141 and Japan 104.

These 500 MNEs account for over 90 percent of the world's stock of FDI and nearly 50 percent of world trade.

The significant role of MNEs and FDI flows is very profound, as noted from the fact that global FDI inflows rose rapidly and faster than global GDP and global exports during the last two decades. In particular, global FDI inflows over the period 1991–2000 increased 4.8 fold, as compared to the previous ten year period, and surpassed the 4.5 fold increase attained in the 1970s and the 1980s. The dramatic increase in FDI over the last decade was based on globalization and economic integration, technological improvements and lastly, on liberalization of various regimes with the abolishment of monopolies and barriers.

The transition economies presented an opportunity for MNEs to create new markets and extend their productive base. Extending the arguments about less developed countries advanced by Hymer (1972 and 1979) to transition economies, the penetration by MNEs implies uneven development, self-perpetuating dependency and inequality. Those experiencing freedom from despotic rule by communist party run transition economies, are also experiencing an erosion of power of the nation-state, as are all nation-states in the globalized world, with growing inability to pursue autonomous economic-political-ideological policies (Bitzenis and Marangos, 2005).

Globalization, FDI, Industry Policies and Transition Reforms

FDI can play a key role in improving the capacity of the host country to respond to the opportunities offered by global economic integration, a goal increasingly recognized as one of the key aims of any development strategy and an increased growth rate. The globalization concept implies that a growing share of FDI is worldwide in scope, with transition countries in particular attracting increasing percentages of FDI. However, this did not happen in reality. Globalization in terms of openness of borders, abolition of currency restrictions, liberalization of trade and prices, technological and transportation advances, facilitates decisions for FDI and creates opportunities for efficient, less risky and less costly FDI projects. On the other hand, FDI inflows and outflows by MNEs, and the consequent direct and indirect effects of FDI on the host countries' economy, may be viewed as a vehicle for globalization. Still, there are many countries that opened their economies to trade and received FDI inflows. However, as mentioned before, the share of foreign direct investment is not the same in all countries, and FDI inflows in less-developing or poor countries show little growth or no growth at all (Bitzenis, 2003 and 2004). The limited extent of liberalization reforms or the ineffective transition programs, the increased and high competitive worldwide investment environment, which offers various alternative opportunities to the MNEs, together with the changing opportunities that a country has to offer through time, and the different ways in which MNEs evaluate those opportunities, led us to conclude that globalization and transition reforms can help countries in order to attract FDI flows, and become market economies.

The isolated transition economies lagging in economic growth and level of living standards are unable to adopt new technologies and improve their infrastructure. These countries must focus their attention as fully as possible on the world economy, participate in the globalization procedure, open and liberalize their economies, and attract FDI inflows. Otherwise, there is no way they will ever escape their present state of lagging growth. The interest of MNEs is not concentrated on one part of the world in constant terms, but instead follow opportunities in different areas (Latin America, the UK and Ireland, Spain, Greece, Eastern Europe, CIS, SE Asia, etc.) at different periods of time. Each host country offers its comparative locational advantages and incentives for FDI (Bitzenis, 2004). The MNEs evaluate these incentives and select the most appropriate country for their investment. From world-wide statistical information, one finds countries with near to zero FDI inflows, and simultaneously others that hold a high percentage of the total amount of FDI inflows. For example, there is limited Western investment interest in Central and Eastern Europe, considering the fact that only 3 percent of world-wide FDI outflows reach this region. Since 90 percent of the world-wide volume of FDI belongs to the MNEs, their attitude towards it may reflect the nature of global FDI (Bitzenis, 2005).

The Central and East European region (CEE) received during the entire transition period (1989–2003) more than $225 billion USD. At the same time, the Commonwealth of Independent States (CIS) received around $75 billion USD and the South East European region (SEE) in the same period, received less than $40 billion USD. Moreover, FDI per capita on average, during the transition period in a country from the CEE, is between $200–500 USD, while at the same time in a SEE country, the FDI per capita per year is less than $100 USD, with the only exception being Slovenia and Croatia ($250 USD for each one). The South East European countries, except for Slovenia, lag behind most of the other CEE countries, since they have not yet recovered economically, neither in GDP nor in industrial output (most of the SEE countries did not even reach the levels of GDP they had in 1989).

Industry policy refers to whatever governments do to develop or support various industries in order to maintain global competitiveness of their economies and their companies. Industry policies in advanced economies have focused mainly on the improvement of firm performance through addressing market failures, expanding technological capabilities, and paying greater attention to the quality of investment and human resources (UNIDO, 1995). Industry policies in developing and transition economies have focused on market reforms, trade liberalization, privatization, a significant increase in the private sector, absorption and attraction of technology, internationalization of production, openness of the country (as this is measured by the ratios FDI/GDP and trade/GDP) and, on an increase in competitiveness of the country (country's comparative advantage).

As mentioned in Bitzenis and Marangos (2005), the transition process incorporates an industry policy. Governments prefer to attract foreign investment projects in specific sectors of the economy. So, in this way, there is specific industry growth based on privatization deals of state-owned enterprises (SOEs) offered by the government, and through the increase of the private sector with the creation of new enterprises based on significant incentives offered in order to improve and facilitate entrepreneurship and private ownership. Thus, most of the Central and East European economies and especially the South East European economies have, as their target, the services sector and have moved far from their initial levels of industrial production that they had in 1989. For example, Albania reached only 28 percent of its level of industrial production in 2003 (compared to the level that Albania had in 1989) when at the same time its GDP level in 2003 was 123 percent of its level in 1989. This resulted due to the new industry policy towards the services sector, where there is a competitive advantage for Albania.

To sum up, the transition economies presented an opportunity for multinationals to become MNEs in new markets and extend their productive base. The transition process involved stabilization, liberalization of the domestic and external economy, structural and institutional reform, privatization and restructuring of the state-owned enterprises, the creation of a sound business environment in order for new private companies to be established with the ultimate aim of developing national comparative advantages and integrating these economies through international trade and investment. But integration, especially during the early stages of transition, took the form of imports, not exports, due to the limited competitiveness of the countries' production and the output collapse, as well as capital inflows acting as foreign direct investment (FDI), partially for purchasing state enterprises, and the remainder as joint ventures and Greenfield FDI. On the other hand, as most of the transition economies, especially the South East European and the CIS, struggled to achieve the institutional prerequisites for EU accession, the differentiated outcomes of the transition process increased. Thus, we have two gear economies, even in the CEE region: the advanced Central European economic members of the EU; the 'moving towards' members of those South-East European countries towards EU membership, and the lagging countries of the Commonwealth of Independent States, with GDP levels less than that at the start of transition.

Conclusion

The dramatic increase in FDI over the last decade was based on globalization and economic integration, technological improvements, and on liberalization of various regimes with the abolishment of monopolies, and barriers.

The globalization concept implied that a growing share of FDI is worldwide in scope, and transition countries in particular should attract an increasing percentage of FDI. However, this did not happen in reality. It can be argued that there is a regional concentration of FDI, which can be seen from the examples of Greek MNEs becoming dominant entrepreneurs in the Balkan region, the Austrians in Slovenia and Croatia, the Nordic countries (Sweden, Norway, and Finland) in the Baltic region (Estonia, Lithuania and Latvia), Germany, France, and the UK in the ex-Visegrad countries (Poland, Hungary, the Czech Republic, and Slovakia) and the UK, France, Germany and Netherlands in advanced economies such as the Belgian one, Spain in Latin America, the USA in Canada and Mexico, Japan in China, and in the whole SE Asia, etc.

Globalization, which the transition economies struggled to become a part of, in its economic form envisages an interdependent world economic system dominated by global corporations not identified with any individual country. At the same time the multinational corporations became more powerful, since 90 percent of world-wide volume of FDI belongs to multinationals, their attitude towards it may reflect the nature of world FDI, while the 'drivers' of globalization are only managers from within large corporations.

The limited extent of liberalization reforms or ineffective transition programs; the increasing and highly competitive worldwide investment environment, which offers various alternative opportunities to the MNEs, together with the changing opportunities a country has to offer through time, along with the different ways in which MNEs evaluate those opportunities, lead us to conclude that globalization and transition reforms can help countries to attract FDI flows and become market economies.

The isolated transition economies lag in economic growth, are unable to adopt new technologies and improve their infrastructure. Furthermore, they display a low level of living standards. These countries must simply focus their attention as fully as possible on the world economy, participate in the globalization procedure, open and liberalize their economies, and attract FDI inflows. Otherwise, there is no way in which they will ever escape their present state of lagging growth.

Finally, the transition process incorporates an industry policy. Governments prefer to attract foreign investment projects in specific sectors of the economy. In this way, there is specific industry growth through privatization deals of state-owned enterprises (SOEs) offered by the government, and through creation of new enterprises based on significant incentives offered in order to improve and facilitate entrepreneurship and private ownership. Thus, most of the Central and East European economies, especially the South East European economies, have targeted their economies to the services sector and moved away from their initial levels of industrial production they had in 1989.

Lastly, globalization is not a new phenomenon, but just a new episode, something that is much more pervasive, deeper, and different from previous episodes or phases. Some researchers accept that globalization is an established process, that it is unstoppable and irreversible due to liberalization of international trade, goods and services, the free market, significant growth of services sectors, especially ones dealing with knowledge and information, rapid growth of a new generation of technology, the high degree of openness and the huge and fast circulation and distribution of information, mainly through the Internet. A major debate is being carried out regarding the question of benefits and the cost of globalization. However, summarizing both supporter and opponent arguments for and against the globalization process, globalization can not be classified as either bad or good. It is its evaluation that matters most, because challenges and threats are subject to continuous changes.

References

Apodaca, C. (2002), 'The Globalization of Capital in East and South East Asia', *Asian Survey*, Vol. 42, No. 6, pp. 883–905.

Bitzenis, A. (2003), 'Universal Model of Theories Determining FDI. Is There Any Dominant Theory? Are the FDI Inflows in the CEE Countries and Especially in Bulgaria a Myth?', *European Business Review*, Vol. 15, No. 2, pp. 94–103.

Bitzenis, A. (2004), 'Is Globalization Consistent with the Accumulation of FDI Inflows in the Balkan countries? Regionalization for the case of FDI inflows in Bulgaria', *European Business Review*, Vol. 16, No. 2, pp. 1–23.

Bitzenis, A. (2005), 'Company Oriented Investment Interest and Cross-border Transactions under Globalisation: Geographical Proximity Still Matters', *European Business Review*, Vol. 17, Issue 6, pp. 547–565.

Bitzenis, A., and J. Marangos (2005), 'The Transition Process in the Globalization Debate: The Role of Multinational Enterprises and FDI Flows', *Special Issue of Contributions to Political Economy*, 'Globalization, Localization and Global Governance'.

Brewer, T.L. and S. Young (1997), 'Investment Incentives and the International Agenda', *The World Economy*, Vol. 20, No. 2, pp. 175–198.

Farrell, D., J.K. Remes, and H. Schulz (2004), 'The Truth About Foreign Direct Investment in Emerging Markets', *McKinsey Quarterly* [online], 1, pp. 25–35; Available at <http://www.epnet.com>.

Floyd, D. (2001), 'Globalisation or Europeanisation of Business Activity? Exploring the Critical Issues', *European Business Review*, Vol. 13, No. 2, pp. 109–113.

Fortanier, F. and M. Maher (2001), 'Foreign Direct Investments and Sustainable Development', *Financial Markets Trends*, OECD, No. 79, pp. 51–107.

Friedman, T. and I. Ramonet (1999), 'Dueling Globalization: a Debate Between Thomas L. Friedman and Ignacio Ramonet', *Foreign Policy*, No. 116, pp. 110–127.

Hymer, S.H. (1972), 'The Multinational Corporation and the Law of Uneven Development', in L.N. Bhagwati (ed.), *Economics and the World Order* (London, UK: Macmillan).

Hymer, S.H. (1979), 'The Multinational Corporation and the International Divison of Labour', in Cohen, R.B., Felton, N., Van Liere, J and Nkosi M. (eds) *The Multinational Corporations: A Radical Appriach. Papers by Stephen Herbert Hymer* (Cambridge, UK: Cambridge University Press).

Kleinknecht, A. and J. Wengel (1998), 'The Myth of Economic Globalization', *Cambridge Journal of Economics*, Vol. 22, pp. 637–647.

Moore, K. and A. Rugman (2003), 'US Multinationals Are Regional Not Global', *Business Strategy Review*, Vol. 14, No. 4, p. 2.

Pitelis, C. (1996), 'Effective Demand, Outward Investment and the (Theory of the) Transnational Corporation: An Empirical Investigation', *Scottish Journal of Political Economy*, Vol. 43, No. 2, pp. 192–206.

Rugman, A. (2001), 'The Myth of Global Strategy', *International Marketing Review*, Vol. 18, No. 6, pp. 583–588.

Rugman, A. (2003), 'Regional Strategy and the Demise of Globalization', *Journal of International Management*, Vol. 9, No. 4, pp. 409–417.

Rugman, A. and R. Hodgetts (2001), 'The End of Global Strategy', *European Management Journal*, Vol. 19, pp. 333–343.

Stiglitz, J.E. (2003), 'Globalization and Growth in Emerging Markets and the New Economy', *Journal of Policy Modeling*, Vol. 25, No. 4, pp. 505–524.

Tanzi, V. (2004), 'Globalization and the Need for Fiscal Reform in Developing Countries', *Journal of Policy Modelling*, Vol. 26, pp. 525–542.

UN/ECE (2000), *Globalization: A European Perspective* (Geneva:UN/ECE Publication).

UNCTAD (1996), *The Least Developed Countries: 1996 Report* (Geneva and New York: United Nations).

UNCTAD (1997), *World Investment Report 1997* (Geneva and New York: United Nations).

UNCTAD (2001), *World Investment Report 2001* (Geneva and New York: United Nations).

UNCTAD (2003), *Foreign Direct Investment and Performance Requirements: New Evidence from Selected Countries*, United Nations; Available at <http://www.unctad.org/en/docs//iteiia20037_en.pdf>.

UNCTAD (2004), *World Investment Report 2004* (Geneva and New York: United Nations).

UNIDO (1995), 'Industrial Policy Reforms: The Changing Role of Governments and Private Sector Development', *Global Forum on Industry, Perspectives for 2000 and Beyond*, New Delhi, India, 16-18 October 1995, pp. 1–19.

Wade, R.H. (2004), 'Is Globalisation Reducing Poverty and Inequality', *World Development*, Vol. 32, No. 4, pp. 567–589.

Chapter 2

International Expansion Strategies: A Novel Framework and its Application to the Ten New EU Countries

Dirk Panhans and Lutz Kaufmann

Introduction

Ten new countries joined the European Union (EU) in May 2004. Barriers to trade and to foreign direct investment (FDI) had been falling long before then, starting in 1991 with the collapse of the Warsaw Pact and the newly gained independence of the Baltic States and Slovenia. On their way towards accession, the eight formerly Eastern Block states, Cyprus, and Malta continuously opened their markets. With the entry into the EU most trade and investment barriers fell altogether. This has opened up new opportunities for foreign companies both from the EU and from third countries.

There are various forms of international expansion. Eastern Europe can serve as an independent business system in and of itself, an export market for German products, or a prolonged work bench for the European market. On the one hand, stand-alone businesses comprise all functions from research and development to procurement and production to sales. On the other hand, sales offices only have operations at the very end of the value chain, including at times after sales services, distribution, marketing and refurbishing. Finally, affiliates that function as a prolonged work bench may comprise single functions at any point of the value chain and must therefore have resource interdependencies with its parent company.

Established frameworks are not able to adequately capture these alternatives. There is extensive literature on international expansion strategies; for an overview see Harzing (2000). Yet most of it are modifications or empirical tests of one of the three typologies provided by Perlmutter (1969), Stopford and Wells (1972), and Barlett and Ghoshal (1989, tested for example by Roth and Morrison, 1990, Leong and Tan, 1993, Ghoshal and Nohria, 1993, Harzing, 2000). While each of these typologies have their specific merits, neither of them differentiates between strategies that are directly measurable, scalable and action-oriented. Most typologies merely categorize strategies, which impedes to identify gradual differences to competitors (benchmarking) or over time (longitudinal analysis). Also, the lack of measurability prevents the comparison of strategic posture with macroeconomic indicators, which could help to easily assess geographic differences or emerging shifts in strategic posture. Moreover, most existing typologies are not scaleable and thus do not allow for the measurement or formulation of differentiated strategies on the functional, regional or product level. Finally, most typologies are not action-oriented. Like Perlmutter (1969), some are merely descriptive and do not at all allow for prescriptive strategy recommendations based on situational variables. Others like Bartlett and Ghoshal's (1989) do not answer the basic configurational questions of where to locate value creation, what resource-interdependencies to establish between different locations, and how to structure the ownership of these locations (Root, 1988). Due to the lack of a measurable, scalable and action-oriented typology, we have conceived a novel framework. It aims at addressing three audiences. Managers can use this new framework to benchmark themselves against competitors and to evaluate future expansion strategies. Policymakers can use it to determine how competitive their region is and how to further attract foreign companies. Academics can use it to focus their empirical work on practically relevant aspects and to test their hypotheses concerning international expansion strategies in a research efficient manner.

Findings of our research project are already available for China, India, Brazil and the US (see Kaufmann et al. 2005, 2006a-c). This article tries to generate first insights on the business activities of foreign companies in the new EU member states. On the *exploratory* side, it is analysed what strategies are directed towards the new EU countries, specifically how they differ from strategies employed elsewhere, how they differ between the new EU countries, how they differ between the home countries of involved companies, and how they differ between various industries. This will be a novelty, as previous empiricism either did not describe strategies towards a specific target region (as empiricism based on Barlett and Ghoshal 1989) or did only focus on mainly market-seeking strategies (as Dunning 1980). On the *confirmatory* side, hypotheses regarding the consistency of our novel framework are tested that concern the impact of country-specific advantages ('aces') and disadvantages ('barriers') on strategic choice. As this project is still at an early stage, this article gives first indications rather than definite evidence.

The chapter is structured as follows. Next section presents the new framework, then we outline the methodology that enables the measurement of the expansion strategies directed towards the new EU countries, and present the exploratory findings of what strategies foreign companies use towards the new EU countries and provides first confirmatory indications regarding the determinants of strategic choice. Finally, we conclude with summarizing remarks and points out recommendations for future research.

Theory

Our aspiration is to establish a framework that differentiates between strategy terms that are directly measurable, scalable and action-oriented. We will first explain what dimensions define our strategy terms before we describe the resulting generic strategies, the concept of mixed strategies, the determinants of strategic choice, and the expected impact of those determinants on strategic posture.

Dimensions

We define our strategy terms along the dimensions proposed by Root (1988): Localization (where to locate value creation), integration (what resource-interdependencies to establish between those locations) and outsourcing (how to structure the ownership of those locations).

Localization describes whether value creation activities are located abroad. Foreign value creation can be performed in various forms, such as licenses and franchises, joint ventures, and wholly owned subsidiaries, which can in turn be created by mergers, acquisitions, or greenfield development (Meissner and Gerber, 1980). The extent of localization is typically reflected in statistics on direct foreign investments.

Integration describes whether there are resource-interdependencies with and between foreign affiliates. With no integration at all, each foreign affiliate operates as a stand-alone business. There are no cross-border interdependencies, so each foreign affiliate needs to provide all business functions by and for itself. With full integration, there are intensive dependencies between corporate group members (Welge, 1989). A foreign affiliate may receive substantial provisions from corporate headquarters or from other foreign affiliates, so it is no longer necessary to provide all business functions by and for itself. Also, a foreign affiliate may provide products or services for headquarters or other foreign affiliates that results in the specialization of some business functions, product ranges or regional scope. Integration across borders does not only describe the company-internal trade of unfinished or finished goods that is reflected in import and export statistics, but it also includes the company-internal exchange of research data and product developments, the shared utilization of management know-how and internal services as well as the shared use of business connections, rights and brands. Strictly taken, the mere establishment of cross-border controlling or the return of profits to the parent-company already constitutes a marginal form of cross-border integration.

Outsourcing describes the ownership structure of the foreign entities. The ownership may range from wholly owned subsidiaries to equity joint ventures to minority investments to portfolio investments to complete outsourcing. Outsourcing may apply to support functions (Meier et al., 1997) but also to production itself (Picot, 1991) or to any other function such as research and development, procurement, or sales (Hanser, 1993).

Generic Strategies

Combining these three dimensions creates the value creation cube depicted in figure 2.1. Inside firm boundaries (i.e., in the front of the cube), we differentiate between the international expansion strategies of Export Orientation, Business Transfer and Global Integration. Outside firm boundaries, we differentiate between Export Partnering, Licensing and Franchising and Foreign Subcontracting. The remaining two strategic postures, not shaded in figure 2.1, refer to purely domestic strategies, namely national focus and national subcontracting. As they do not have any international aspect to them, we will not analyze them any further. In addition to these purely external expansion strategies, companies may also establish partial forms of ownership, or so-called joint ventures. Similar to our intra-firm strategies, joint ventures may aim at exports, the transfer of entire business systems or the selective value creation for third markets.

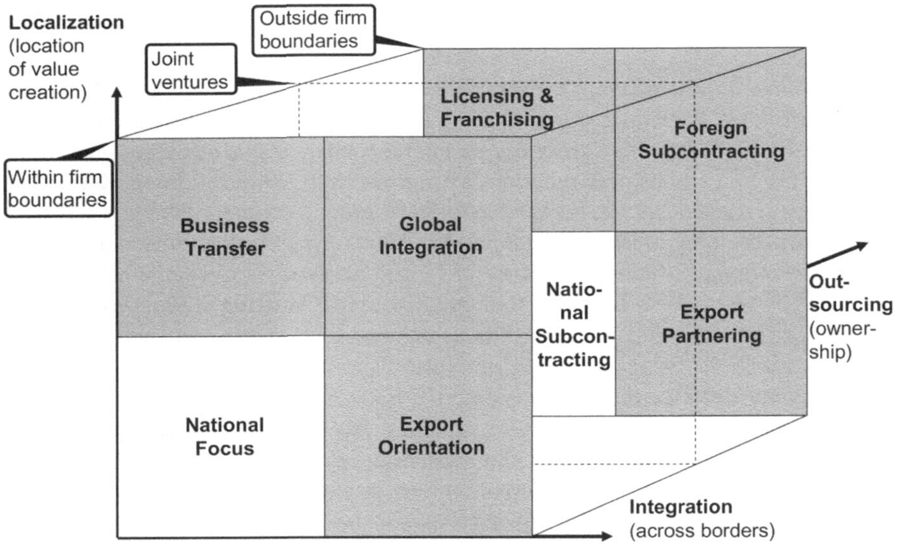

Figure 2.1 International expansion cube

Export Orientation means that the foreign country is utilized primarily as a sales market for German exports. This strategy is located in the lower right-hand front of the cube. There is only marginal value creation in the host country (low localization), as all products sold in that market are exported by the German parent company (high integration). If sales are not conducted through an intermediating trading company, the company itself has full ownership over these sales activities (low outsourcing). The foreign affiliate is hence a sales office, strongly dependent on the parent company and consisting only of marketing, sales and in some cases also after-sales services. Export Orientation is clearly a market-oriented strategy. It is most likely to be used by Bartlett and Ghoshal's (1989) international company, to employ Stopford and Wells's (1972) area division and to take Perlmutter's (1969) ethnocentric view.

Business Transfer means that the host country is treated as an isolated market where the company's basic business concept is replicated. This strategy is located in the upper left-hand front of the cube. All value creation takes place locally (high localization), within firm boundaries (low outsourcing), and cross-border transactions are restricted to control and governance issues (low integration). The foreign affiliate is hence an independent, fully-fledged, stand-alone business system, consisting of all business functions including not only marketing and sales, production and procurement but also research and development and its own internal support functions. Business Transfer is also a primarily market-oriented strategy. It is most likely to be used by Bartlett and Ghoshal's (1989) multinational company, to employ Stopford and Wells's (1972) product division and to take Perlmutter's (1969) polycentric view.

Global Integration is characterized by a close integration of the foreign affiliate into the company's worldwide value creation network. This strategy is located in the upper right-hand front of the cube. The foreign affiliate is majority-owned (low outsourcing) and specializes on some specific business functions, product groups or has a regional mandate (high localization). It exports products or services for processing or sales elsewhere in the world and in return receives products or services it cannot generate itself from other group members (high integration). Hence the affiliate has a contributing function and is strongly interdependent with the company's worldwide network (Malnight, 1996). In contrast to the expansion strategies explained before, Global Integration is characterized by globally distributed, interdependent resources and activities. With this strategy, a company locates each functional unit where it can reap economies of location best, connects these units located all over the world, and thus bundles volumes across national borders (Hedlund, 1986, Barlett and Ghoshal, 1989, White and Poynter, 1990). The choice of location depends on location-specific resources, such as low factor costs (e.g., textile manufacturing in low cost countries), qualifications and externalities (e.g., pharmaceutical research clusters), or proximity to natural resources, suppliers, and other strategic resources. This strategy is mostly resource- or efficiency-seeking and allows the combination of firm-specific with country-specific advantages (see Rugman and Verbeke, 2003). This strategy is most likely to be used by Bartlett and Ghoshal's (1989) multinational company, to employ Stopford and Wells's (1972) product division and to take Perlmutter's (1969) polycentric view. A prominent example of this strategy is the relocation of production facilities to low cost countries. Although the term global may suggest that operations span multiple continents (Rugman and Verbeke, 2004), we use this term also for any cross-border integration, and also for those within a continent or region.

Export Partnering is the counterpart to Export Orientation outside firm boundaries (high outsourcing). This strategy is located in the lower right-hand back of the cube.

As part of an export partnership, local trading firms take on the responsibilities for sales and marketing of goods exported to the country (high integration, low localization). This strategy is primarily used in those export markets where market volume is of lesser importance, where a lot of local marketing know-how is needed, or where it is difficult to gain access to local sales channels.

Licensing and Franchising corresponds to Business Transfer outside firm boundaries (high outsourcing). This strategy is located in the upper left-hand back of the cube. Through external partners, it applies the domestic business system in foreign markets, i.e., the entire value chain is replicated in the foreign country (high localization). Because the local business system is largely self-sufficient, exchanges with the German parent company are low (low integration). The only difference to the Business Transfer strategy is that control is enforced by contracts and not by ownership.

Foreign Subcontracting corresponds to Global Integration outside firm boundaries. This strategy is located in the upper right-hand back of the cube. Specific company functions are transferred to a foreign partner (high outsourcing and localization). Similar to Global Integration, foreign economies of location are being utilized to produce goods and services for third countries (high integration). One common form of subcontracting is passive job processing. Here, locally-produced, unfinished goods are shipped to a foreign subcontractor for additional finishing steps and are then, in turn, sold back or re-imported (Kaufmann, 2001, pp. 44–45).

This systematization reflects two major research streams of international business literature: Localization and integration refer to the research stream concerning forms of international expansion (e.g., Barlett and Ghoshal, 1989), whereas outsourcing reflects the research stream concerning the boundaries of a firm (e.g., Buckley and Casson, 1976). Please note that these dimensions also correspond to the strategies Dunning (1977) uses in his eclectic paradigm. He differentiates between the strategies of contractual resource transfer (outsourcing), exporting (integration) and FDI (localization), whereas we combine these dimensions to derive our strategies. Thus the value creation cube goes beyond Dunning's eclectic paradigm because it combines freely the former three strategies.

Similar to the empirical testing conducted by Dunning (1980) we want to concentrate on the international expansion strategies within the boundaries of a firm where the international expansion cube is reduced to its front matrix. The strategies outside firm boundaries do certainly play a role; according to Buckley and Casson (2003) they are even gaining in importance. Yet for reasons of research efficiency and simplicity, we have focused our entire research project on the intra-firm expansion strategies. The underlying assumption is that the (semi-) external forms of international expansion show similar characteristics. They are, for example, faced with the same aces and barriers as company-internal forms of expansion. The advantages and disadvantages from outsourcing are the only differing elements. We will thus focus on the three intra-firm expansion strategies of Export Orientation,

Business Transfer and Global Integration. With Export Orientation, Eastern Europe primarily functions as an export market for German products. With Business Transfer, the Eastern European affiliate is an independent business system in and of itself. And with Global Integration, the new EU countries may function as a prolonged work bench for the European market.

Mixed Strategies

The three generic strategies presented above are conceptual extreme points. Most companies choose mixed strategies, i.e., different strategies for different host countries, business functions or product groups. Even within each business function, several strategies can apply; for instance, intermediate products are exported from Germany (Export Orientation) but the final assembly takes place in the sales country (Business Transfer). Hence the critical question is what is the share of individual base strategies that contributes to the overall mixed strategy of a company.

Also these shares may well change over time, as the conceptual example in figure 2.2 illustrates. In this illustration, each strategy mix is represented by an individual dot in the matrix: the higher the percentage of a specific strategy, the closer the dot to the corresponding corner of the matrix. The three shaded quadrangles delineate dominant strategies, e.g., all points in the upper left-hand quadrangle represent mixed strategies whose share of Business Transfer is highest. The lower left-hand side remains empty, as we focus on expansion strategies towards the new EU countries and thus abstract away from the strategy of National Focus, which would be located on the lower left-hand side.

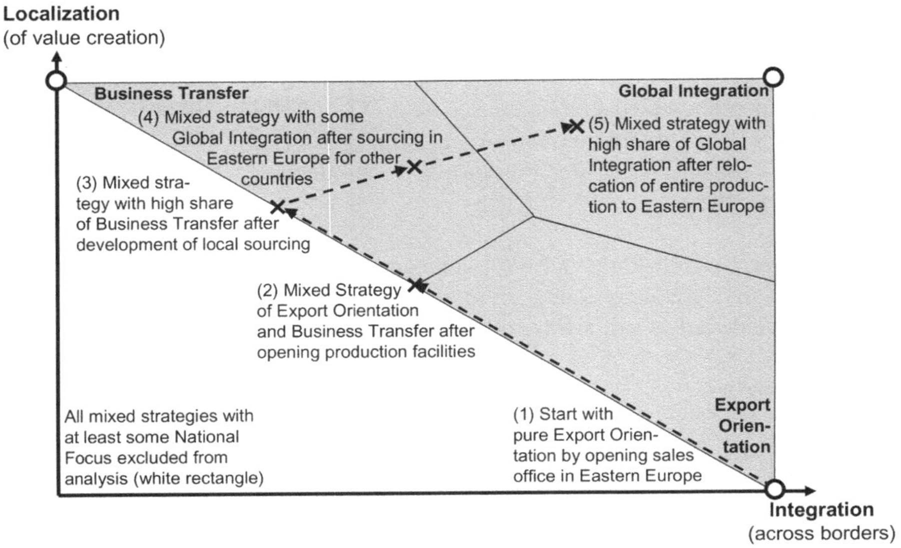

Figure 2.2 Mixed strategies of international expansion

1. When a German company opens a sales office in Eastern Europe, it follows the pure strategy of Export Orientation. This position is mapped in the lower right corner of the matrix because the affiliate is fully integrated (all products and services are provided by the parent company) and does not yet perform any or only minimal value creating activities in Eastern Europe.
2. The company may build up production facilities in Eastern Europe – initially only for the final assembly of unfinished goods from Germany and later for the entire production process. If the local production is purely aimed at the local consumer market (localization) and if R&D and sourcing continue to be provided by the German parent company (integration), this represents a mixed strategy of Business Transfer and Export Orientation. This example will be placed somewhere in the centre of the matrix.
3. The Eastern European affiliate may then establish a local sourcing network, e.g., to take advantage of lower indirect labor costs in sourced products, to fulfill local content requirements or to avoid the costs and time associated with exporting preliminary products to Eastern Europe. The position within the matrix shifts further to the upper left without ever reaching the point of pure Business Transfer as long as R&D results are still provided from Germany.
4. In case the manufacturer decides to use its Eastern European sourcing activities to supply German production facilities, it would be the first move towards Global Integration. Sourcing in Eastern Europe for Germany increases both the share of local value creation and the integration across borders. The Eastern European affiliate would no longer be unilaterally dependent on the parent company (e.g., for R&D). In addition, the parent company would now be dependent on the Eastern European affiliate (e.g., for sourcing).
5. Should the manufacturer decide to transfer the entire production to Eastern Europe to serve the entire European market from there, the degree of Global Integration would rise even more. The company's actions would still be considered a mixed strategy because R&D would follow Export Orientation (as R&D activities would remain in Germany) and parts of production would follow Business Transfer (because some production would serve the local sales market).

This example is to illustrate that most companies follow mixed strategies and that these shares may gradually change over time. Our statements about the application of individual strategies will always refer to their share within a mixed strategy.

Aces and barriers

Every company should consider its motives for entering the new EU countries carefully. Is it to address one of the fastest growing markets in the world and to increase sales volume? Or is it primarily to benefit from low labor costs? So what are the motives to conduct business in Eastern Europe? We categorize these motives into four different 'aces' that companies can play during their international expansion.

The first two aces, market opportunities and economies of location win the trick on the output or input side through the utilization of local advantages on the sales or factor markets. The other two aces, economies of scale and scope, trump through positive efficiency effects of international expansion.

Market opportunities represent local advantages on the sales market. The target market can hold interest because of its size or growth but also, for example, because of anti-cyclical market characteristics or the presence of sophisticated lead customers. The Eastern European market may also be of interest due to companies' desires to simply follow their existing corporate customers to Eastern Europe or to gain a first mover advantage in market penetration. Even though market opportunities are the most intuitive ace of international expansion, they are definitely not the only one.

Economies of location reflect country-specific advantages of the factor market. This includes, for example, lower labor, real estate and sourcing costs as well as lower tax rates but potentially also local technological know-how, higher education levels, agglomeration advantages in industry clusters or better access to capital. Economies of location can only translate into a real competitive edge for a company if those advantages are transferred across borders again. This is because economies of location are of no competitive advantage in relationship to other local companies. Ghemawat (2003) refers to this as the arbitrage function of a firm. The two aces discussed so far relate to factor and sales markets.

Economies of scale are efficiency effects that result from bundling volumes across borders. It is not automatic that the development of new markets will result in economies of scale. If the foreign affiliates are self-sufficient, bundling effects are not substantiated. One kind of economies of scale is the distribution of fixed costs across a larger production volume. For example, the development of a new drug by a German company would often not be profitable if it would be sold solely on the German market. But fixed R&D costs may be retrieved by selling the drug also in other markets. Economies of scale may also arise in form of more efficient technologies for an increased production volume, in form of increased process know-how over time (so-called learning curve effect) or in form of added negotiation power with suppliers or other market participants (see Buckley and Casson, 1976; Caves, 1971). Hence this ace makes it advantageous for companies to locate specific process steps to only one location where other markets can be served from this site. Pharmaceutical companies with centralized research facilities often play this ace. Other examples can be found in the electronics industry, especially semiconductors, where scale economies are essential to achieve cost advantages in centralized production.

Economies of scope are efficiency effects that result from a geographical spread of activities. Examples for geographical economies of scope are risk minimization through a regionally diversified business portfolio, the build-up of real options for future expansion, learning effects from cultural interaction and exchange and the opportunity to spread cross-country projects across different time zones (Tallman and Fladmore-Lindquist, 2002). We do not consider, however, horizontal economies of scope (by product diversification) or vertical economies of scope (by front- or backward integration) as they do not relate to international expansion.

Behavioral aspects, coincidence and luck are also often cited as reasons for choosing international expansion strategies and target countries. For instance, top managers' personal preferences, or perhaps influences from relatives or friends in the region, may drive the decision for a particular location. In addition, ignorance of other options or power struggles within organizations may lead to suboptimal expansion decisions. Furthermore, the bandwagon effect may misdirect an international expansion. That is, companies may have expanded to a country simply because 'everyone was doing it!'. We will set such behavioral aspects aside and focus rather on rational drivers for international expansion. Our framework is meant to be prescriptive rather than merely descriptive. In other words, in order to construct a hands-on tool for decision makers, we refrain from the distracting influence of behavioral aspects and instead concentrate on rational decision requirements as seen from a company perspective.

The four aces are designed to categorize opportunities of international expansion in a mutually exclusive and collectively exhaustive manner. Other benefit categories found in the literature can also be assigned to the four aces. For example, learning effects embody the aspect of market opportunities (learning from the local market), economies of location (utilization of location-specific qualifications or spillover effects in clusters), scale effects (distribution of research and development costs), as well as scope effects (learning across cultures).

If a world without borders and barriers would exist, a company might play these four aces of international expansion to their full extent. The decision for a particular location (where value is created) would be entirely independent of the sales market (where products are eventually sold). Naturally, reality paints a very different picture. But why? The answer here is that strategic choices are restricted by trade and investment barriers. For reasons of clarity, we use the terms trade barriers and investment barriers in a broad sense. They also include barriers of non-material integration (such as restrictions on the exchange of research findings) and investment barriers other than capital restrictions (such as barriers to the delegation of employees to establish foreign entities).

Trade barriers may hinder cross-border integration. These can be transportation and communication costs, tariffs, quotas, national regulations, and heterogeneous customer preferences. For example, despite substantial economies of scale, most commodity chemicals are only produced on a national or at most on a regional scale, due to high transportation costs.

Investment barriers complicate or even prevent foreign value creation. Barriers include discrimination against foreign firms, general disadvantages within the host environment as well as control and governance issues of transferring processes or knowledge (Kim et al., 2003).

Impact of Aces and Barriers on Strategic Posture

How do these aces & barriers affect strategic choice, i.e. what strategies help to play certain aces and which barriers have to be overcome to pursue a certain strategy? Figure 2.3 illustrates the expected relationship between aces and barriers on the one hand and strategic posture on the other hand.

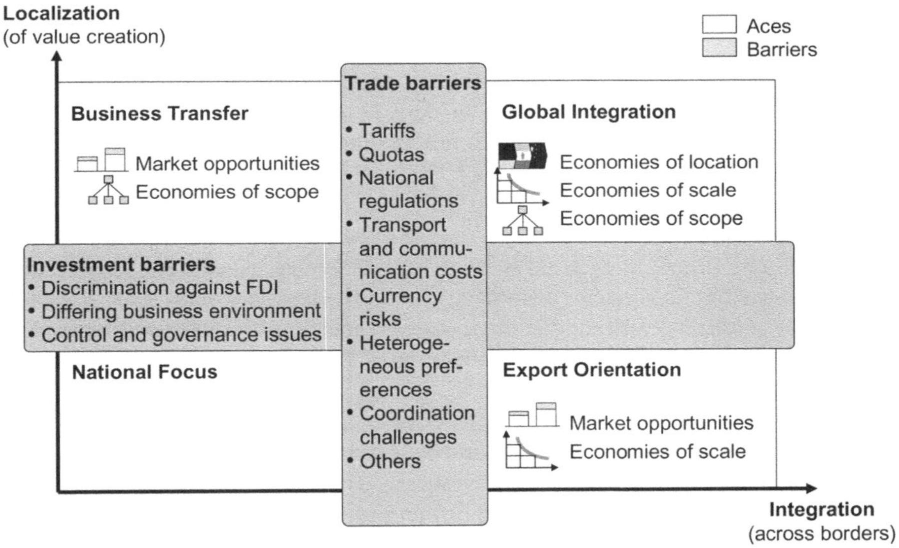

Figure 2.3 Effect of aces and barriers on strategic posture

Export Orientation combines market opportunities with economies of scale and is exposed to trade barriers. Economies of scale are not directly seen at the foreign affiliate but rather realized at the German headquarters by bundling the value creation for both countries at one location. For example, fixed costs such as in R&D can be distributed across the entire production volume, resulting in lower unit costs. Trade barriers are a major concern for export oriented companies, e.g., they are exposed to tariffs, hidden trade barriers, transportation costs and currency risks. Thus the strategy of Export Orientation is only chosen if trade barriers are comparatively low. Investment barriers do not affect purely export oriented companies. High investment barriers may only result in the evasion of Business Transfer and hence in the indirect effect that companies flee into the alternative of Export Orientation.

Business Transfer profits from market opportunities and economies of scope, while being subject to investment barriers. Similar to Export Orientation, the development of new markets is the primary goal. Yet, in contrast, Business Transfer does not lead to new economies of scale because separate capacities supply the market. On the contrary, if the foreign capacities are initially smaller than those in the parent company, the affiliate has to overcome diseconomies of scale. In return, economies of scope will result from the geographical spread of activities arise. Investment barriers reduce the attractiveness of Business Transfer as trade barriers reduce the attractiveness of Export Orientation. Hence comparatively high investment barriers keep companies from following a Business Transfer strategy, while comparatively high trade barriers make companies evade the Export Orientation strategy, resulting in a higher share of Business Transfer (Corden, 1967).

Global Integration benefits from economies of scale, scope and location while being exposed to both, trade and investment barriers. Economies of scale can be realized at the foreign affiliate because volumes are bundled between the host country and additional sales markets. As the specialization of affiliates necessitates a presence in many countries, economies of geographical scope arise. In turn, this provides opportunities such as real options for future expansion or learning opportunities across cultures. Global Integration is the only strategy that benefits from economies of location because local factor advantages need to be tapped (localization) and then exported to third countries (integration) in order to constitute a competitive advantage relative to other companies. In the pure form of Global Integration, local market opportunities play no role whatsoever because products are sold to third markets. There are at most secondary market effects, as more efficiently produced products become more competitive in existing and new markets. Global Integration is subject to trade and investment barriers, as it requires companies to build a substantial presence in the host country (localization) and to export products and services to third countries (integration). In effect, Global Integration is only applied in countries with substantial economies of location and low barriers to trade and investment.

According to this framework, these opportunities and barriers determine the choice of strategic posture. Some of them are largely country-specific, such as market opportunities, economies of location, trade barriers, and transfer barriers. Others are largely independent from country characteristics such as economies of scale and scope. According to the concept of fit, companies should adapt their strategies towards a region to the aces and barriers it provides. Economies of scale and scope are neglected from analysis. This leaves to be tested what impact market opportunities, economies of location, trade barriers and investment barriers have on the strategies of Export Orientation, Business Transfer, and Global Integration.

Methodology

In the previous paragraph, a new framework has been introduced that allows for the direct measurement of the expansion strategies towards the new EU countries. This section will describe the data sources that are used and the conceptualization of variables that makes our framework measurable by the given data. We take a macroeconomic perspective, basing our analysis only on aggregated data. We do so because such aggregated data is more comprehensively available and gives a better overview over trends than single company data (Sethi et al., 2003). For an overview of data used see table 2.1.

Concerning the *measurement of strategies*, a multitude of sources is consulted. For Export Orientation, imports by the new EU countries are taken as a proxy. These imports consist of the exports of foreign companies towards the new EU countries and exports of foreign affiliates of companies with a home-base in the accession countries towards their parents. Yet the second category seems negligible in size, as the stock of outward FDI is still low for the new EU countries. Therefore the proxy should be sufficiently good. Business Transfer and Global Integration are both measured by the sales of foreign affiliates located in the new EU countries. Whereas Business Transfer corresponds to the local sales of those affiliates, Global Integration corresponds to their exports towards their home country or third countries. For Poland, Hungary, the Czech Republic, and Slovenia, this data is available in the World Investment Directory (UNCTAD, 2004a). Updated and completed data is found at the statistical offices or national banks of those countries. For all other countries, the sales and exports of foreign affiliates is extrapolated from data of German foreign affiliates in the new EU countries. This is achieved by using the reciprocal of the share of German companies on the total inward FDI stock as a factor.

Concerning the *measurement of opportunities and barriers*, each variable is supported by three items. This only represents a selection from a multitude of possible items. For trade barriers open and hidden trade barriers are considered. Hidden barriers are based on a survey conducted by the World Economic Forum (2002). Also investment barriers are measured by various items from that survey. Opportunities of market expansion are measured by market size, market growth and buyer sophistication. For market size the logarithm of gross domestic product (GDP) is taken, for market growth the change in GDP. Economies of location are measured by technological sophistication, the wage level, and the corporate tax rate. Because the wages are in absolute values, again the logarithm is taken. Please note that productivity levels are not incorporated in the analysis, as country-level productivity is often irrelevant for company-level new investment decisions.

For the *exploratory* part, the absolute figures for Export Orientation, Business Transfer, and Global Integration are for convenience reasons transformed into a sum (the total of foreign activities) and shares (the distribution of strategies). For the home country perspective on expansion strategies, Poland is chosen as the host country because it is the largest country in terms of attracted foreign activity. For the industry perspective Slovenia is chosen due to the industry detail available.

Table 2.1 Data sources

	Variable	Item	Country	Source	Editor
Strategies	Export Orientation	*Imports by accession countries*	*all*	*Statistical Yearbook 2003 for* Foreign Countries	*Federal Statistical Office* Germany (2004)
	Business Transfer and Global Integration	Sales and exports by foreign affiliates	PL, HU, CZ, SL	World Investment Directory Statistical yearbook of Poland 2003 Statistical yearbook of Hungary 2003 Foreign Direct Investment 2002 Direct Investment 1994–2002	UNCTAD (2004a) Central Statistical Office (2004) Central Statistical Office (2004) Czech National Bank (2004) Bank of Slovenia (2004)
		Sales of German affiliates abroad	all but PL, HU, CZ, SL	Kapitalverflechtung mit dem Ausland (Capital linkages with abroad)	German Central Bank (2004)
		Inward FDI stock from Germany	all but PL, HU, CZ, SL	Handbook of Statistics 2003	UNCTAD (2004b)
		Total inward FDI stock	all but PL, HU, CZ, SL	World Investment Report 2002	UNCTAD (2002)
Opportunities and barriers	Trade barriers	Import duties	all	World Development Indicators 2001	World Bank (2002)
		Hidden trade barriers	all but CY, MT	Global Competitiveness Report 2001–2002	World Economic Forum (2002)
		Irregular payments in exports and imports			
	FDI barriers	Intellectual property protection			
		Favorism in decisions of government			
		Business cost of corruption			
	Market opportunities	Market size (GDP)	all	Handbook of Statistics 2003	UNCTAD (2004b)
		Market growth (GDP growth)			
		Buyer sophistication	all but CY, MT	Global Competitiveness Report 2001–2002	World Economic Forum (2002)
	Economies of location	Technological sophistication			
		Wages	all	Statistical yearbook on candidate countries 2003	Eurostat (2004)
		Corporate tax rate	all but SL	World Development Indicators 2001	World Bank (2001)

For the *confirmatory* part only a single regression analysis is used in this article due to the early stage in the research process and the low number of observed countries. A proper multiple regression analysis for the structural model coupled with a factor analysis for the measurement model will be conducted at a later point of time. Thus here, single items are regressed against single strategies. For each regression, the correlation coefficient is displayed and a F-test is performed to describe the significance of the result. In cases where data is not available for all ten new EU countries, this is respected in the calculation of significance level. All correlations significant at <0.01, <0.05 und <0.20 are marked. The tolerance of 0.20 is used to account for the low number of data points with only ten accession countries.

Results

First, exploratory results are aimed at better understanding the strategies of foreign companies towards the new EU countries. Then, a confirmatory analysis is to test the expected impact of the barriers and opportunities on strategic posture.

Exploratory Results

Figure 2.4 illustrates the position of the ten new EU countries in the world with respect to the total volume of attracted foreign activities and the distribution of strategies directed towards the region. All ten accession countries taken together attract a total volume of 367 billion USD in 2001, which consists of all exports by foreign companies towards the new EU countries and all local sales and exports by foreign affiliates in the accession countries. For comparison, the 12 largest countries in terms of attracted foreign activity are listed.

It can be seen that even taken together the new EU countries are relatively small in terms of attracted foreign activity. Also it can be seen that the share of Export Orientation towards the accession countries is much higher than on world average, much to the expense of Global Integration. This means that on average the new EU countries still function mainly as an export market rather than a value creation platform. This is partly due to the proximity to established sites in Western Europe. But it is also partly due to the relatively small domestic markets of some of the accession countries, as some industries require a minimum efficient scale that cannot be reached by domestic demand only. Yet the high levels of current FDI inflows into these countries suggest that Business Transfer and Global Integration may grow faster than Export Orientation.

Also note the low levels of Global Integration directed towards the US, which is due to the large domestic market and relatively high factor costs. Also note the very low levels of Business Transfer and Global Integration directed towards Japan, which due to high informal investment barriers.

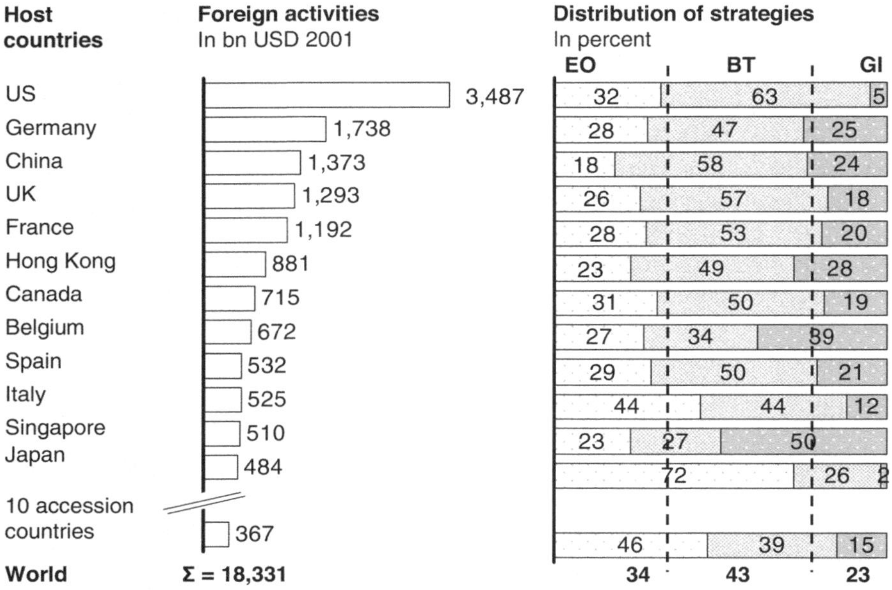

Figure 2.4 Comparison of new EU countries with the world, 2001

Figure 2.5 compares the new EU countries with each other. Poland, Hungary, and the Czech Republic are the largest countries in terms of attracted foreign activity, making up for nearly 80 percent of all accession countries. These three countries also exhibit the highest shares of Business Transfer, as large markets tend to reach minimum efficient scales easier by domestic demand. In smaller countries like Lithuania or Estonia, the domestic markets may not be big enough to justify a separate business system there, so demand is largely satisfied by Export Orientation.

Also note the high shares of Global Integration attracted by Estonia and Hungary. Estonia early opened up its investment and trade regime and especially attracts companies from the geographically and culturally close Finland, which use Estonia as an export platform for automotive parts, IT and communication technology, and lately also shared services. Hungary profits from early preferential agreements with the EU and the establishment of industrial free trade zones that simplify production for exports. Especially foreign automotive and electronics companies use Hungary as an export platform as depicted in figure 2.6.

According to the World Investment Report (UNCTAD, 2002), exports from Hungary were mainly in primary products, manufactures based on primary products, and low tech back in 1985. Today, automotive and electronics alone make up for more than half of Hungarian exports. It is interesting to note that the exporters are not Hungarian companies but affiliates of foreign companies from all over the world. Not only European companies use Hungary as a production platform, but also US

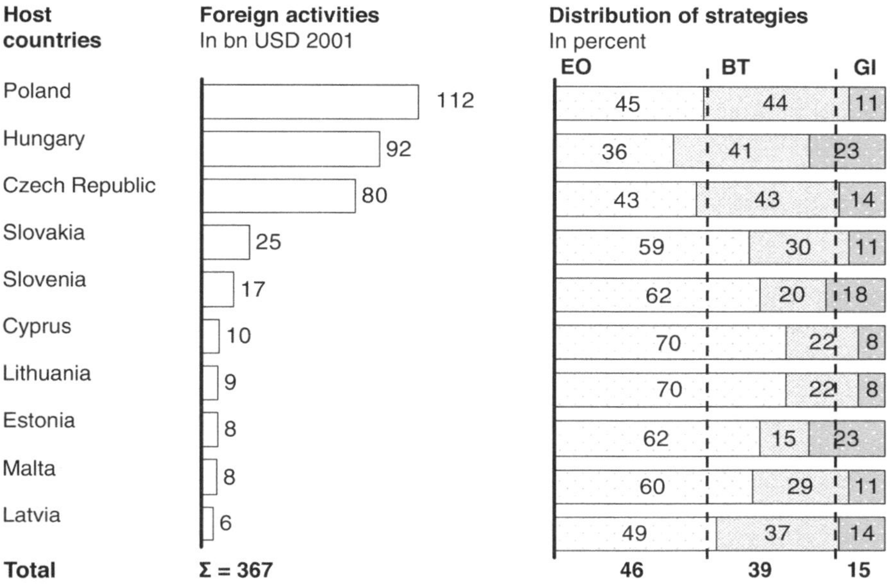

Figure 2.5 Comparison between new EU countries, 2001

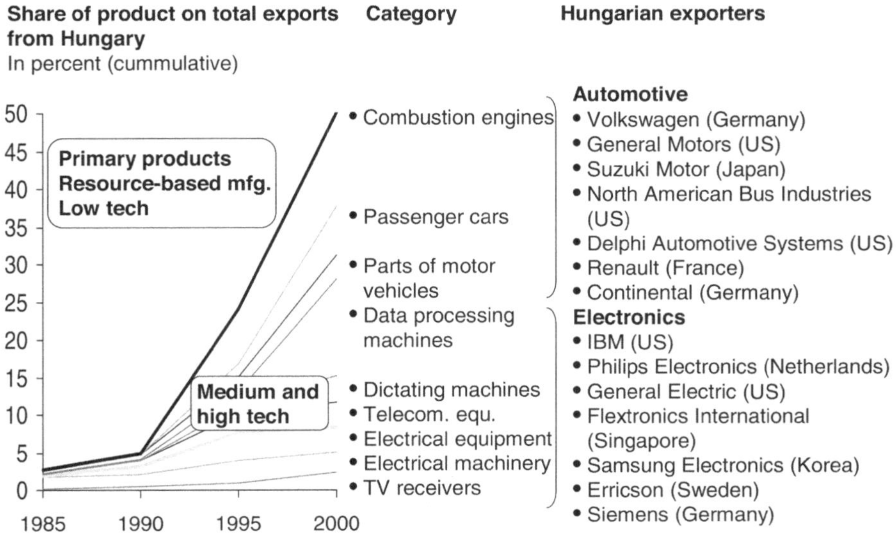

Figure 2.6 Export platform Hungary

and Asian companies do so to combine the good production conditions of Hungary with its proximity to the large EU-15 market.

Figure 2.7 depicts the countries of origin of companies active in Poland. Companies from Germany, the Netherlands, and France alone make up for nearly half of total foreign activity. Overall EU companies have a strong presence in Poland due to the geographical proximity and the low hurdles within the common market. The high share of Business Transfer from the Netherlands may be a distortion as some foreign investors use the Netherlands as an investment vehicle. Comparing the other largest host countries Germany, France, and the US the data suggests that geographical proximity has a positive impact on the share of Export Orientation. Also Russia stands out with its very high share of Export Orientation, which may be due to the overall low investment activity of Russian companies. Also note that the share of Global Integration is largely the same for companies from different home countries. Yet the meaning of Polish operations may be different for German and U.S. companies: Whereas German companies may tightly integrate Polish operations into their domestic value creation system, US companies may use Poland as a stand-alone platform for the EU-15 market.

Figure 2.8 displays the top 12 industries of foreign activity in Slovenia. Similar to Estonia and Hungary mentioned earlier, automotive and electronics are the areas of highest foreign involvement. Yet Slovenia functions mostly as a sales market for foreign companies. Especially in the manufacturing industries the share of Export Orientation towards Slovenia is exceptionally high, which is somewhat compensated

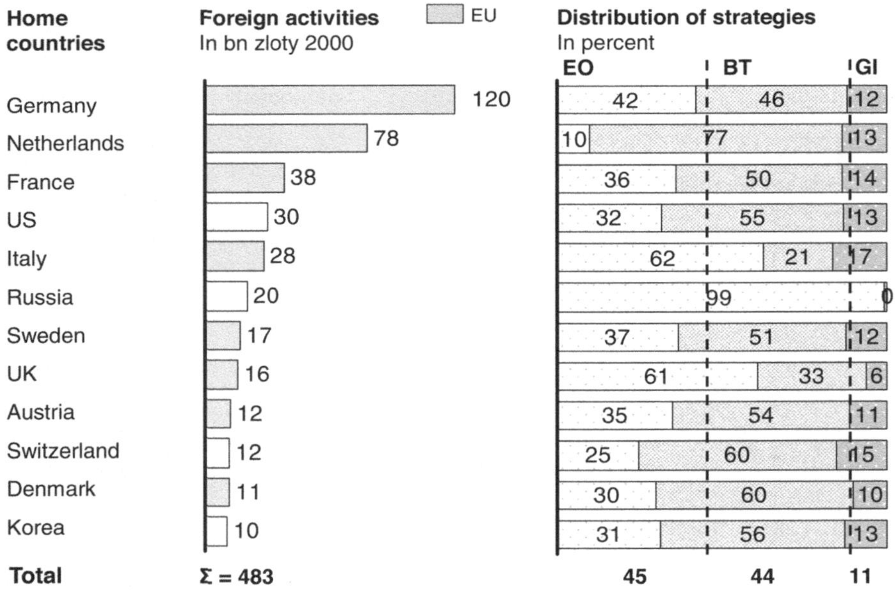

Figure 2.7 Home countries of foreign companies active in Poland, 2000

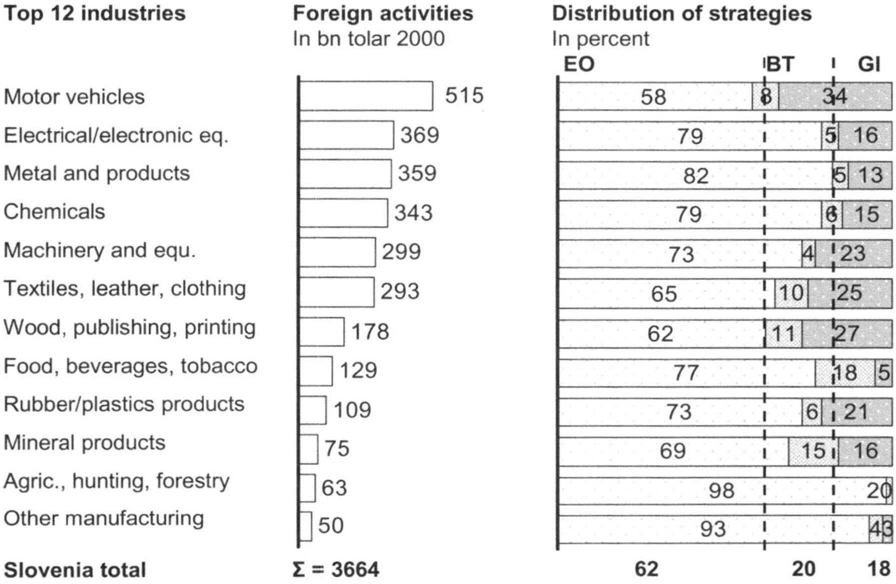

Figure 2.8 Industry Split of Foreign Companies Active in Slovenia, 2000

by higher shares of Business Transfer in services (not seen in the figure). Also noticeable is the high ratio of Global Integration to Business Transfer in many manufacturing industries. This means that because the host market lacks sufficient market size, companies invest in Slovenia mostly for exports. In machinery and equipment, for instance, more than 80 percent of production by foreign companies is exported again. Also note that especially scale industries show high levels of Export Orientation, as for example electrical and electronic equipment, metal and metal products, and chemicals.

Confirmatory Results

To confirm the expected impact of the barriers and opportunities on strategic posture, various items of barriers and opportunities are for the ten new EU countries regressed with the shares of strategies of attracted foreign activity. The result is depicted in table 2.2.

Regression Analysis

Trade barriers are expected to have a negative impact on Export Orientation and Global Integration. This expectation is supported by the regression analysis. Hidden trade barriers negatively impact Global Integration at a significance level of <0.01. For a detailed analysis, see figure 2.9. The three countries identified earlier for

Table 2.2 Regression Analysis

	Item	Strategies EO	BT	GI
Trade barriers	Import duties	−0.21	0.37	−0.26
	Hidden trade barriers	0.28	0.14	−0.85***
	Irregular payments in exports and imports	0.58*	0.68*	−0.20
FDI barriers	Intellectual property protection	0.53*	−0.23	−0.62*
	Favoritism in decisions of government	−0.60*	0.75**	−0.30
	Business costs of corruption	0.57*	−0.22	−0.71**
Market opportunities	Market size	−0.67*	0.70**	0.06
	Market growth	−0.32	0.09	0.51*
	Buyer sophistication	−0.29	0.22	0.15
Economies of location	Technological sophistication	−0.57*	0.29	0.58*
	Wages	−0.29	0.21	0.21
	Corporate tax rate	−0.15	−0.11	0.54*

Significance level: *<0.20, **<0.05, ***<0.01

being subject to high levels of Global Integration – Estonia, Hungary, and Slovenia – are also the countries with the smallest hidden trade barriers. Similarly, irregular payments in exports and imports have a negative impact on Export Orientation. That means that companies actually transfer value creation to those countries to avoid the attrition associated with trade. Interestingly, these hidden barriers have a clearer impact on strategic posture than straightaway import duties.

Investment barriers are expected to have a negative impact on Business Transfer and Global Integration. This expectation is supported by the regression results of barriers concerning intellectual property protection and business costs of corruption. Both have a negative impact on Global Integration and a positive one on Export Orientation. Thus companies are avoiding investments into countries with poor property protection and high levels of corruption to prevent technological drainage. Contrary to the expectations, favoritism in decisions of government officials positively correlates with Business Transfer and negatively with Export Orientation. This may be because favoritism requires companies to become insiders to gain government contracts. An exporter with only a sales office in the host country probably does not have the same buy-in with local officials as a foreign affiliate that employs many locals and brings technology into the country.

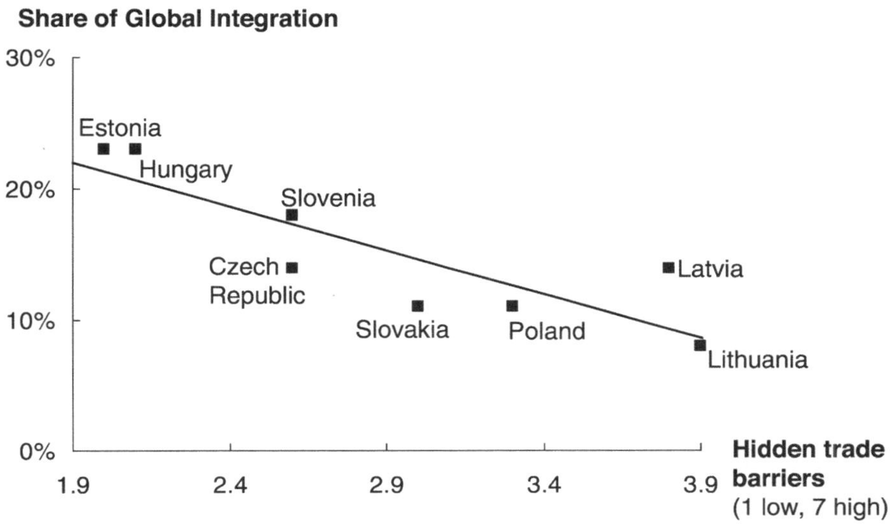

Figure 2.9 Impact of hidden trade barriers on Global Integration

Market opportunities are expected to have a positive impact on Export Orientation and Business Transfer, whereas Global Integration should be independent of host country market opportunities because products are sold abroad. This expectation is only partially supported. Market size has a strong positive effect on Business Transfer, yet correlates negatively with Export Orientation. This is because Business Transfer and Export Orientation substitute each other. At large, companies either export to a country if it lacks sufficient scale, or transfer their businesses there and produce on site. Market growth surprisingly shows a positive correlation with Global Integration. Yet this may be due to reverse causalities, as export platforms can help to stimulate economic growth in the host country. Buyer sophistication shows no significant relationship to any strategy, indicating that premium market segments may not be the main concern of foreign companies in the accession countries.

Economies of location are expected to have a positive impact only on Global Integration. As expected, high levels of technological sophistication and low corporate tax rates significantly correlate with Global Integration. Moreover, high levels of technological sophistication are negatively correlated with Export Orientation, which means that companies prefer exporting to markets that are technologically behind. Surprisingly, no relation between the wage level and Global Integration could be found. This means that the quality of labor is more important for foreign companies than its price.

Overall the expectations from the model concerning the determinants of strategic choice are largely supported by the analysis: For each barrier and opportunity, at least one variable shows the expected relationship on a significant level. Further testing with more items and countries is, however, necessary to conduct a proper structural equation analysis supporting the framework.

Implications and Extensions

A directly measurable, scalable and action-oriented framework has been developed that allows to measure international expansion strategies and to test the determinants of strategic choice. A first application of this framework to macroeconomic data provides a rough overview over strategies employed by foreign companies towards the ten new EU countries and gives some preliminary support for the consistency of the framework.

On the *explorative* side, the analysis shows that overall, companies employ more Export Orientation towards the accession countries than on world average. This can partly be explained by the small market sizes of the new EU countries, partly by the proximity to established production sites in Western Europe. Especially Estonia, Hungary, and Slovenia have been successful in attracting automotive and electronics companies pursuing Global Integration. This success can be traced back to especially open trade and investment regimes in those countries. A breakdown by home countries suggests that proximity favors Export Orientation. Similarly, a breakdown by industries indicates that especially scale industries in manufacturing tend to pursue Export Orientation.

On the *confirmative* side, the validity of the framework concerning the determinants of strategic choice is supported at large. Moreover it is found that hidden trade barriers have a stronger impact on strategic choice than straightforward import duties. Contrary to expectations it is found that companies meet problems of government favoritism by trying to become insiders via Business Transfer. Also, Business Transfer strongly depends on market size. Global Integration is favored by economies of location, such as technological sophistication and low corporate taxes. Surprisingly, low wage levels alone are not sufficient to attract Global Integration.

While our research project is still in an early stage, we hope to have made some informative contributions for all three audiences. For *managers* of foreign companies it may have been insightful that small countries such as Cyprus or Lithuania are mainly served by Export Orientation, whereas larger countries such as Poland, Hungary, or the Czech Republic are common targets for Business Transfer. Also, it may have shown them the attractiveness of Hungary, Estonia, and Slovenia for Global Integration. *Policy makers* from the new EU countries may have learned about the importance of keeping their corporate tax rates low. Also, the analysis may have shown them that further technological development seems to be vital for further attracting foreign companies, as most of the new EU countries cannot compete on wages alone with the new low-cost frontier of South Eastern Europe (SEE), the Coalition of Independent States (CIS) and Turkey. *Academics* may have learned about the convenience of the new framework for the direct measurement of international expansion strategies. Also, the confirmatory testing may have added to the face-validity of the framework and thereby contributed to existing research.

Further research is needed to fully utilize the potential offered by the new model. While addressing the strategies of foreign companies towards the new EU countries, this analysis raises further questions concerning the development of strategies over time, the resource-interdependencies of foreign affiliates at various stages of the value chain, and the impact of strategic choice on performance. Moreover, a proper structural equation analysis based on more items and countries is needed to confirm the consistency of the framework.

A longitudinal analysis based on macroeconomic data could be performed to understand the changes in employed strategies over time. Then it could even be observed how the strategies have adapted to decreasing barriers over time. An analysis on the company-level could add extra insight into the roles that foreign affiliates in the accession countries play within their group network. Until now, trade has been taken as a proxy for integration. Yet intra-company trade of intermediate or final products is only one form of cross-border integration. Also other forms of integration are worth studying, such as the provision of internal support functions or the company-internal exchange of research and development findings.

A proper structural equation modeling could support the validity of the model. Therefore, variables need to be supported by a more comprehensive list of items, and more data points need to be added. The confirmatory analysis could also be extend to examine the effect of strategic choice on performance. There is plenty of contradicting literature on the performance of foreign operations (Ruigrok and Wagner, 2003), so incorporating expansion strategies as an independent variable may be enlightening.

References

Bank of Slovenia (2004, ed.), *Direct Investment 1994–2002*, Ljubljana.

Barlett, C.A. and Ghoshal, S. (1989), *Managing Across Borders. The Transnational Solution*, Boston.

Buckley, P.J. and Casson, M.C. (1976), *The Future of the Multinational Enterprise*, London.

Buckley, P.J. and Casson, M.C. (2003), 'The Future of the Multinational Enterprise in Retrospect and in Prospect', *Journal of International Business Studies*, Vol. 34, No. 3, pp. 219–222.

Caves, R.E. (1971), 'Industrial Corporations: The Industrial Economics of Foreign Investment', *Economica*, Vol. 38, pp. 1–27.

Central Statistical Office Hungary (2004, ed.), *Statistical Yearbook of Hungary 2003*, Budapest.

Central Statistical Office Poland (2004, ed.), *Statistical Yearbook of Poland 2003*, Warsaw.

Corden, W.M. (1967), 'Protection and Foreign Investment', *The Economic Record*, Vol. 43, pp. 209–232.

Czech National Bank (2004, ed.), *Foreign Direct Investment 2002*, Prague.

Dunning, J.H. (1977), 'Trade, Location of Economic Activity and the MNE: A Search for an Eclectic Approach', in Ohlin, B. (1977, ed.), *The International Allocation of Economic Activity*, London, pp. 395–418.

Dunning, J.H. (1980), 'Toward an Eclectic Theory of International Production: Some Empirical Tests', *Journal of International Business Studies*, vol. 11, nr. 1, pp. 9–31.

Eurostat (2004, ed.), *Statistical Yearbook on Candidate Countries 2003*, Luxembourg.

Federal Statistical Office Germany (2004), *Statistical Yearbook 2003 for Foreign Countries*, Wiesbaden.

Ghemawat, P. (2003), 'Semiglobalization and International Business Strategy', *Journal of International Business Studies*, Vol. 34, No. 3, pp. 138–152.

Ghoshal, S. and Nohria, N. (1993), 'Horses for Courses: Organizational Forms for Multinational Corporations', *Sloan Management Review*, Vol. 34, pp. 23–35.

Hanser, P. (1993), 'Marketing-Outsourcing: Schlankheitskur mit Risiko', *Absatzwirtschaft*, Vol. 36, No. 8, pp. 34–39.

Harzing, A.-W. (2000), 'An Empirical Analysis and Extension of the Bartlett and Ghoshal Typology of Multinational Companies', *Journal of International Business Studies*, Vol. 31, No. 3, pp. 101–120.

Hedlund, G. (1986), 'The Hypermodern MNC: A Heterarchy?', *Human Resource Management*, Vol. 25, No. 1, pp. 9–35.

Kim, K., Park, J.-H. and Prescott, J.E. (2003), 'The Global Integration of Business Functions: A Study of Multinational Businesses in Integrated Global Industries', *Journal of International Business Studies*, Vol. 34, No. 7, pp. 327–344.

Kaufmann, L. (2001), *Internationales Beschaffungsmanagement – Gestaltung strategischer Gesamtsysteme und Management einzelner Transaktionen*, Wiesbaden.

Kaufmann, L. et al. (2005), *China Champions: How German companies can successfully integrate China into their global strategies*, Frankfurt.

Kaufmann, L. et al. (2006a), *Investmentguide Indien: Erfolgsstrategien deutscher Unternehmen auf dem Subkontinent*, Stuttgart.

Kaufmann, L. et al. (2006b), *American Allstars: Success Strategies of German Companies in the United States*, Frankfurt.

Kaufmann, L. et al. (2006c), *Brazilian Brilliance: Success Strategies of Foreign Companies in the United States*, Frankfurt.

Leong, S.M. and Tan, C.T. (1993), 'Managing Across Borders: An Empirical Test of the Bartlett and Ghoshal [1989] Organizational Typology', *Journal of International Business Studies*, Vol. 24, No. 9, pp. 449–464.

Malnight, T.W. (1996), 'The Transition from Decentralized to Network-Based MNC Structures: An Evolutionary Perspective', *Journal of International Business Studies*, Vol. 27, No. 1, pp. 43–65.

Meier, A., Stuker, C. and Trabucco, A. (1997), 'Auslagerung der Personaldienstfunktion: Machbarkeit und Grenzen', *Zeitschrift Führung und Organisation*, Vol. 66, No. 3, pp. 138–145.

Meissner, H.G. and Gerber, S. (1980), 'Die Auslandsinvestition als Entscheidungsproblem', *Betriebswirtschaftliche Forschung und Praxis*, Vol. 32, No. 3, pp. 217–228.

Perlmutter, H.V. (1969), 'The Tortuous Evolution of the Multinational Company', *Columbia Journal of World Business*, No. 1, pp. 9–40.

Picot, A. (1991), 'Ein neuer Aufsatz zur Gestaltung der Leistungstiefe', *Zeitschrift für Betriebswirtschaft*, Vol. 43, No. 4, pp. 336–357.

Root, F.R. (1988), 'Some Taxonomies of International Cooperative Arrangements', in Contractor, F.J. and Lorange, P. (eds), *Cooperative Strategies in International Business*, Toronto, pp. 69–80.

Roth, K., Morrison, A. J. (1990), 'An Empirical Analysis of the Integration-responsiveness Framework in Global Industries,' Journal of International Business Studies, vol. 21, no. 3, pp. 541-561.

Rugman, A.M. and Verbeke, A. (2003), 'Extending the Theory of the Multinational Enterprise: Internalization and Strategic Management Perspectives', *Journal of International Business Studies*, Vol. 34, No. 3, pp. 125–137.

Rugman, A.M. and Verbeke, A. (2004), 'A Perspective on Regional and Global Strategies of Multinational Enterprises', *Journal of International Business Studies*, vol. 35, nr. 1, pp. 3–18.

Ruigrok, W. amd Wagner, H. (2003), 'Internationalization and Performance: An Organizational Learning Perspective', *Management International Review*, Vol. 43, No. 1, pp. 63–83.

Sethi, D. et al. (2003), 'Trends in Foreign Direct Investment Flows: A Theoretical and Empirical Analysis', *Journal of International Business Studies*, Vol. 34, No. 7, pp. 315–326.

Stopford, J.M. and Wells, L.T. (1972), *Managing the Multinational Enterprise. Organization of the Firm and Ownership of the Subsidiaries*, New York.

Tallman, S. and Fladmore-Lindquist, K. (2002), 'Internationalization, Globalization, and Capability-Based Strategy', *California Management Review*, Vol. 45, No. 1, pp. 115–135.

UNCTAD (2002, ed.), *World Investment Report 2002*, Geneva.

UNCTAD (2004a, ed.), *World Investment Directory*, URL: www.unctad.org/ Teplates/ Page.asp?intItemID=2980&lang=1 (as of June 2004).

UNCTAD (2004b, ed.), *Handbook of Statistics*, Geneva.

Welge, M.K. (1989), 'Organisationsstrukturen, differenzierte und integrierte', in Macharzina, K. and Welge, M.K. (eds) (1989), *Handwörterbuch Export und Internationale Unternehmung*, Stuttgart.

White, R. and Poynter, T.A. (1990), 'Organizing for Worldwide Advantage', in Barlett, C., Doz, Y. and Hedlund, G. (eds), *Managing the Global Firm*, New York.

World Bank (2002, ed.), *World Development Indicators 2001*, Washington.

World Economic Forum (2002, ed.), *Global Competitiveness Report 2001–2002*, Davos.

Chapter 3

How International Trade Ties Influence Democratization: The Case of the Post-Soviet States

Mikhail Balaev and Caleb Southworth

Introduction

After the collapse of the Soviet Union in 1991, many analysts argued that Russia attempted to maintain some semblance of its former imperial power through political intervention, military threats, international aid and, especially, through trade relationships with its former autonomous republics (Bugajski, 2004; Bukkvoll, 2004; Lo, 2003; MacFarlane, 2003; Mihkelson, 2002; Smolansky, 1999; Simonia, 1995). There are numerous examples of Russia's attempts to influence domestic and international politics of the new independent countries.

In 1993, Moscow introduced special tariffs in order to force Moldova to join the Commonwealth of Independent States (CIS); throughout the 1990s, Russia was periodically cutting, or threatening to cut, the energy supplies to Ukraine, demanding at first that Ukraine ratify a number of CIS agreements and then join the Common Economic Space between Russia, Belarus and Kazakhstan (which Ukraine eventually joined in 2004); in 1997 Yeltsin forfeited the energy debt of Belarus in exchange for creating a formal union between the two countries.

The formal dissolution of the USSR. resulted in the official formation of fifteen independent states with different political systems ranging from highly authoritarian to reasonably democratic. Some of these states have legal guarantees concerning independence of the media and personal freedom of expression. Researchers have hypothesized that such ties with Russia, along with Soviet-era economic and political relationships, could explain the sort of political regime that developed in the post-Soviet period (Bugajski, 2004, pp. 29–49). A majority of other social science researchers also tend to depict Russia as the central player in the post-communist world, using the arguments concerning economic dependence of the post-communist countries on Russia (Strachota, 2002; Checkel, 1995).

The research question for this chapter concerns the relationship between trade ties to Russia and the possible development of democratic political regimes in the 14 former Soviet republics. Specifically, we analyse the trade ties of 14 post-Soviet countries to Russia for the period from 1995 to 2003. These are then compared to the freedom indicators, being press freedom and measures of individual rights. Finally, we draw conclusions about the relationship between post-Soviet countries and the Russian Federation, and the extent of democratic development in these former Soviet states. To presage our main finding, unlike many analysts of Russian geopolitics, we find that systematic examination of the data on trade relationships between Russia and its former republics shows little impact on political outcomes.

Russia's Political and Economic Influence in Successor States

The originating question for this chapter is: What are the social origins of democracy? More specifically, what are the origins, sources, and restrictions of democratic development of the post-Soviet states? When considering a period of more than 70 years of suppression of democratic freedoms and liberties in the USSR, one knows that waives of mass euphoria and uplifting of democratic beliefs emerged after the declaration of independence in each country of the former Soviet Union. This suggests that such countries contained fertile soil for further democratic development. Democracy, however, came neither easily nor quickly. Tajikistan, for example, fell into a prolonged period of civil war. Belarus and Turkmenistan developed an extreme form of authoritarian government with presidential personality cults. The Baltic States managed to develop a more-or-less democratic system, but with policies that excluded much of their Russian national population from full citizenship rights (Commercio, 2004). What accounts for such structural differences?

The western media often portrayed the political events and outcomes in the former Soviet states as pro-Russian and, oppositely, pro-Western, considering 'pro-Russian' outcomes as less democratic and 'pro-Western' outcomes as more democratic (*The New York Times*, December 27, 2004, p. A1; December 9, 2004, p. A16). Such reporting maintains Cold War logic, that Russia is the successor of the Soviet empire, with similar ambitions and a similar sphere of influence within the former partner states. Some researchers also describe the political processes within the former Soviet states in a similar way. Bugajski (2004, p. 109), for instance, writes:

> In the Kremlin's view, former Soviet borders, including the outside borders of the Baltic republics, retain a measure of validity as the major parameters of exclusively Russian influence and a barrier against Western penetration.

After the breakup of the USSR, the Russian Federation lacked direct political control, such as the ability to veto political leaders and did not have occupying military forces with which to influence the political processes in the newly independent countries.[1] If the main working hypothesis of experts is that Russia still

1 By the time the new independent countries officially declared their independence and were recognized internationally, Russia had withdrawn the majority of its troops in exception of Tajikistan, where the Russian troops have been guarding the border with Afghanistan and

does influence the political processes in these countries, the precise mechanisms through which that influence operates still need to be specified. We identify two mechanisms through which the Russian Federation affects the domestic political process in other countries: political propaganda and international trade.

While this chapter focuses on trade relationships, briefly examining Russia's political propaganda in the newly independent states will help put that mechanism in its proper context. Political propaganda takes various forms. Russia has supported specific political parties and candidates through endorsements, and used bellicose rhetoric against opposition parties while lauding political causes deemed pro-Russia. It also broadcasts its two main state-owned television stations (ORT or 'societal Russian television' and RTR or Russian Tele-Radio) to 10 of the 15 new states (www.internews.ru). While estimates vary widely, ORT is thought to reach nearly 200 million viewers, RTR another 140 million, and state radio and other small channels such as St. Petersburg's government-run Channel-5 another 90 million (Internews Russia).

Other viewers worldwide receive these channels via cable, an option that is particularly common in these former Soviet states. Television and radio are important tools to frame political debate and advocate for causes and electoral candidates. Still, one weakness of such a channel of influence is that it can be cut-off, as in the Baltic States, or reduced to limited hours, the situation in many of these countries. Moreover, overt political advocacy thus far has been limited to relatively fair political contests, something rare in this set of countries. The Georgian Rose Revolution in 2003, Ukrainian Orange Revolution in 2004 and the recent public protests of the parliamentary elections in Kyrgyz Republic, show that a major obstacle to fair democratic elections was not external influence, but internal corruption, fraud and other major violations that took place, during the elections. While framing of political discourse on television and radio is an important axis of influence, we do not analyse further the actual influence of Russian political propaganda on the democratization of post-Soviet countries.

Russia has sought to augment political and cultural efforts to shape Soviet successor states with its economic power, particularly trade ties linked to energy and raw material export. Most of the post-Soviet countries have remained dependent on Russia for energy, mainly oil and gas, and electricity. There are exceptions, but these are minor in scale: Turkmenistan is rich in natural gas; Azerbaijan has a large share of oil in the Caspian Sea, and, to a lesser extent, Uzbekistan has, though largely undeveloped, resources of natural gas. Russia used import tariffs to put economic pressure on most of the former Soviet states to force these independent countries

---

still constitute a major military force in the country. In addition to the official participation of Russian military forces in Transnistrian region of Moldova, there was an unofficial participation of Russian military in operations in Georgia and during Azerbaijan-Armenian conflict. However, with the resolution of the latter two conflicts and the cessation of the civil war in Tajikistan, Russia had very minimal military influence on any of the post-Soviet states.

into the newly created Commonwealth of Independent States. Even after the obvious failure of CIS to establish itself as a military, economic or even political alliance, the individual economic relations between Russia and the other members of CIS were considered central to international relations (*The Economist*, Vol. 343, Issue 8018, May 24, 1997, p. 47).

The notion of economic dependence on Russia is often discussed in literature. Smolansky (1999, pp. 49, 58) argues that because 'Russia has been Ukraine's largest supplier of fuel, largest creditor, and largest trading partner' '... Ukraine's very existence as an independent state is at stake'. The main hypothesis in the extant literature is that there is a direct relationship between the amount of international trade between Russia and its successor states, on the one hand, and political outcomes, on the other.

> *Hypothesis 1: Post-Soviet states with strong trade ties to Russia are less democratic than those with weak trade ties.*

Furthermore, Bugajski (2004) suggests that by increasing its exports of oil and natural gas and the import of agricultural products from the partner countries, Moscow is trying to increase the economic dependence of the former Soviet states on Russia. Elaborating on this idea we would expect that increased economic dependence of one country on another would result in reduced general trade openness of the former. That is, there exists a trade off between developing trade with Russia and trade with the world market in general; the former comes at the expense of the latter.

> *Hypothesis 2: In the economies of post-Soviet states, there is an inverse relationship between trade openness with Russia and trade openness with the world market.*

Analysis of Data on Trade Ties and Political Freedoms

At this point, we need to introduce the main measures of our concepts of trade and freedom.[2] We use the 'Press Freedom' indicator as published by the Gannett Foundation's Freedom House to assess the extent of democratic development. Press Freedom is not the only important characteristic of a democracy, but it is a basic one. Freedom House also publishes a general freedom indicator, but the Press Freedom variable is superior as it has a more nuanced set of components and a variable scale from 0 to 100 rather than 1 to 7. The Press Freedom Indicator is based on three categories: the legal environment, the political environment, and the

2 The analysis uses the following sources for our data collection: 'Freedom of the Press' indicators (published by the Freedom House, www.freedomhouse.org/research/pressurvey.htm); World Development Indicators (published by World Bank, http://www.worldbank.org/data/onlinedatabases/onlinedatabases.html); 'Russia in Figures' statistical bulletin (published by Russian Federal State Statistics Service, also at http://www.gks.ru); Statistical Office of Estonia (http://www.stat.ee); Central Statistical Bureau of Latvia (http://www.csb.lv); Statistics Lithuania (http://www.std.lt).

economic environment. The data for the computation of the index is derived from various sources: correspondents, the findings of human rights and press freedom organizations, the reports of governments and multilateral bodies, domestic and international news media, International Freedom of Expression exchange (IFEX) network. The Press Freedom and General Freedom measures are highly correlated in all the post-Soviet countries, and all the years have a correlation coefficient close to 1.0, which means that these indexes measure the same thing.

The extensiveness of trade ties to Russia is defined as the percentage of the trade turnover with Russia divided by the overall foreign trade turnover of the country:

$$\text{Trade ties to Russia} = \frac{\text{Export to Russia} + \text{Import from Russia}}{\text{Total Export} + \text{Total Import}} * 100\%$$

This definition allows us to assess the magnitude and the influence of Russia as a trade partner, net of the effect of change in the general trade openness of the country. The general trade openness of a country is defined as a percentage of its foreign trade in GDP:

$$\text{Trade openness} = \frac{\text{Total Export} + \text{Total Import}}{\text{Gross Domestic Product}} * 100\%$$

Although contemporary economists have debates over this method to measure trade openness of a country (for example, see Lloyd and MacLaren, 2002), the severe limitations of the available data on most of the post-Soviet countries prevent us from employing more sophisticated measurements of trade openness.

We collected the following data for the period from 1995 to 2003: countries' gross domestic product (GDP), GDP per capita (purchasing power parity), total exports, total imports, exports to Russia, imports from Russia, freedom indicators. All monetary variables are denominated in millions of USD. The summary of the data is presented in Figure 3.1.

The scatter plot represents the relationship between trade ties to Russia on the x-axis and countries' freedom on the y-axis. The scale for the Press Freedom indicator is counter-intuitive: zero is the highest degree of press freedom and 100 is the lowest degree of press freedom. (We follow the convention of the Freedom House so that our results can be compared with other research using this measure.) Each observation in the scatter plot refers to a particular country in a particular year from 1995 to 2003. Visually, Figure 3.1 shows that the relationship between trade and press freedom has different trajectories in different countries. Spatially, we can identify three clusters: the Baltic states (Estonia, Latvia, and Lithuania), Belarus and Moldova, and the rest of the countries, particularly those of Eurasia. The remainder of this analysis examines the direct relationship between each country's trade with Russia and whether the extensiveness of this trade affects democratic development.

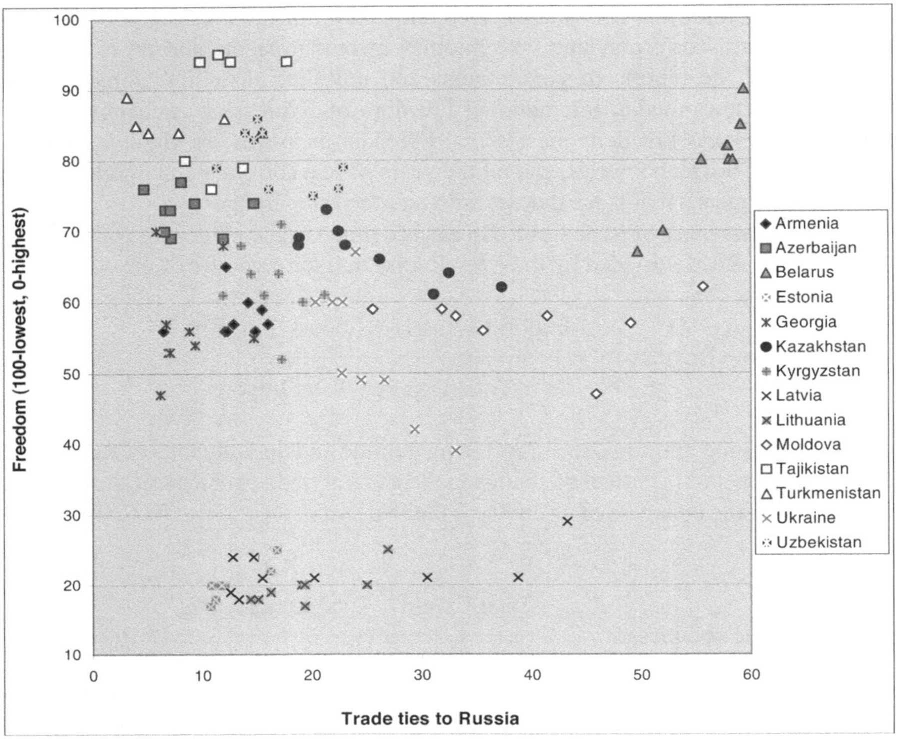

Figure 3.1 Post-Soviet states' freedom and trade ties to Russia

In Table 3.1 we summarize the total change in both variables for the period from 1995 to 2003 as the percent change. The percent change in trade ties to Russia shows the change in the percent of foreign trade with Russia in overall foreign trade between 1995 and 2003. A positive percent change in Press Freedom indicators shows a decrease in freedom of the press. Conversely, negative percent change in the Press Freedom indicator shows that the media has become more independent in the country in 2003 than it was in 1995.

Table 3.1 shows that between 1995 and 2003, Russia became a less important trade partner in all former Soviet states except Belarus and Georgia. This fact is especially striking considering that the large increase in trade to Russia for Georgia (60.4 percent) represents the increase in absolute value from only 5.8 percent, being the lowest in 1995, to only 9.4 percent, being the third lowest in 2003, thus making Russia far from being an influential trade partner for Georgia despite the highest percent change of trade ties to Russia. The change in the Press Freedom indicator offers us a different picture. Besides Estonia, Latvia, and Lithuania, the increase in press freedoms within a post-Soviet state (that is, negative percent change in the Press Freedom indicator) was observed in Georgia and Tajikistan. Changes in these scales can be grouped into three categories:

Table 3.1 Trade and Press Freedom in Former Soviet States, 1995 and 2003

	Trade ties to Russia			Press Freedom indicator		
	1995	2003	% change	1995	2003	% change
Armenia	16.0	12.2	–23.9	57	65	14.0
Azerbaijan	7.2	7.1	–0.7	69	73	5.8
Belarus	49.7	57.9	16.6	67	82	22.4
Estonia	16.8	10.7	–36.1	25	17	–32.0
Georgia	5.8	9.4	60.4	70	54	–22.9
Kazakhstan	31.1	21.4	–31.3	61	73	19.7
Kyrgyzstan	17.3	17.2	–0.2	52	71	36.5
Latvia	43.3	13.3	–69.3	29	18	–37.9
Lithuania *	26.9	14.4	–46.6	29	18	–37.9
Moldova	45.9	25.6	–44.3	47	59	25.5
Tajikistan **	11.6	10.9	–5.7	93	76	–18.3
Turkmenistan ***	15.4	3.2	–79.3	84	92	9.5
Ukraine	29.4	24.0	–18.3	42	67	59.5
Uzbekistan	22.9	15.1	–34.1	79	86	8.9

* For Lithuania the initial period used is 1996.
** For Tajikistan the initial period used is 1997.
*** For Turkmenistan the percent change calculated as of 2001.

1. Increase (more than 10 percent increase in the trade ties or less than 10 percent decrease in the Press Freedom indicator);
2. No change (between negative 10 percent and positive 10 percent change in both variables);
3. Decrease (less than 10 percent decrease in the trade ties or more than 10 percent increase in the Press Freedom indicator).

Table 3.2 presents a cross tabulation of the categories of 'democracy', measured in press freedom, and 'trade ties', measured in trade volume with Russia.

According to Hypothesis 1 we should expect to see the post-Soviet countries mainly located in the cell 3,1 (increased democracy and decreased trade ties to Russia) and in the cell 1,3 (decreased democracy and increased trade ties to Russia). Only four countries are consistent with the hypothesis: Estonia, Latvia, and Lithuania in cell 3,1 and Belarus in cell 1,3. All the other cells are unexplained by the hypothesis. Note, that the table represents the change in the two variables between 1995 and 2003 therefore it does not include the period of the Orange Revolution in Ukraine in 2004 and Tulip Revolution in Kyrgyz Republic during 2005, where both will likely increase the level of democracy in both countries. While the Baltic States show very

Table 3.2 Democratic Change and Trade Ties between Russian and Former Soviet States

		Trade ties to Russia			
		Decreased	Same	Increased	Total
	Decreased	Armenia Kazakhstan Moldova Ukraine	Kyrgyzstan	Belarus	6
Democracy	Same	Turkmenistan Uzbekistan	Azerbaijan	–	3
	Increased	Estonia Latvia Lithuania	Tajikistan	Georgia	5
	Total	9	3	2	14

similar relation between the two variables, the Central Asian countries (Kazakhstan, Kyrgyzstan, Tajikistan, Turkmenistan, and Uzbekistan), often portrayed as having many common characteristics, show very different patterns. Overall, both qualitatively and quantitatively ($P = 0.856$) this table does not support Hypothesis 1. Moreover, cell 1,1 contains four countries (Armenia, Kazakhstan, Moldova, and Ukraine) they have hardly anything in common. These countries exhibit the same relation of the two variables: decrease of trade ties to Russia corresponds to the decrease in the country's democracy. The dissimilarity of these countries further suggests that there might not be a direct causality between the two variables of interest. Rather, both are affected by different omitted variables specific for each country. Based on Table 3.2 it appears that trade ties to Russia do not have a direct effect on the countries' extent of democratic development.

Table 3.3 represents a different approach to analysing the relationship between the two variables. We combined the data for different years for each country. This means each year becomes an instance of the connection between trade and press freedom, i.e. a case in the data set gives the trade and press freedom measures for Azerbaijan in 1995 and another case contains the measures for the same country in 1996 and so on. Medians of trade ties and press freedoms are then calculated over these country-years.

According to Hypothesis 1 we should expect most of the observations to fall within either cell 1,2 (trade ties above the median and freedom below the median) or cell 2,1 (trade ties below the median, freedom above the median). Table 3.3, however, shows no such relationship. In fact, having trade ties to Russia above

Table 3.3 Country–Year Analysis of Press Freedom and Trade Ties to Russia

		Trade ties to Russia		
		Below the median	Above the median	Total
Freedom	Below the median	33 54.1%	29 48.3%	62 51.2%
	Above the median	28 45.9%	31 51.7%	59 48.8%
	Total	61 100%	60 100%	121 100%

the median level, a country is more likely to have above median press freedoms. In contrast, countries with trade below the median are also likely to be below the median on press freedom. Thus, Table 3.3 does not support Hypothesis 1.

Table 3.4 represents the major political events and facts about each country that are of importance for our analysis. In the three binary variables 1 indicates presence of the variable on at least one occasion and 0 indicates absence. We hypothesize that less democratic countries are more likely to experience either of the political events

Table 3.4 Political Events in Post-Soviet Countries since the Declaration of Independence in the early 1990s until the Present

	Number of the heads of state	Violent succession	Civil war/ military conflict	Ethnic conflict
Armenia	2	0	1	1
Azerbaijan	3	1	1	1
Belarus	2	0	0	0
Estonia	2	0	0	0
Georgia	3	1	1	1
Kazakhstan	1	0	0	0
Kyrgyzstan	1	1	0	0
Latvia	2	0	0	0
Lithuania	3	0	0	0
Moldova	3	0	1	1
Tajikistan	1	0	1	0
Turkmenistan	1	0	0	0
Ukraine	3	0	0	0
Uzbekistan	1	0	0	0

described in the table and to have only one head of state since the declaration of independence in early 1990s.

We cross-tabulated each variable in Table 3.4 on the countries' trade ties to Russia in 2003, the most recent year for which there are complete data. Below we present these four tables.

Table 3.5 Analysis of Number of Heads of State and Trade Ties to Russia

		Trade ties to Russia		
		Below the median	Above the median	Total
Heads of state	One	2 28.6%	3 42.9%	5 35.7%
	More than one	5 71.4%	4 57.1%	9 64.3%
	Total	7 100%	7 100%	14 100%

Table 3.6 Analysis of Violent Successions and Trade Ties to Russia

		Trade ties to Russia		
		Below the median	Above the median	Total
Violent succession	Absent	5 71.4%	6 85.7%	11 78.6%
	Present	2 28.6%	1 14.3%	3 21.4%
	Total	7 100%	7 100%	14 100%

As we observe, none of these tables indicate a clear relationship between trade ties to Russia and the political events specified.

Lastly, we produced two multidimensional scaling scatter plots. In Figure 3.2 we used trade ties to Russia, trade openness of the country and its Press Freedom indicator, and in Figure 3.3 we used only trade openness of the country to the world market and its Press Freedom indicator (all the data used in MDS scatter plots are

Table 3.7 Analysis of Civil Wars/Military Conflicts and Trade Ties to Russia

		Trade ties to Russia		
		Below the median	Above the median	Total
Civil war/ military conflict	Absent	4 57.1%	5 71.4%	9 64.29%
	Present	3 42.9%	2 28.6%	5 35.7%
	Total	7 100%	7 100%	14 100%

Table 3.8 Analysis of the Ethnic Conflicts and Trade Ties to Russia

		Trade ties to Russia		
		Below the median	Above the median	Total
Ethnic conflict	Absent	4 57.1%	5 85.7%	10 71.4%
	Present	3 42.9%	1 14.3%	4 28.6%
	Total	7 100%	7 100%	14 100%

for 2003, except Turkmenistan that has the latest data for 2001). The dimensions in these plots are calculated to minimize 'lack of fit' among these variables. Essentially, they map patterns of similarity and difference among the countries and depict that in a two-dimensional graph.

The only noticeable change in the location of the observations is for Belarus. Not all other countries changed their location on the graph after the variable of trade ties to Russia was excluded. The interpretation of these two figures is that the net effect of trade ties to Russia concerning freedom of the media in all the post-Soviet countries, except Belarus, is minimal. Based on the results of our analysis, we did not find any support for the Hypothesis 1.

This leads us to our second hypothesis. First, we summarize the data for each country's trade openness and trade ties to Russia in Figure 3.4.

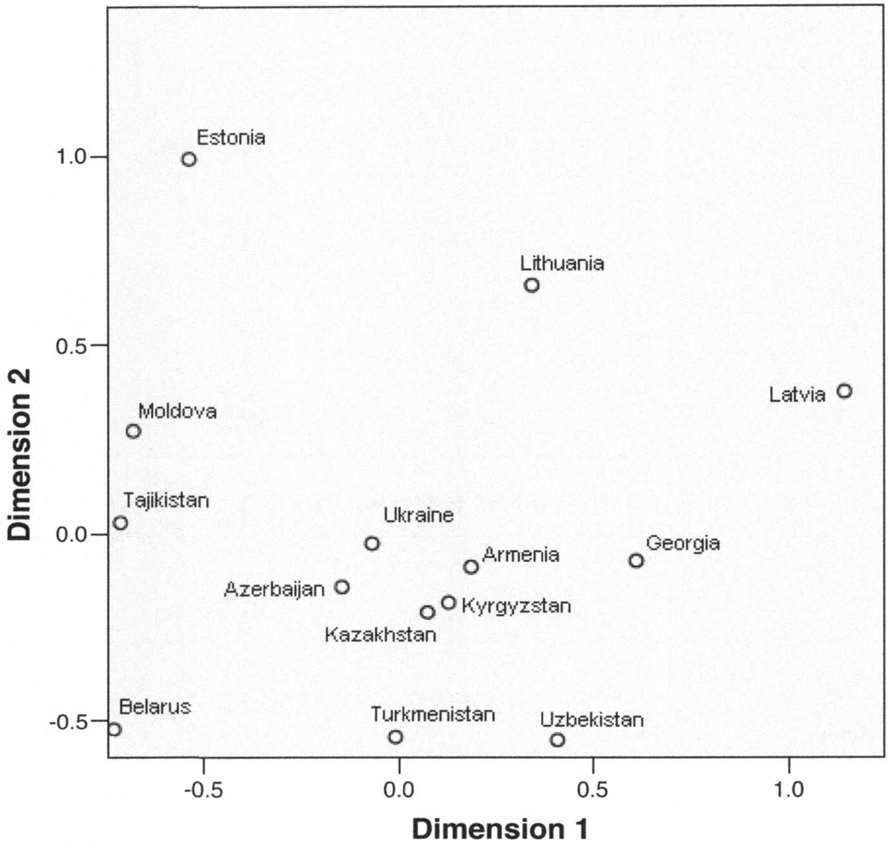

Figure 3.2 Trade Ties to Russia, Trade Openness and Press Freedom

The scatter plot offers a picture that is rather opposite to the assumption of Hypothesis 2. Based on this hypothesis we would expect the countries with stronger trade ties to Russia to have lower trade openness. Furthermore, over time with strengthening or weakening of the trade ties to Russia we would expect to see decreased or, conversely, increased trade openness. The observations for each country, however, do not offer such a picture. Finally, we have cross-tabulated the two variables (combined period from 1995 to 2003, above and below corresponding medians) that are presented in Table 3.9.

Based on Hypothesis 2 we would expect to see the majority of the observations split between the cell 1,2 (trade ties to Russia above the median, trade openness below the median) and the cell 2,1 (trade ties to Russia below the median, trade openness above the median). Table 3.9 shows us a picture opposite to the one we would expect based on Hypothesis 2. In fact, a country that has stronger trade ties to

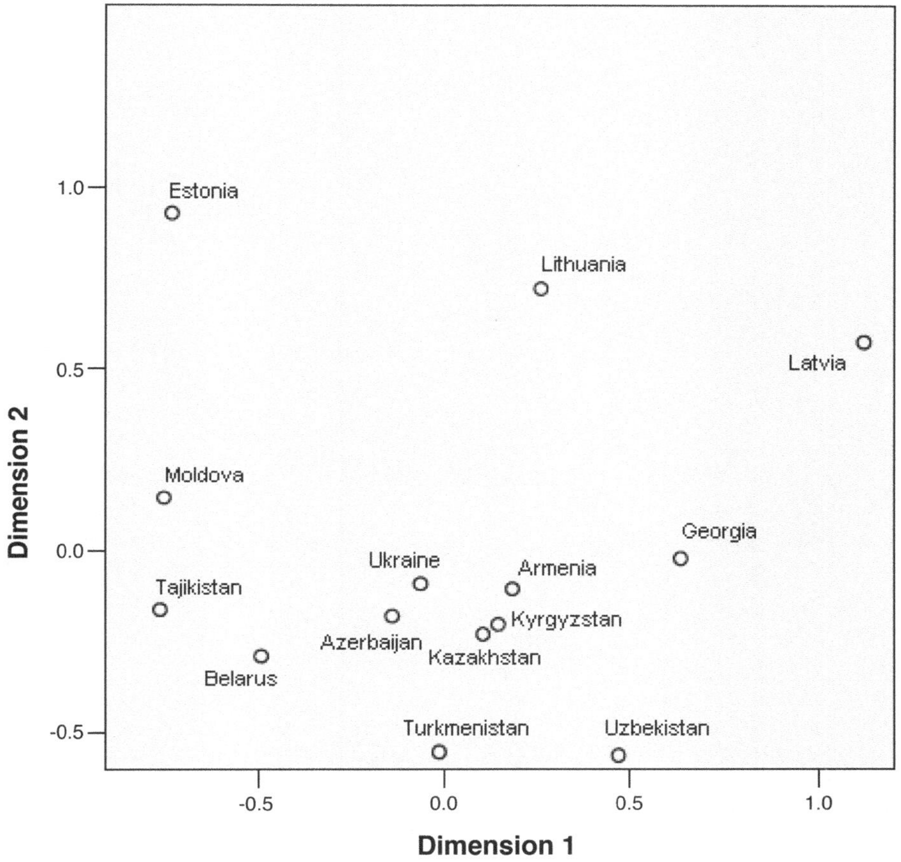

Figure 3.3 Trade Openness and Press Freedom

Russia is more likely to have higher trade openness. On the contrary, if a country has weaker trade ties to Russia, it is more likely to have lower trade openness. Based on the results of our analysis we did not find any support for Hypothesis 2.

Conclusion

The formal death of the Soviet empire was proclaimed on December 25, 1991 with the resignation of Mikhail Gorbachev and self-dissolution of the Supreme Soviet. Since then, both Kremlin watchers in the media and experts within the social sciences viewed many of Russia's economic and political maneuvers as attempts to maintain its imperial sphere of influence. In its attempt to regain its perceived lost importance and international prestige, Russia tried to use its economic ties to

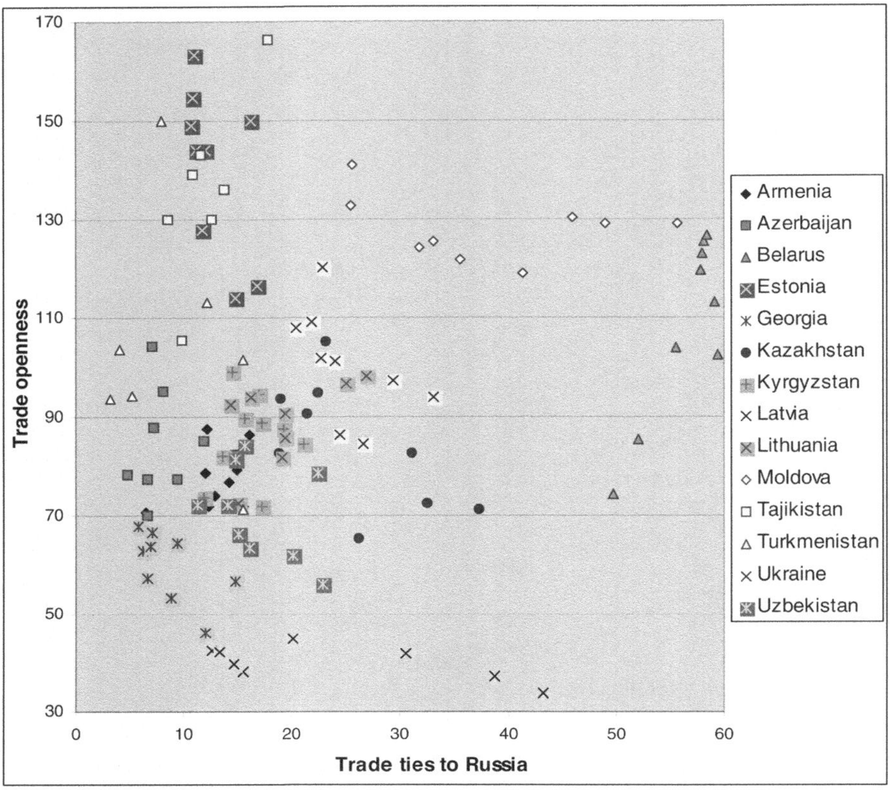

Figure 3.4 Trade Ties to Russia and Trade Openness of the Former Soviet States

Table 3.9 Country–Year Analysis of Trade Openness and Trade Ties to Russia

		Trade ties to Russia		
		Below the median	Above the median	Total
Trade openness	Below the median	47 74.6%	14 22.2%	61 48.4%
	Above the median	16 25.4%	49 77.8%	65 51.6%
	Total	63 100%	63 100%	126 100%

consolidate political power around Moscow. Such attempts, however, appear to have had limited success.

In our analysis, we have found no evidence of a connection between foreign trade and the extent of democratic development of the independent countries. A single exception is Belarus, where the amount of trade with Russia correlated to the freedom indexes. However, establishing causality in that case is problematic due to other variables that are not present in the analysis. It is likely that rather than being a result of strong economic dependence on Russia, a highly authoritarian state instead kept the trading relationship with Russia in place. A series of major political decisions by governments of some of the former Soviet states further undermined the ability of Russia to use trade to affect the political process. It was a bitter surprise and disappointment for the Russian government and many Russian politicians, when the government of Azerbaijan turned to Western countries and corporations for assistance in exploration of the Caspian Sea oil basin. Moscow also vigorously opposed the creation of a US military base in Uzbekistan at Karshi-Kanabad during the US–Afghan war without avail.

Although Central Asian countries have authoritarian governments with undemocratic political processes and few guarantees of individual or press freedoms and liberties, these governments are the products of social, political, and cultural features of the region. This is opposite from the general, globalizing nature of world trade. Despite increased trade openness and an increasing amount of cultural and political information, these countries have not been part of the wave of democratization. Because the data showed no correlation between the freedom indexes and trade ties, we conclude that trade with Russia does not have an evident effect on political development within Central Asia. The Rose Revolution in Georgia in 2003, Orange Revolution in Ukraine in 2004, and the most recent political events in Kyrgyz Republic further suggest that political processes in former Soviet countries is rooted within these countries and unlikely to be affected by trade or political ties to the Russian Federation.

The Russian government has offered oil and natural gas to its former republics at below market prices in an attempt to influence both political and economic policy. As a mechanism of political influence, however, import and export policy proved to be a crude instrument, at least as measured by press freedoms. While Russia achieved a few political victories – either through increasing export prices for oil and gas or introducing special tariffs on the imports from neighboring states – the process of opening of these economies to a freer international market gradually made the post-Soviet countries less dependent on Russia. This improved their economic situation in general. Stronger economic independence and introduction of the institutions for a market economy made the Baltic states more democratic, and created the potential for further democratic development in countries like Ukraine and Georgia. Closer ties between the European Union and post-Soviet states appear to be a matter of time. Although Moscow opposes this process, Russia thus far has not found sufficient economic or political leverage to affect this global process of integration.

References

Bugajski, J. (2004), *Cold Peace: Russia's New Imperialism*,Westport, CT: Praeger.

Bukkvoll, T. (2004), 'Private Interests, Public Policy: Ukraine and the Common Economic Space Agreement', *Problems of Post-Communism*, Vol. 51, No. 5, pp. 11–22.

Checkel, J. (1995), 'Structure, Institution, and Process: Russia's Changing Foreign Policy', in A. Dawisha and K. Dawisha (eds), *The Making of Foreign Policy in Russia and the New States of Eurasia* (pp. 42–65), Armonk, NY: M. E. Sharpe.

Chivers, C.J. (2004), 'Pro-West Leader Appears to Win Ukraine Election', *New York Times*, December 27, p. A1.

Chivers, C.J. (2004) 'Ukraine's Sharp Turn Toward the West', *New York Times*, December 9, p. A16.

Commercio, M.E. (2004), 'Exiles in the Near Abroad: The Russian Minorities in Latvia and Kyrgyzstan', *Problems of Post-Communism*, Vol. 51, No. 6, pp. 23–32.

Lo, B. (2003), 'The Securitization of Russian Foreign Policy under Putin', in G. Gorodetsky (ed.), *Russia Between East and West: Russian Foreign Policy on the Threshold of the Twenty-First Century* (pp. 12–27), London, UK: Frank Cass.

Lloyd, P.J. and D. MacLaren (2002), 'Measures of Trade Openness using CGE analysis', *Journal of Policy Modelling*, Vol. 24, pp. 67–81.

MacFarlane, N.S. (2003), 'Russian Policy in the CIS under Putin', in G. Gorodetsky (ed.), *Russia Between East and West: Russian Foreign Policy on the Threshold of the Twenty-First Century* (pp. 125–131), London, UK: Frank Cass.

Mihkelson, M. (2002), 'Russia's Policy Toward Ukraine, Belarus, Moldova, and the Baltic States', in J. Bugajski (ed.), *Toward an Understanding of Russia: New European Perspectives* (pp. 97–115), New York, NY: Council on Foreign Relations Press.

'Russia's Old Imperial Map is Still Shriveling', *Economist*, Vol. 343, Issue 8018, May 24, 1997, p. 47.

Simonia, N.A. (1995), 'Priorities of Russia's Foreign Policy and the Way It Works', in A. Dawisha and K. Dawisha (eds), *The Making of Foreign Policy in Russia and the New States of Eurasia* (pp. 17–41), Armonk, NY: M.E. Sharpe.

Smolansky, O.M. (1999), 'Fuel, Credit, and Trade: Ukraine's Economic Dependence on Russia', *Problems of Post-Communism*, Vol. 46, No. 2, pp. 49–58.

Strachota, K. (2002), 'Russian Policy in the Caucasus and Central Asia.' In J. Bugajski (ed.), *Toward an Understanding of Russia: New European Perspectives* (pp. 117–134), New York, NY: Council on Foreign Relations Press.

Other Sources

Central Statistical Bureau of Latvia, http://www.csb.lv

Freedom House (2004), Freedom of the Press 2004: A Global Survey of Media Independence (Oxford, UK: Rowman & Littlefield).
Freedom House. http://www.freedomhouse.org/research/pressurvey.htm
Internews Russia. http://www.internews.ru/report/tvrus/tv32.html
Russia in Figures 2004, Russian Federal State Statistics Service. Moscow: Goskomstat.
Russian Federal State Statistics Service. http://www.gks.ru
Statistical Office of Estonia. http://www.stat.ee
Statistics Lithuania. http://www.std.lt
World Development Indicators. World Bank. http://www.worldbank.org/data/onlinedatabases/onlinedatabases.html

Chapter 4

The Making of the Concept of the EU–Russia Common Economic Space

Evgeny Vinokurov

Introduction

The Concept of the EU–Russia Common Economic Space (CES[1]) was adopted on the EU–Russia Summit in Rome (November 5–6, 2003). It states that 'Russia and the EU are geographically close, have complementary economic structures and assets, and have strong mutual interest in further economic integration'. As the existing potential of economic cooperation is not fully used (Art. 8), there is a need to bring partners closer together on the way to economic integration. A significant spread between the high flight of politics and the day-to-day bottlenecks is observed now. It is argued (Hamilton, 2003) that there is a worrisome discrepancy between the discussions envisaging EU–Russia Common Spaces aiming at the deeper integration in the medium- and long-term term and difficult negotiations on such down-to-earth matters as the extension of Partnership and Cooperation Agreement (PCA), Kaliningrad cargo transit, or import quotas.

In the 2000s, Russia has found itself on the outskirts of the European integration. There is a growing danger that Russia will be further marginalized. Due to many economic, political and historical reasons, it is likely that the new member states would favor a tougher EU stand on Russia. Besides, the EU has already started re-coupling the economic issues of the EU–Russian dialogue with the political issues of democracy, human rights, and the war in Chechnya. Furthermore, Russia's strive to preserve its influence in the CIS states and build on the CIS economic and political integration may lead to the potential clash with the EU on the issue of the compatibility of the Russian EU and CIS integration.

1 There is a good deal of terminological confusion. The initially launched idea was that of the Common European Economic Space. The same term has been used in the title of the Concept. However, in the meantime the term 'Common Economic Space' (CES) asserts itself in the official discourse. The CES should refer to the contents of the Saint-Petersburg declaration plus related issues, most importantly energy. We use this term consistently throughout the chapter. It is not to be confused with the Single Economic Space of Belarus, Kazakhstan, Russia, and Ukraine launched in 2003.

Against this background, the CES Concept represents a major piece of official conceptual thinking, which aims at bringing the Union and Russia closer together on the economic side, with various linkages to other fields of cooperation. The analysis of the Concept itself and of the way it evolved may be instrumental for our understanding of the nature and prospects of the Russia-EU relations. Furthermore, there are important issues linked to the conceptual framework of the EU–Russia Common Economic Space that are crucial for the eventual success. The definition of the CES is provided in the text of the Concept Paper:

> the CES means an open and integrated market between the EU and Russia, based on the implementation of common or compatible rules and regulations, including compatible administrative practices, as a basis for synergies and economies of scale associated with a higher degree of competition in bigger markets. It shall ultimately cover substantially all sectors of economy (CES Concept, Art. 12).

The task of the Concept was to create an appropriate model for this project of EU–Russian economic integration. This model should combine the issues of potential economic efficiency with existing political possibilities and constraints on both sides. The basic choice is between horizontal and vertical approaches. Under the horizontal approach, the sides choose to integrate 'across-the-board' incorporating the principle of the four freedoms enshrined in the Single Market. As the movement of labor has never been an issue in EU–Russian relations, three freedoms remain. First, free movement of goods and services, second, free movement of capital, and, third, free movement of persons. Meanwhile, the vertical approach would mean the decision to draft a number of sector-specific agreements. We analyse the approach incorporated in the CES Concept and argue that the Concept contains an original model that combines horizontal and vertical approaches.

Furthermore, another issue needs to be resolved on the conceptual level. The experiences of both the European Economic Area and the EU–Swiss agreements have shown that economic integration with the EU could cause a severe policy-taker problem on the opposite side. The EU insists that the free access to the Single market should be coupled with the corresponding obligations so as not to create unfair advantages for the non-EU producers. Under the existing agreements, the EU counterparts are obliged to follow changes in the EU *acquis* to a certain extent, adopting new directives in their own legislation as they come up. If it will be the case also with the CES, Russia will be exposed to the policy-taker problem, that is, it will have to follow the developments of the EU legislation. In the chapter, we analyse the CES Concept from this point of view as well.

This chapter concentrates on the Russian approaches to the economic integration with the EU. The chapter has the following outline. It starts with the description of the process leading to the CES Concept, delineating its phases, main activities, and the working mode. It illustrates an essentially top-down nature of the process on the Russian side, with the dominant role of the role of the governmental bureaucracies. It goes on to assess the impact that several economic studies have made on the negotiations on the Russian side and the final content of the Concept. The conclusion is drawn that this impact was limited. It is argued further that the Concept of the CES represents an original model in itself, combining the elements of the European Economic Area (EEA) and Swiss models; that is, it unites both horizontal and sectoral approaches. On this basis, drawing on the experience of the EEA and EU-Swiss agreements, we go on to discuss the potential policy-taker problem that may arise for Russia.

Phases of the Development of the CES

We start with delineating the major steps and phases of the negotiations leading to the CES Concept Paper and beyond. The *phase 1* started during the EU–Russia Summit in May 2001 when Romano Prodi threw in the idea of a Common European Economic Space in discussions with Vladimir Putin. The latter responded positively, indicating Russia's interest in closer economic cooperation. A High-Level Group (HLG) was created under an appropriate mandate at the *phase 2*. It took a year to set up an HLG to lead the work on the concept. During the Summit in October 2001, the parties agreed to establish a joint HLG to elaborate the Concept. The designated co-chairs were Russian Deputy Prime Minister Khristenko and Commissioner Chris Patten. In March 2002, the Cooperation Council of the Partnership and Cooperation Agreement provided the HLG with a mandate to elaborate the CES Concept. In the *phase 3*, the sides negotiated the concept. The deadline set by the mandate was October 2003, that is, in one and a half years, or three summits away. In fact, the first Khristenko-Patten meeting already took place in the second half of 2001. At its second meeting in March 2002, the HLG adopted a work plan for the next 18 months. To fulfill the task of assessing the potential impact of a CES, a number of economic assessment studies were commissioned separately by Russia and the EU. The negotiations have resulted in the CES Concept, which was agreed upon by the parties as Annex I 'The Common European Economic Space (CEES) Concept Paper' (CES Concept, 2003) to the Joint Statement of the 12th EU–Russia Summit in Rome on the November 5–6, 2003 ('Joint Statement' 2003).

The current phase (*phase 4*) is an intermediary, however an important one. As Russia's WTO accession is widely perceived to be a prerequisite for the CES talks to continue, waiting for the WTO accession is one of the reasons why the CES Concept was knowingly formulated rather broadly. Besides, it was also the reason for mentioning the term free trade so as not to create additional difficulties in Russia's negotiations with non-EU members of the WTO. In principle, the CES development process goes along three tracks. Art.19 names (1) market opening, (2) regulatory convergence, and (3) trade facilitation. The work on the concrete contents along the first track of market opening depends directly on Russia's membership in the WTO. Many of the issues of trade facilitation are also linked to the adoption of the WTO regulations (e.g. customs and customs procedures). However, the work on the regulatory convergence and infrastructure may be continued in the absence of Russia's WTO membership.

In the future, it is possible to foresee *phase 5*, with a new mandate for a new HLG to operationalize the Common economic space. Russia's WTO accession is a likely requirement for this work to begin.

In late April 2004, the European Commission submitted to its Russian counterparts a proposal for an Action Plan. Based along the lines of the Concept, this document aims at specifying more concrete objectives and measures to achieve them. The proposal concerns not only the CES but also all the four Common Spaces. In this way, the Commission tries to couple the Spaces together, linking, for example, the progress on the market opening with the progress on the visa-free regime. There are two reasons for adopting this approach. First, it goes along the lines of the Commission's Communication on relations with Russia underlying that the EU–Russia partnership must be based on shared values and common interests (EU Commission, 2004). It thus couples an economic cooperation with the issues of human rights, democratic rule, and the war in Chechnya. Second, the Commission wants to see a coherent approach so as not to create a considerable discontinuity of advancements in economic and JHA matters that are linked to each other. Russia disagrees with the approach and insists on de-coupling these and other issues. Thus, Russia insists on having four separate roadmaps (a separate one for each Space) instead of an overarching Action Plan. Separate roadmaps should serve the purpose of de-coupling various issues. Technically, the Commission does not mind four separate roadmaps but would like to advance the coherency.

The EU–Russian negotiations, based on the CES Concept and the Commission's proposal for an Action Plan, led to the four Road Maps, which were agreed on by the sides during the May 2005 Summit in Moscow. The Road Map for the Common Economic Space is the longest one, comprising 19 pages out of 52 in total. It reiterates the Concept in the preamble in stating that the goal of the CES is to create an 'open and integrated market between the EU and Russia' (Road Map 2005, 1). Further, it proceeds with the standard EU accession agenda, including regulatory convergence in various sectors (telecom, financial services, automotives, medical devices, textiles, and pharmaceuticals), public procurement, intellectual and industrial property rights, trade facilitation and customs, etc. Telecommunication and transport networks are covered in a separate sub-section stating the objective of the creation of the EU–Russian information society area. Separate sub-sections are devoted also to the cooperation on space, environment, and energy within the Energy Dialogue. Free trade is not mentioned a single time: the overall framing and the context imply that a free trade area is not on the agenda. The words dominating the document are 'dialogue', 'cooperation', 'harmonization', and 'convergence'. While the former two are vague and often used to cover the emptiness of contents, the latter two terms evade mentioning the vector of convergence, that is, the question on who ought to converge on whom. Meanwhile, it might represent the major problem of the eventual EU–Russian regulatory integration. The vagueness and ambiguity of the Road Map let Emerson characterize the current state of affairs as the 'proliferation of the fuzzy' (2005, 1). In fact, a standard road map provides not only the objectives and actions but also time schedules to realize them. The latter element is completely lacking in the Road Map as well as in the other three Road Maps forming the package of the 15th Summit.

The CES is perceived as a central element in the EU–Russian integration. In other words, there is a widely shared implicit as well as explicit understanding that the CES is the central one out of four envisaged Common Spaces. Other Common Spaces envisaged in the Joint Statement of the 12th EU–Russia Summit in November 2003 are the common space of freedom, security and justice; the common space of external security; and the common space of research and education. The economic space is the only one for which a separate Concept exists. Despite the fact that processes and negotiations run on their separate tracks, other spaces are connected to the economic issues raised in the CES and would benefit from the advances in the economic sphere. For example, the Common Space of freedom, security and justice would directly benefit from any advances made on the related aspects of movement of people (Art.18 of the CES Concept). The issue of the free movement of persons, naturally falling within the scope of the JHA common space, has been prioritized in 2003–2004. However, even this issue is closely linked to the successfully facilitated economic cooperation. The external security represents an exception, as there are no direct links between the CES and the external security matters.

Although the idea of a Common Economic Space came out as a surprise in the EU–Russia Summit in May 2001, similar ideas were envisaged in the Partnership and Cooperation Agreement (PCA). The PCA's Art.1 lists among the main objectives the creation of the necessary conditions for the future establishment of an FTA covering substantially all trade in goods as well as for the freedom of establishment of companies, cross-border movement of services and of capital movements. The idea of a free trade zone has come up in the EU Common Strategy towards Russia in 1999 as well. In fact, the Concept of the CES reiterates the basic idea of the free movement of goods, services, capital and persons, with the labor being excluded from the list. Is the CES an 'old wine in a new bottle'? On the one hand, the answer is yes, because the Concept follows the ideas worded by the ten-year old PCA. On the other hand, the CES Concept goes an important step forward conceptualizing the way towards achievement of these objectives, with Russia's WTO membership being now in sight.

One reason why it took a year to issue an appropriate mandate for negotiators to begin their work is that the conceptual framework of the CES was unclear. There were no concrete and rigid initial positions or conceptions of a desirable outcome. Not only the potential concrete contents remained unknown, but also the general contours of the to-be-created Concept remained vague. The common shared understanding was severely limited to a simple but vague idea that the CES should represent an FTA *plus*. In addition, there was a perception that it should represent a WTO+ in two senses, first, being deeper than the WTO, and, second, taking place after Russia's WTO accession. Another reason for a leisurely procedure was the lack of urgency due to the distant perspectives of Russia's WTO accession.

Generally, the work on the Concept was organized in the view of the regular EU–Russia summits as well as Khristenko-Patten meetings, which also took place on a semi-annual basis. Negotiations and talks proceeded from summit to summit and from HLG to HLG meetings resolving difficulties and gaining new momentum at these points. In fact, the process has proceeded in semi-annual intervals from the very beginning: while the idea was made public at the Summit in March 2001, the decision to create the HLG was made in October 2001, and its mandate was issued in March 2002. Besides, the mandate for the HLG was set for one and a half years of work. Although it is common for such deadlines to be broken, it nevertheless served as a reference point for the negotiators in their attempts to produce a finished paper.

These peculiarities of the work organization led to two important consequences. Firstly, the negotiators structured their work schedules and proceedings in order to fit into the schedule of the regular meetings at a higher level. Secondly, and more importantly, due to regular semi-annual Khristenko-Patten meetings the negotiations were able to surpass and to move from the deadlocks. The HLG has helped to overcome serious problems, which otherwise might have lead to blocking the negotiations in their totality. It is likely that without such regular meetings of the higher government officials (such as both Patten and Khristenko were at the time) the negotiators would have lacked the 'level' necessary to reconcile their positions.

The elaboration of the Concept and the respective negotiations were structured on several levels with various goals and competences. First, at the top, there were semi-annual Khristenko-Patten meetings. Second, Expert groups on either side mastered the day-to-day work. Third, in addition, the CES-related questions were occasionally discussed during the meetings of the EU Trade Commissioner, Pascal Lamy, and Russia's Minister for economic development and trade, German Gref. It was intended to lend the high-level support to the mainstream process within the HLG.

The main bulk of work – that is, developing the positions of the parties, elaborating the concept and reconciling the final text – was done by expert groups on both sides. While on the EU side these were the European Commission officials, Russia's Expert group was composed of the governmental officials of both the Ministry of Economic Development and Trade (MEDT) and the Ministry of Foreign Affairs (MFA). It is peculiar to the internal composition of the Russian group that the representatives of the MEDT and not MFA dominated it. The majority of the members of the group) belonged to the MEDT, with Deputy Minister Maxim Medvedkov (who is also the main Russian negotiator at the WTO accession talks) and the Head of the Trade Policy Department Elena Danilova leading the work. Moreover, the MEDT officials assumed a pro-active position on the contents of the Concept, whereas the MFA officials, most notably the Russian Mission to the EU, however important to the elaboration of the text, rendered more technical and formal support.

Impact of Economic Studies and Assessments[2]

It is a common rule in the business of negotiating a trade agreement that the parties conduct or commission to an external institution one or more economic assessments, which should provide them with a clearer view on the benefits and drawbacks of a potential agreement. The negotiations on the CES Concept were not an exception to the rule, as both parties commissioned several economic studies. The CES Concept states that

> economic impact assessment studies, conducted separately by the Parties, clearly demonstrated the positive benefits of CES, and, at the same time, highlighted shortcomings in certain areas, which should be addressed in the future work on the CES (Art. 8).

We will go deeper into details and answer the question of what impact the conducted economic assessment studies have had on the Russian position.

Several economic studies were made. First, the MEDT organized a large number of expert working groups on various sectors and issues, such as customs, standards, automotive industry, banking, telecommunications, insurance, etc. The task assigned to experts was to estimate the consequences of a deeper economic integration with the EU in prospective sectors. The leading institutes of the Russian Academy of Sciences served as a core source of experts. Second, the European Commission commissioned an economic assessment study to the Centre for European Policy Studies (CEPS) in Brussels (Brenton, 2002). Third, the White Book 'Common Economic Space: Prospects of Russia–EU Relations' was published by the Russian–European Centre for Economic Policy (RECEP) in Moscow. The EU within the TACIS framework funded RECEP's activities. Both EU and Russian experts took part in working on the White Book (Samson and Greffe, 2002). Lastly, the Russian Union of Industrialists and Entrepreneurs (RUIE) has prepared and provided the MEDT with a compilation of useful materials relating to the CEES matters.

The most comprehensive economic studies were conducted by CEPS and RECEP. They can be summarized as follows. The CEPS study focuses on the potential effects of a free trade agreement (FTA). The principal conclusions are that the economic impact of a Russia–EU FTA, which is both broad, in terms of sector coverage, and deep, in terms of addressing regulatory constraints upon trade, will be largly relative to an agreement that is limited to the removal of tariff restrictions on trade in goods. A broad and deep FTA could have a profound effect on the level of income and the rate of growth in Russia through increasing flows of trade, investment and technology, via improvements in the efficiency of services and by providing a foundation for the locking in and intensification of market reforms. A limited free trade agreement might increase economic welfare in Russia by about 0.1 percent, whereas a comprehensive FTA could raise real incomes by more than

---

2 The contents of this section are built on a set of interviews with the Russian officials and experts who took part in the negotiations on the CES concept. The interviews were conducted in February–March 2004.

13 percent. In the latter case, Russian exports to the EU would increase by over 100 percent and could rise by a factor of more than three. Despite large changes in trade flows, changes in production are expected to be relatively small; hence, the economic adjustment to an FTA will be slight. However, these substantial economic impacts in Russia will only arise if the agreement enables Russia to successfully lock-in economic reforms (Brenton, 2002).

Macroeconomic modeling by the authors of the RECEP White Book led them to the conclusion that a strong potential for trade through the CES exists. Gravity measurements showed that mutual trade between the EU and Russia could be multiplied by several times. Realization of this potential would not be detrimental to trade between Russia and other CIS countries. The White Book argues further that institutional adjustments are necessary for the Russian economy to be competitive and sustainable, irrespective of the type of integration. Better adjustment between capital, investment, and better implementation of property rights are of major importance for the Russian economy. The CES must be viewed as a way to support such a process. The study shows that convergence towards market-friendly institutions, which exist in the EU, could alone produce an 80 percent increase in trade between Russia and the EU (Samson and Greffe, 2002).

RECEP's econometric explorations correlate to the conclusions made by CEPS working group: the best concept for the CES is one that combines effects of trade liberalization with productivity effects of internal adjustment due to strong FDI flows. The economic efficiency of such a CES for Russia is manifest, since it will lead to the highest GDP increase, strong expansion of imports and exports, a higher share of manufactured goods in exports, and improved welfare in Russia.

Conditionality of economic success and the concentration on the long-term implications coincides with the world experience of regional integration agreements (RIAs). As such, RIAs are examples of the second best, the impact of which on economic welfare is ambiguous. Despite an enormous theoretical, empirical and historical-descriptive literature, no consensus on the desirability of RIAs has emerged (Schiff and Winters, 1997). Given the ambiguity of the static welfare impact of RIAs and their generally small estimated size, many commentators have appealed to dynamic effects such as those on FDI, economies of scale, and convergence to justify them. This is also the case with the economic studies made of the CES. Both CEPS and RECEP studies appeal to dynamic effects, with the static ones being small or even negligible. One of the problems of the practical usage of the CEPS study is that it was conducted on a very high level of aggregation, which does not allow observing implications for specific sectors. The RECEP study went deeper into the structure, incorporating specific studies on the gas, automobile, and aluminium industries as well as financial services and banking.

In 2002, in the initial stage of working under the HLG mandate, the MEDT organized a number of expert groups on various sectors and issues. The list of sectors and industries included agriculture, automotive industry, banking, insurance, space launching, and telecommunications. The list of related issues included, among others, customs regulations and procedures, standards, public procurement, technical regulation and conformity assessment. Thus, the industries and issues that are the most sensitive to a prospective Russia–EU economic integration were chosen for an expert analysis. The expert groups were composed of academics from the leading institutes of the Russian Academy of Sciences. Neither ministry officials nor representatives of the Russian business community were included in these groups (unless indirectly involved through academic circles). In view of the initial task, which was to estimate the consequences of deeper economic integration with the EU in prospective sectors, the working groups concluded that they bore much similarity. While in the short-term a certain degree of negative impact is feasible in many industries and sectors of the Russian economy, the consequences in the medium term are likely to be positive in many sectors. In the long term, the impact would be positive on virtually all issues and in all industries that were assessed by the expert groups.

Interviews done by the author with the Russian officials and experts who took part in the negotiations on the CES Concept and the analysis of the Concept itself lead to the conclusion that the impact of the economic assessments on the negotiations and the Concept's final text varied from one study to another and was in many cases rather limited. On the Russian side, the conclusions drawn by the expert groups under the aegis of the MEDT have won the most attention. The principal conclusion that a CES would be beneficial for the Russian economy was taken on board. The results of the general equilibrium trade modeling as well as the gravity modeling carried out by CEPS and commissioned by the EU counterpart have also influenced the decision-making on the Russian side. As the Commission in drafting the Concept and in discussing the Concept used the findings, the Russian experts received the message, which seemed not to contradict their own findings. Meanwhile, RECEP's White Book was not given much weight on the Russian side. It was perceived as a confirmation of the assessments done by the MEDT's expert groups. A somewhat critical attitude towards RECEP as the working body financed by the European Union seems to have contributed to the insignificant impact of this major work. To complete the picture, the compilation prepared by the RUIE was read and perceived as a useful supplementary material.

Overall, the economic assessment studies rendered some influence on the Russian position and on the final text of the Concept. It can be observed, for example, in the attention that the Concept devotes to such instruments as regulatory convergence and trade facilitation, which are introduced on equal terms with market opening (Art. 19). Increased cooperation in the upgrading and enhancement of infrastructure networks is also seen as crucial to the establishment of the framework conditions for increased economic cooperation (Art. 20).

A conclusion can be drawn that the more theoretic the studies were the less impact they rendered. One of the reasons can be that the negotiators were constrained in several respects. They had to comply with other objectives of Russia's multi-vectored economic foreign policy, most notably with its CIS vector. Besides, they acted under the constraints of governmental politics. Another probable explanation is that the theory runs a few steps ahead whereas the negotiators had to tackle on-the-ground problems. Henceforth, the practitioners were inclined to let the conceptual framework to evolve systematically. Nevertheless, the inherent task of the Concept was to create a framework for further practical contents, leaving elaboration of details for future work. Due to its very nature, the CES Concept was supposed to envision the idea and to foresee the deepening and widening of the EU–Russian economic cooperation for a long time to come.

Top-down Approach, the Role of Bureaucracies and the Russian Business Community

When analysing Russian foreign policy, it is important to account for a major formal and informal role of the President in the hierarchic governmental structure. From the viewpoint of the bureaucratic politics model, even in the system of decision-making dominated by one person, he/she does not make decisions alone, but collectively, surrounded by other high-level actors, aides, and consultants. The individuals and organizations, who act as agents, are active participants of the process. Thus, they are also ' players' who do not just represent a mechanical device but affect the outcome in a variety of ways (Allison and Zelikow, 1999).

So far, the CES process has been based on a strong top-down approach with the dominant role played by the governmental bureaucracies. It was initiated from the very top during the EU–Russia Summit in May 2001. Further, the Concept was written and negotiated exclusively by the governmental officials (of MEDT and MFA) with almost no participation of the business community and with limited interest from the public. The only economic field of the Russia–EU cooperation where the bottom-up approach has been quite strong is the energy dialogue, where big business players have been able and willing to exert influence at the level of decision-making in the presidential administration and in the government. The Energy dialogue is, however, excluded from the CES at present, although Art. 17 of the Concept declare an intention to integrate its results into the CES in due course.

The survey made by *Eurochambres* in co-operation with the Russian Chamber of Commerce reveals that the CES has not been on the agenda of the Russian business community (*Eurochambres*, the Russian Chamber of Commerce, 2003). Their counterparts in the EU have acknowledged that they had some idea about the concept of CES and the on-going discussions. The general reaction has been supportive of the idea and optimistic about the impact this initiative could have on the potential lowering of the barriers to trade between the EU and Russia. The EU business representatives cited such benefits as general improvement of the economic relations between the EU and Russia, convergence in the regulatory areas, removal of non-tariff barriers to trade, and faster economic development in Russia. Harmonized and simplified customs procedures as well as more transparent and less bureaucratic administration are mentioned among the specific benefits by the EU business representatives. The security of supply of natural resources and enhanced possibilities for investment in Russia were also mentioned as potential benefits of the CES. Some respondents underlined that the idea was still vague and highly political, therefore significant progress was required to turn the idea into a workable action plan. At the same time, the Russian respondents were almost unanimous in stating that they had no information on the initiative from either side in the EU–Russia dialogue. Among those who did provide comments some businesspersons believed that the CES concept could become feasible only after Russia's accession to WTO. An opinion was also expressed that the CES would result in an even stronger shock than the WTO accession (*Eurochambres*, the Russian Chamber of Commerce, 2003).

The lobbying activities of the Russian business community are concentrated on the WTO negotiations. Russia's large businesses have been lobbying hard not only to keep higher levels of tariff protection but also to retain regulatory restrictions for foreign presence in the financial services. In the bilateral relations with the EU, most attention has been devoted to the specific down-to-earth issues such as the EU import quotas on steel, chemical products, and alike. By contrast, the CES negotiations did not attract as much attention from the Russian business community. A skeptic position of larger companies in metallurgy and chemicals channeled through the Union of Industrialists and Entrepreneurs was the only known major case of involvement. Their position is consistent with pressures that these sectors put in the framework of the WTO accession.

There might be two explanations for the non-involvement of the Russian business community. Firstly, the businesses did not assign significant importance to the negotiations on the CES Concept because of its conceptual and preliminary character. Secondly, the CES development remained an internal governmental affair. The public discussion on the issue was very modest, and the business community remained largely uninformed. This situation is worrisome. The CES discourse on the Russian side seems to run detached from the grass-root level of firms and households. As an essentially governmental undertaking, the CES might find itself in the situation of an insufficient support or even of a persistent opposition from the business side at the time of discussing the concrete contents of the CES.

Model for the CES and the Policy-taker Problem

The Concept states that the CES means 'an open and integrated market' which 'shall ultimately cover substantially all sectors of economy' (Art. 12). The CES is understood as an objective rather than a process. In other words, integration is seen as a certain degree of movement along the three freedoms (movement of goods and services, of capital, and of people); however, the degree of integration is ambiguously defined. The list of individual priority sectors and the degree of the possible depth of the integration within them are also left open-ended. In fact, the term 'free trade' does come up in the Concept explicitly. However, there is an implicit understanding that the CES would not – in the foreseeable future and in the current framework – move further than an FTA supplemented by a deeper degree of integration in individual sectors. The Russian President confirmed this view in one of his speeches shortly after the CES Concept was agreed upon in Rome. In his words:

> we consider the main guideline is to create a zone of free trade with increased cooperation in individual priority sectors. This primarily concerns energy and transport, science and education, ecology and telecommunications (Putin, 2003).

At the present time, there are two cases of deep and comprehensive integration agreements of the EU with non-EU states, the EEA and Switzerland. Vahl mentions that the EEA and the Swiss agreements represent two conceptually different approaches towards the goal of ensuring access to the EU market for companies and their products across a wide range of sectors, i.e. their inclusion in the Single Market (Vahl, 2004). The EEA is based on a comprehensive horizontal approach incorporating the principle of the four freedoms enshrined in the Single Market, whereas the EU-Swiss arrangement is in fact a bundle of sector-specific agreements. These alternative approaches have also been considered at the CES. According to Vahl (2004, 17):

> whereas the EU initially preferred a 'horizontal' approach focusing on harmonization 'across-the-board'. Russia favored a 'sectoral' (or 'Swiss') approach, with sector-by-sector harmonization depending on the different effects of liberalization on competitiveness in specific sectors.

The CES is expected to cover both horizontal and sectoral targets. A number of areas have been considered for prioritized action: standardization, technical regulation and conformity assessment, customs, audit and accounting, public procurement, competition, financial services, telecommunications, cooperation in space launching, and other sectors/issues (Art. 15). Thus, the CES Concept effectively employs a combined approach uniting both the horizontal base (with the reference to the overarching freedoms) and sectoral issues. The horizontal approach lays the foundation for the Concept, although it is defined broadly and restricted to the relevant fields of economic activity. It is incorporated in the Concept in a specific broad way. Art.18 of the Concept suggests that the CES should focus on four main areas of economic activity: first, cross-border trade of goods; second, cross-border trade of services; third, establishment and operation of companies (including issues related to movement of capital); and, fourth, related aspect of movement of persons. The horizontal approach is combined with the sectoral one, as the Concept assigns priority to an open list of individual sectors and issues. Thus, the Concept of CES represents an original model in itself, combining the elements of the EEA and Swiss approaches.

Russia does not intend to apply for the EU membership, even in a long-term perspective. If Russia's foreign policy is to be conducted in compliance with this objective, it becomes a necessity to create such a model of EU–Russian relations that would allow for an economic integration of the European Union with Russia as a non-member. While Russia is willing to adjust its legislation according to its pragmatic commercial interests (Mau and Novikov, 2002), it will try to avoid the situation of being dictated to from Brussels. There are several reasons for that, among which are both the subjective national pride and the objective presence of the vital interests in the Pacific and in Central Asia. The key term in this discussion is ' the policy-taker problem'. As such, it was encountered by both Switzerland and the non-EU members of the European Economic Area (EEA), most notably the latter ones. Meanwhile, it has become a serious issue for Switzerland, too.

The question arises whether the model envisaged in the CES Concept can help avoid the policy-taker problem on the Russian side. The authors of the White Book on EU–Russia Common Spaces argue that the CES would be better defined as a co-development path,

> something much more sophisticated than a traditional free-trade area, although the latter dimension is very important, and it is something radically new, which cannot be reduced to a customs union or recognition of the EU *acquits communitarian* (Samson and Greffe 2002, p. 17).

The co-development path can however take various conceptual forms. Besides, it depends on both partners in the process; in other words, there are certain limits, guidelines, and reference points set both by the Russia and the EU.

The EEA implies a comprehensive adoption of the EU *acquits* in exchange for good market access and the right to participate in the EU decision shaping up to a certain extent. At the same time, it makes the non-EU members of the EEA follow changes in the EU *acquits*, adopting new directives in their own legislation as they come up ('backlog implementation'). Thus, Norway and EEA members are exposed to the policy-taker problem: they are obliged to follow the changes in the EU legislation while possessing only limited leverage on the EU's internal affairs.

The sect oral model employed in EU-Swiss agreements after Switzerland left the EEA in 1992 aspires to allow to choose those areas and *acquits* chapters which the state is willing to adapt while leaving aside those that it does not want to take on board ('cherry-picking'). The EU, however, has not been willing to let the non-EU countries enjoy the advantages of such partial integration into the Internal Market without taking the costs of other chapters. This led to the specific arrangements of the EU–Swiss agreements. Emerson, Val, and Woodcock (2002), comparing the various options, EEA and the EU–Swiss agreements in particular, came the conclusion that the latter provides for no substantially better regime with regard to the policy-taker dilemma. On the contrary, while exposing Switzerland to much of the EU internal legislation, this model provides substantially less access to decision shaping. For example, the EU–Swiss model has a high degree of harmonization required before mutual recognition; besides, it potentially exposes Switzerland to the EU competition policy. On the other hand, while Norway and other EEA states can participate in the Commission working groups and expert groups, Switzerland has no access to the EU internal decision shaping except via some multi-level channels. The short answer to the question whether the type of arrangement as with the Swiss model can provide a sufficient degree of market access while retaining more policy autonomy appears to be negative (Emerson, Val, and Woodcock, 2002). The EU market access for Swiss producers is guaranteed only when Switzerland adopts the EU *acquits*. Mutual recognition only applies in the so-called harmonized sectors in which Switzerland has fully adopted the EU regulations.

Mau and Novice (2002) argue that Norway (that is, the EEA option) may serve as the model for Russia in its relations with the EU, albeit with qualifications. At the same time, Mau and Novice go through the chapters of the EU *acquits* trying to figure out which chapters could be beneficial for Russia (and therefore shall be adopted) and what chapters could be detrimental to the Russian economy and therefore shall not become subject of the EU–Russian integration. This approach is questionable. First, as said above, the EEA model would expose the country to the policy-taker problem. The latest internal political developments in Norway show growing dissatisfaction with the EEA and growing support for the EU membership. It indicates that the policy-taker problem might become a trap forcing Norway to become an EU member to be able to exert some influence of the Union's policy-making and, thus, to avoid policy-making being a one-way street. Russia would want to avoid that, unless there is an intention to move Russia gradually and imperceptibly in the direction of the EU membership. Second, the divisibility of the Internal Market *acquits* may be questioned. To what extent can the Internal Market *acquits* be 'sliced up' and to what extent can the horizontal approach be eroded by the exclusion of certain areas? The experience of both the EEA and the EU–Swiss agreements shows that this is hardly possible. The EU pursues the policy of linking the advantages of the access to the Internal Market to the relevant costs. For example, the EU would demand the adoption of the environmental directives so as not to allow for unjust advantages for non-EU producers. Therefore, Russia would be pressed by the EU to balance advantageous and disadvantageous chapters.

In view of this discussion, it is worth mentioning that the EU–Chile trade agreement rather than the EEA or the EU–Swiss bundle of sect oral agreements served as an informal technical reference point (not as a model, though) for the CES Concept negotiators. It took ten years for Chile and the EU to negotiate this very comprehensive trade agreement. The negotiators in the CES case shared the perception that a prospective EU–Russia CES agreement should be more compact.

This informal reference to the EU–Chile agreement is interesting because Chile in fact manages to cooperate successfully with both the EU and NAFTA at the same time. This is close to what Russia wants, that is, to be able to pursue independent policies on the post-Soviet space and in the Pacific region. In fact, the EU–Chile Association Agreement contains not only a comprehensive FTA for goods that goes far beyond the respective WTO commitments but also goes far in the direction of free trade in services and free movement of capital. Besides, it contains elements of cooperation on customs procedures, sanitary and phytosanitary issues, standards, technical regulations, and conformity assessment as well as intellectual property rights. There are a number of priority sectors, such as wines and spirits for which a separate agreement is included. The agreement guarantees a non-discriminatory access to telecommunication networks. It also opens up the public procurement markets. Thus, in some respects it goes beyond the envisaged scope of the CES. At the same time, the EU-Chile relationship does not imply a direct implementation of the EU directives in the national legislation to sustain the conformity with the European *acquis*.

So, could the EU–Chile Association Agreement serve as a model for the EU–Russia CES? The EU Commission would argue that it is not the case because of the completely different structure of the EU–Russian relations, geographic proximity, and corresponding sets of interests. The direct neighborhood is a crucial factor as it defines the scope and vectors of cooperation. Unlike in the Chile case, the contents of the EU–Russia CES should prioritize such vitally important issues as energy, transport, and integration of infrastructure. On all of these issues, the regulatory convergence that would assure a certain degree of legislative homogeneity is essential for successful cooperation. An integration of infrastructure in particular calls for a relatively horizontal approach. The need for a regulatory homogeneity on the potential common electricity market can serve as a vivid example. What Chile has with the EU is an FTA, albeit a comprehensive one, and not a common economic space implying an integration of neighbors.

Is the original model of the CES Concept, combining the elements of the EEA and 'Swiss' approaches, capable to provide a satisfactory solution to the policy-taker challenge? The broad definitions of the CEES Concept do not allow answering this question with confidence at the present time. The situation with the policy-taker problem will depend on the more concrete contents of the CEES, which are still to be elaborated. The CEES Concept in its present form provides for a large degree of flexibility, which can be interpreted as strength and a weakness at the same time. On the one hand, it allows Russia to be sensitive about the policy-taker dilemma; on the other hand, the Concept is defined too broadly, balancing on the verge of being devoid of substance. As the Chilean experience seems to be inapplicable to the neighborly complexity of the EU–Russian relationship, the analysis of the EU's external economic integration agreements with the EEA and Switzerland gives a hint showing that the policy-taker problem is likely to become a major hurdle on the way Russia's comprehensive integration with the EU.

Conclusion

The CES process has been based on a strong top-down approach with the dominant role played by the governmental bureaucracies. After being initiated at the very top, the Concept was written and negotiated on the Russian side exclusively by the governmental officials with a very limited participation of the business community and with a limited interest from the public. The impact of the economic assessment studies prepared by the academia was also limited. This creates a situation when the discourse is concentrated on a detached governmental level, with the business communities and public not informed, not participating, and therefore indifferent to the process and its outcome. This problem is yet to be overcome for the EU–Russian CES to be successful in the future.

The Concept specifies that the CES should move along the lines of the three freedoms (goods, services, and capital), supplemented by a higher degree of integration in individual priority sectors. The Concept of CES represents an original model in itself, combining elements of the EE and 'Swiss' models; that is, it unites both horizontal and sectoral approaches. The question remains open whether the model envisaged in the Concept is capable of providing a satisfactory solution. The policy-taker problem represents an important challenge. As the Chilean experience seems to be inapplicable to the complexity of the EU–Russian relationship, the experience of the EEA and EU-Swiss agreements shows that the policy-taker problem would be hard to avoid if Russia strives for a comprehensive integration with the EU.

References

Allison G.T. and P. Zelikow (1999), *Essence of Decision*, New York, NY: Longman.

Brenton, P. (2002), 'The Economic Impact of a EU–Russia Free Trade Agreement', Brussels: CEPS, unpublished.

The Common European Economic Space (CEES) Concept Paper (2003), Annex I to the Joint Statement of the 12th EU–Russia Summit, Rome, 5–6 November. http://europa.eu.int/comm/external_relations/russia/summit11_03/1concl.pdf.

Joint Statement of the 12th EU–Russia Summit (2003), Rome, 5–6 November. http://europa.eu.int/comm/externat_relations/russia/summit11_03/jsp061103.htm.

Emerson M. (2005), 'EU–Russia Four Common Spaces and the Proliferation of the Fuzzy', Brussels: CEPS Policy Brief 71.

Emerson M., M. Vahl, and S. Woolcock (2002), *Navigating by the Stars. Norway, the European Economic Area and the European Union*, Brussels: CEPS Paperback.

EU Commission (2004), *Communication to the Council and the European Paliment on Relations with Russia*, COM 106, 09.02.04.

Eurochambres, the Russian Chamber of Commerce (2003), Survey 'EU–Russia Trade and Investment: Practical Barriers', October, Section 7. www.eurochambres.be.

Hamilton, C.B. (2003), 'Russia's European Economic Integration. Escapism and realities', CEPR Discussion Paper 3840.

Mau, V. and V. Novikov (2002), 'Otnosheniya ES i Rossii: prostranstvo vybora ili vybor prostranstva?' [Relations of Russia and EU: Space of Choice or Choice of Space?], *Voprosy Ekonomiki*, No. 6, pp.133–143.

Putin, V. (2003), 'Speech of the President of the Russian Federation Mr. Vladimir Putin at a meeting with representatives of the European Round Table of Industrialists and the Round Table of Industrialists of Russia and the EU Mission of the Russian Federation to the European communities', Press-release No. 38/03, December 2, 2003, www.russiaeu.org.

'Road Map for the Common Economic Space', Annex I to the *Joint Statement of the 15th EU–Russia Summit*, Moscow, 10–11 May 2005.

Samson, I. and Greffe, X. (2002), *The White Book 'Common Economic Space: Prospects of Russia-EU Relations*', Moscow: Russian-European Centre for Economic Policy.

Schiff, M. and Winters, A. (1997), 'Regional Integration as Diplomacy', Policy Research Policy Paper 1801, Washington, DC: World Bank.

Vahl, M. (2004), 'Whither the Common European Economic Space? Political and Institutional Aspects of Closer Economic Integration between the EU and Russia', in T. de Wilde d'Estmael and L. Spetschinsky (eds) *La politique étrangère de la Russie et l'Europe* (pp. 167–201), Bruxelles: Peter Lang.

Chapter 5

The Dynamics of Innovation in Post-Communist Countries: Opportunities and Challenges

Per Högselius

Introduction

The generation and exploitation of new technologies, processes and products, i.e., innovations, is widely regarded as the principal driving force in all long-term socio-economic development. Future development of today's countries – also in the post-communist world – is therefore likely to be largely determined by their capability to generate and exploit various types of innovations.

The purpose of this chapter is to give an overview of the most important characteristics of post-communist dynamics of innovation in Central and Eastern Europe and to provide a basis for understanding the forces that shape these dynamics. The chapter is structured as follows. Section 2 establishes the general picture of the post-communist position in the world of innovation. In section 3, the developments underlying this overall pattern is introduced by outlining the historical heritage of post-socialist countries in terms of the innovative capabilities that they possessed in socialist times. This forms a suitable point of departure for assessing the post-socialist development. Particular questions that are taken up in the remaining sections then address issues such as the transformation of the socialist R&D complex from the late 1980s and onwards, the challenge of exploiting the inherited competencies from the socialist era, the restructuring of innovation networks, the build-up of linkages to foreign, more advanced systems of innovation, and the prospects for building post-communist 'styles of innovation' that either strive for harmonization with Western styles or rather seek to build innovative strength by developing differing styles.

Can Post-communist Countries Innovate? The General Picture

The general picture of innovative activities in post-communist countries is one where post-communist innovative performance is very weak. While GDP growth has been considerable in most post-communist countries since around 1990, firms in post-communist countries invest, on average, only about half of their GDP into R&D as do typical OECD countries. There are a few encouraging examples of countries that show signs of slowly catching up with the more advanced economies along this measure – notably Slovenia, Russia and the Czech Republic. Other post-communist countries, however, such as Slovakia, Hungary, Romania and in particular Poland, are rapidly falling behind and the gap to the more advanced countries has been constantly expanding in recent years, as shown in Figure 5.1.

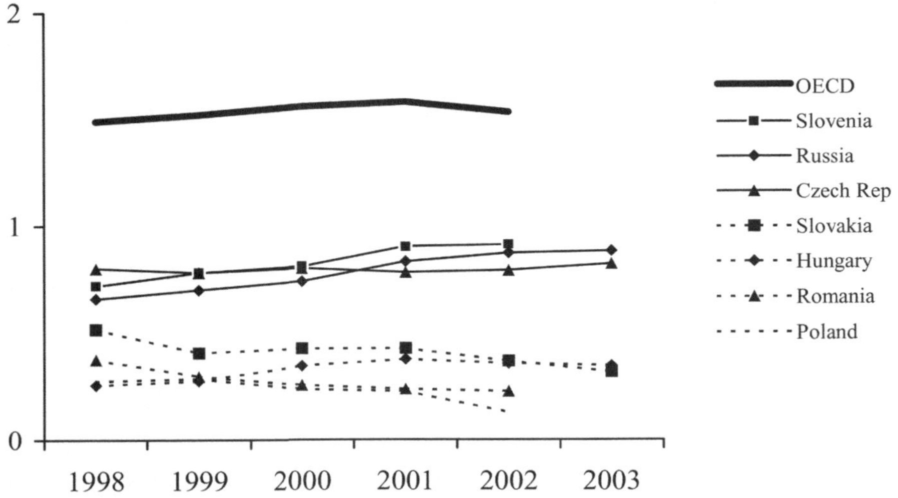

Figure 5.1 Business Enterprise Expenditure on R&D for OECD and Selected Post-Communist Countries, 1998–2003 (percentages of GDP)

In terms of innovative outcomes, the difference between post-communist countries and the more advanced Western countries is even more dramatic – a fact that signals the inefficiency of R&D for innovation. For example, within the European Union, the new Eastern EU member states are on average only about 4 percent as active in patenting new inventions as are the Western member states (measured *per capita*). In other words, for every single patent that a post-communist firm applies for in the European Patent Office, a corresponding Western firm applies for no less than 25 patents. Moreover, there is no sign that this enormous gap is closing (see Figure 5.2).

These aggregate and simple figures tell us that post-communist economies can hardly be said to be innovation-driven to any significant extent. It is obvious that economic growth is based rather on relatively non-innovative activities related to production, which have an advantage due to the typical low-cost environment in post-communist countries.

On the other hand, public policies in the CEE countries already contain a strong commitment to the establishment of advanced innovation-driven economies with strong systems of innovation and R&D bases, where education, science and technology would represent the main driving forces of socio-economic change.

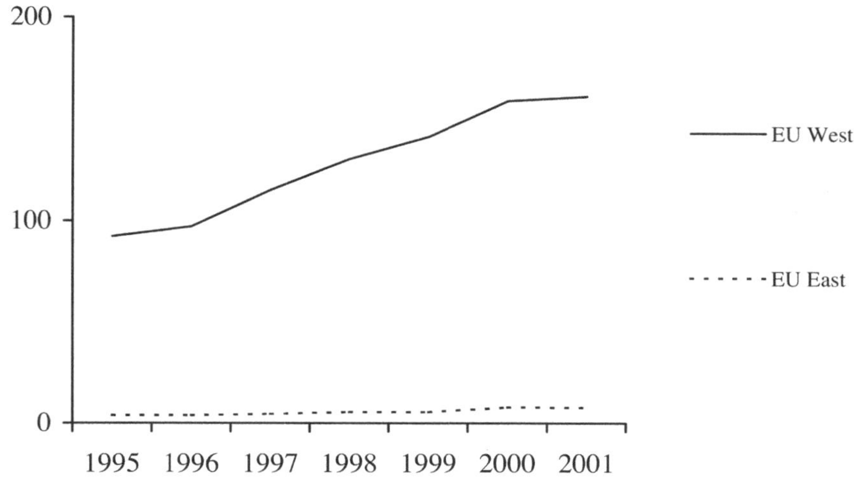

Figure 5.2 Patent Applications to the European Patent Office, 1995–2001 (per million inhabitants)

Drawing as far as possible on their problematic but advanced industrialized and technified Soviet-era pasts and taking advantage of the recent establishment of open capitalist systems, post-communist countries have set out to establish themselves among the most advanced economies. There is a strong belief in these countries that this can be achieved within a foreseeable future. From this perspective, it is, despite the low levels of innovation, important to gain an understanding of the underlying dynamics of post-communist innovation and how post-communist systems of innovation are being transformed currently. In the following sections, I will introduce some aspects of this theme.

Historical Background: Patterns of Innovation Under Communism

Technological change and innovation in the Cold War era constituted paramount societal concerns equally within capitalist and socialist civilizations. In both these worlds technology was seen as the ultimate key to civil and military progress, and technological achievements became the criterion along which the level of societal development was to be measured and evaluated in the ideological struggle. At the same time, however, technological and innovative activities in the East and West were only weakly *connected* to each other. Technologies, organizations, and institutions in the East and West developed according to radically different logics, and the interactions among these elements across the East–West interface were almost negligible in comparison to the interactions within the Eastern and Western worlds themselves. Although the Iron Curtain and institutions such as Cocom did not fully prevent ideas and artefacts from being transferred – in both directions – across the East–West divide, their principal impact was undeniably to reinforce separation and differentiation in terms of innovation, and environments for innovation, in the socialist and capitalist worlds. This meant that socialist and capitalist systems of innovation could not be seen simply as variations on a common theme. Rather, they worked according to fundamentally different logics.

From an East–West perspective on innovation, one of the most interesting studies on this subject is the explicitly comparative analysis by Hanson and Pavitt (1987) on the characteristics of research, development and innovation in the East and West. Building on the emerging modern insights from studies on innovation, they suggested a *systemic* perspective to understanding the differences between innovation in East and West. They concluded, in general, that the East European systems of innovation, including those which were undergoing 'market socialist' reform in the 1980s, so far showed a very weak performance, and that this weak performance was closely linked to the *central planning* of innovative activities. Surveying the existing literature on the subject, Hanson and Pavitt pointed, above all, at the *fragmentation* of the innovation system as inhibiting vital learning processes, especially inter-organizational learning. They also identified strongly *linear* characteristics of the East European innovation models, which in the 1980s still persisted despite a strong consciousness about the problems associated with such models and numerous attempts to reform the innovation systems in this respect. Further, referring to evolutionary insights into the economics of innovation, Hanson and Pavitt pointed at the critical lack of *variety* and redundancy and of appropriate *selection* environments.

These overall characteristics of innovation under socialism should be somewhat further commented on and put in relation to developments in Western and newly industrializing countries. From a systemic perspective, an important consequence of central planning of innovation was that the relationships between actors were not allowed to emerge and evolve in any spontaneous way, i.e., based on the ideas and needs of the actors themselves. This was because the very emergence of organizational structures and networks, similarly to technological priorities and product ranges, was subject to central planning. In the West, too, relationships between and within innovating organizations are recognized as extremely difficult to build and to manage, but in the centrally-planned systems of the Eastern bloc, an artificial separation of different organizational units from each other was *consciously* created and enforced. Actors were highly specialized in a functional sense, with separate organizations responsible for different stages of the innovative process. Thus in the Soviet system, which was largely adopted by most of the other Eastern countries, the Academy of Sciences with its hierarchies (and to a smaller extent the system of higher education) was the main producer of basic research, while more mission-oriented R&D was carried out by branch R&D organizations and project-design and product-design bureaux. Similarly, there were also specialized construction and installation organizations, which were typically more prominent in socialist than in capitalist systems of innovation. To the extent that R&D was carried out *in-house* in the Western sense, i.e., within production enterprises themselves, it was strongly limited to routine tasks such as testing, or incremental adaptations necessary to make technologies developed externally work (Hanson and Pavitt, 1987, p. 22).

These separate organizations, with their responsibilities for different stages of the innovative process, found it hard, and were not encouraged, to interact directly with each other. Buyers and sellers seldom met, and partnerships between organizations had to be approved by central authorities, which typically also decided who was to cooperate with whom (Hanson and Pavitt, 1987, p. 29). It was often regarded as sufficient to transfer knowledge and ideas between different units in highly codified forms, notably through blue-prints and physical capital. Important relationships and feed-backs were therefore typically missing, and inter-organizational learning, which plays such a crucial role in the modern economy, was severely hampered. In particular, the Eastern countries faced serious problems with respect to the integration between *R&D* and *production*. This was and is also a well-known problem in Western systems, but whereas in the West R&D is to a great extent an in-house activity and therefore carried out in relative proximity to other activities, Soviet-style R&D was almost exclusively extramural (i.e., firm-external) and thus often carried out at both organizational and geographical distance from production units.

In an interesting way, the commitment to central planning also meant that the organization of innovation did not necessarily take into consideration that different industries might require different organizational forms and different institutional set-ups. In studies on innovation in capitalist market economies, it has been convincingly shown that the nature of technologies tend to strongly influence the organization of innovation and thereby give rise to sector-specific patterns (Pavitt, 1984; Malerba, 2002). Innovation in the automotive industry in capitalist systems is thus likely to be organized in a very different way compared to innovation in biotechnology, in banking, or in scientific instruments. In capitalism, innovation follows different logics in different sectors, whereby the differences largely focus on the features of the specific technologies. In centrally-planned systems of innovation, in contrast, sectoral patterns appear to have emerged not primarily in response to the nature of *technologies*, but rather in response to ideological and other *institutional* considerations. In practice, this meant that sectoral differences hardly emerged at all, as the ideologically preferred type of organization rested almost exclusively on a scale-intensive pattern. Small firms, which play such vital roles in capitalist economies, were not allowed to emerge to any significant extent and could therefore hardly play any active role in socialist systems of innovation. It should be noted, however, that this was not a consequence of central planning itself, but rather of the ideological preferences of the planners. With a different ideological view or with a more modern understanding of the process of innovation, sectoral patterns may have emerged in a different way in the centrally-planned systems of innovation.

The most important consequence of the absence of small firms in socialist systems was probably the lack of 'specialized suppliers'. These are of key importance in capitalist systems of innovation, contributing crucially to the development and diffusion of pervasive capital goods technologies, from machine tools, to control instrumentation, computer-aided design, robots, software, etc. (Hanson and Pavitt,

1987, p. 15). Innovation in these technologies have been considerably driven by strong interactions between small supplier firms and the users of the technologies (von Hippel, 1988). In Soviet-type systems these key technologies were, in accordance with the ideological preferences, supplied by large organizations. Similarly to other firms, these large suppliers found it very difficult, or even impossible, to interact in a meaningful way with their customers, and user–producer interaction was therefore minimal. The tradition that grew up around this pattern implied that customers did not turn to suppliers for problem-solving and up-grading of processes and products. More generally, producers as a rule did not turn to *any* other organizations.

Also with respect to the evolutionary considerations of mechanisms of *variety* generation and *selection*, socialist systems of innovation differed considerably from capitalist ones. In capitalist economies, any organization may be a source of diversity creation in that it introduces new ideas and actions. In Soviet-style systems, however, this function was strongly limited to the planning authorities and perhaps the Academy of Sciences, which was extremely influential. Other organizations – in particular the production units – found it too difficult and hardly worthwhile to try to make reality of the ideas that might exist. When they did try to, they were not allowed to channel their ideas into the innovative process, neither in-house nor with respect to linkages with relevant external organizations – be they suppliers, customers, research institutes, etc. Instead, they had to turn to the central authorities. The resulting meager feed-backs from own ideas and the depressive wall of bureaucracy that was thus raised between inspiration and innovation effectively eliminated most of the 'intrapreneurial' spirit in socialist organizations. In general, *entrepreneurial activities* were hardly an issue at all, as already hinted at above in the discussion of small firms. In contrast to capitalist systems of innovation, new ideas generated in socialism were seldom allowed to lead to start-ups or spin-offs for economic exploitation of the ideas. Rosenberg (1994) has discussed this further in terms of the lack of *freedom to experiment* in socialist economies.

The stagnation of diversity creation outside R&D organizations was further reinforced by the absence of strong selection mechanisms. Technological and product alternatives were not allowed to emerge in parallel with each other and compete; instead, it was seen as an important task of central planning to select among alternatives at a very early stage. *Redundancy*, in the form of organizations working on technologies with the same or very similar purposes, was equated with an unnecessary waste of resources and was thus strongly discouraged. This resulted in a dramatically decreased variety and made the socialist systems extremely fragile through the resulting dependence upon *very few technological trajectories* in comparison to what is typical in capitalist systems. Moreover, *competition* could only be a political process defined by the negotiations between proponents of different technologies and products. In contrast to capitalist economies, the market hardly played any role in the competitive process in socialist systems of innovation.

Moreover, as a consequence of the predominance of 'soft budget constraints' (Kornai, 1980), the threat of bankruptcy was much weaker in Soviet-type systems than in capitalist economies; not being able to cover costs did, in the socialist context, not necessarily mean that anything had to be changed in an organization, since it was always possible to appeal to superior organizations higher up in the hierarchy that could bail it out of its financial difficulties. The threat of losing status and bonuses meant that managers did have incentives to prevent such situations, but the softer budget constraints under socialism appear to have considerably reduced the willingness to respond to problems by engaging in innovative activities, as there was no capitalist whip that forced them to seek to upgrade processes and products. 'Defensive' and 'imitative' innovation strategies, which are so widespread in the capitalist economies (see Freeman and Soete, 1997, ch. 11), did therefore hardly exist at all under socialism.

Connected to the 'soft' budget constraints was also the *slow diffusion* of innovations through the economy. The enormous efforts in terms of personnel and financial resources devoted to 'pushing' scientific discoveries and technical inventions through the different stages of the innovative process was not matched by any 'pull' from production enterprises. The latter were – for good reasons – often reluctant to change, and the whole way of thinking about innovation was different from typical capitalist technology-based firms, deeply devoted to survival and expansion through Schumpeterian competition. Survival in socialist systems was rather an issue of making existing things work – and this was already difficult enough in East European economies. Innovation, in contrast, was typically something imposed from a distant outside, and the overall experience was that the novelties thus introduced were bound to bring with them enormous new problems in connection to their introduction, rather than any improvements. Thus, the very concept of 'innovation' had *within enterprises* often a clearly negative clang, although at the same time it was *politically* almost equated with the very progress of socialism.

With regard to the *connections* between Western and Eastern systems of innovation, the most important research area in the Cold War period was the study of *technology transfer* in an East–West perspective. For example, Sandberg (1989) studied how, and to what extent, Soviet-style innovation systems were capable of 'learning from capitalists' through technology transfer projects. The major results of this, and other studies, were that imported technologies never acquired a dynamic of their own, but worked as static enclaves in the centrally planned economy. For example, modernizations were made only with new support-package deals, and diffusion to other sectors than the military or space industries were minimal. In view of the picture of socialist systems of innovation as outlined above, this is hardly surprising.

In the Soviet industrialization drive in the 1930s inspiration from, and imitation of, Western technologies played a crucial role. At the time of the Bolshevik revolution, Russia, as well as other East European countries, had been relatively far behind Western Europe in industrial development, and foreign sources of knowledge and technology thus played important roles, just as they had done for the somewhat earlier industrialization of Scandinavia. While the new states created in Central and Eastern Europe after World War I built their industrial development largely on stronger and more direct relationships to the West (including considerable amounts of FDI), the Soviet Union built up an enormous R&D system initially concerned with screening foreign technology and copying it (Hanson and Pavitt, 1987, p. 24). This strategy was strengthened by World War II, which played an enormous role for the transfer of technology to the Soviet Union from Germany in the form of war trophies.

It is an interesting question to what extent the 'imitative' character of the Soviet R&D system later turned more 'creative', with the generation and exploitation of genuinely Eastern technological trajectories. There is no consensus about this in the literature, but there are a number of examples that seem to strengthen both the view that Soviet technology largely continued to imitate Western achievements as well as the view that a number of creative areas did emerge and evolve, with varying success (see e.g., Amann, 1986).

Successes of Soviet and East European achievements in innovation can certainly be traced without much difficulty through Western licensing-in of technologies developed in socialist systems of innovation and through the patenting activities of Eastern countries in the West. During the 1970s, for example, US companies acquired 126 licences from the USSR and Eastern Europe (Amann, 1986, p. 14). In the early 1970s, Soviet and East European patenting in the US and West Germany also grew strongly (the rate of growth was in fact exceeded only by very few countries), but then declined. Hungary, however, continued to show strong growth in US patenting in the 1980s (Hanson and Pavitt, 1987, p. 62).

In contrast to patenting by Western countries, patenting in the capitalist abroad by socialist countries was pursued with the goal to strengthen the above-mentioned licensing-out of technologies, rather than to the direct export of goods (Radosevic and Kutlaca, 1999, p. 96). However, the 126 Soviet licenses documented for the 1970s clearly appear a meagre result from this strategy of exporting technological knowledge. Although they indicate in an interesting way that East–West technology transfer was not a strict one-way street, it is clear that the examples of transfer of socialist technologies to the capitalist world are more to be regarded as exceptions (Amann, 1986, p. 14). This is clearly reflected by the fact that the value of socialist imports of licences widely exceeded that of licence exports (Hanson and Pavitt, 1987, p. 79).

To sum up this section, it can be seen that most authors agree in their overall view that socialist systems of innovation were generally weaker in their generation, exploitation and diffusion of innovation than most capitalist systems of innovation. Today, however, the main interest is not primarily the relative quantitative performance of socialist and capitalist systems. Rather, it is much more important that socialist systems worked and developed according to a completely different set of logics than capitalist systems. Transformation and reorientation is precisely about the difficulties of altering inherited behaviors at the level of individuals, organizations, industries and the whole economy. Many of the peculiarities that have been observed in the post-socialist context, and that in Western eyes appear enigmatic and contradictory, can be understood better if the past, as referred to here, is taken seriously into account.

The Transformation of the Socialist R&D Complex

It is clear that the collapse of socialism in the years around 1990 was a radical turning point with respect to innovative activities. In comparison to the earlier reforms that were attempted during the socialist era, the transition to a capitalist market economy system was a revolution that opened up previously unacceptable perspectives on the ways in which innovation could be made to act as a driving force in economic and societal development. Instead of seeing innovation from a collective point of view as an instrument in the ideological struggle and a tool for progressing towards a higher societal stage, the capitalist view now opened up new perspectives, with innovation largely being seen as the decentralized and uncoordinated weapons of firms in their struggle against each other, that is, innovation as an individualist strategy for survival. However, this revolution could not conceal the fact that the transformation of innovation still had to the take as its point of departure the existing socialist systems of innovation. This has turned out to result in enormous difficulties, as will be discussed below.

Above it was noted that in socialist systems of innovation, innovative activities were typically carried out in organizations that were separate from and external to production enterprises. However, the delivery of R&D 'products' from the extramural R&D organizations were predestined for specific companies; such linkages were, as already discussed, imposed from above through central planning rather than – as in Western contract research – negotiated between buyer and seller in a decentralized way. R&D organizations, therefore, had a secured market for their services. Transition to a decentralized capitalist system implies, at least in theory, that the imposition of a market for R&D results from above is suddenly and entirely removed and that the R&D organizations have to face both an imploding overall market as well as competition from other domestic and, above all, foreign players.

The empirical evidence on the actual effects of these radical changes indicate that the farewell to socialism has as a rule led to a dramatic collapse of large parts of the inherited R&D system (e.g., Radosevic, 1997a). In particular, organizations engaged in *applied* R&D have as a rule not been able, or allowed, to adapt to the new situation, and the base for their funding by the state has usually been withdrawn. Ex-Soviet republics such as Estonia and Latvia have been pointed out as extreme cases of shut-downs, as a large part of their R&D complexes had been subordinate to military ministries; the market for their R&D services was therefore totally eliminated (Dyker and Radosevic, 1999).

Organizations involved in *basic* research, i.e., mainly academies and universities, have faced a relatively more continuous transition in most post-socialist countries, although the financial resources and employment for these organizations have decreased considerably. After 1989 hopes were raised about possibilities of strengthening East European academy-industry links (Dyker and Radosevic, 1999), a trend that could have strengthened the financial situation for university- and academy-based research. But with the almost total disappearance of organizations in the spectrum between basic research and production enterprises, and therefore a problematic lack of important 'bridging' actors, this is obviously contradictory to the actual prospects.

In general, the R&D complex in East European countries has thus been radically downsized. Nevertheless, public research institutes and universities typically continue to carry out a majority of formal R&D. While in most Western countries it is typical for the public sector to contribute with around one-third of total R&D expenditures, with private firms contributing with the remaining two-thirds, the situation is sometimes the reversed in the post-socialist context, where government-financed R&D amounts to up to two-thirds of total R&D expenditures. From a historical point of view, this is hardly surprising, since nearly all innovative activities were extramural in socialist systems of innovation, i.e., R&D and innovation were not carried out by production enterprises. The interesting aspect of the post-socialist development, however, is that there are no clear indications that the pattern has been changing since the early years of transition. If there is any trend at all, it is one towards an *increasing* role of government-financed R&D (in countries such as Hungary, Russia and Slovakia). To the most Western-styled post-communist countries belong in this respect the Czech Republic and Slovenia.

As a matter of fact, the public research sector in the Eastern countries is typically of a comparable size to that of Western countries. Thus, for example, a country such as Poland has actually a higher number of university researchers *per capita* than Germany (OECD, 2004, p. 42). The main problem with government-financed R&D activities is not the quantitative amount of research efforts. The most important challenge rather relates to the relevance and competitiveness of the research carried out from the perspective of the system of innovation as a whole. So far, the public

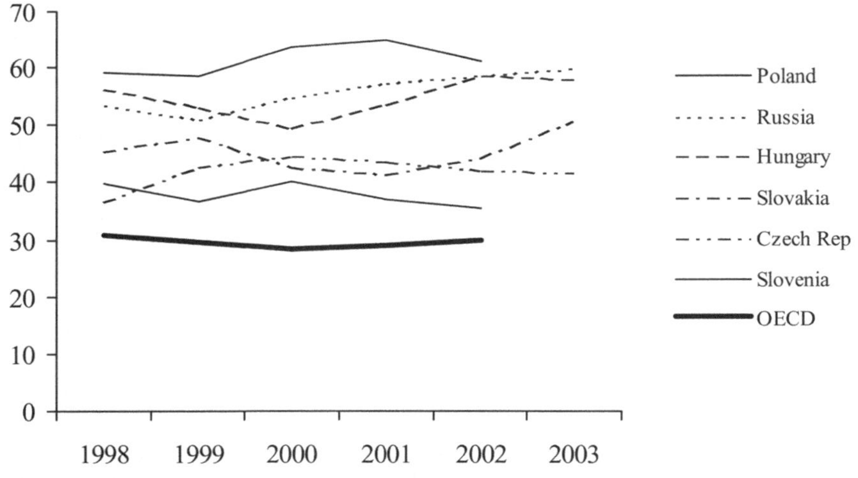

Figure 5.3 Percentage of Total R&D Expenditure Financed by Government, 1998–2003

research system has contributed extremely little to the performance of the system as a whole, in terms of actual commercial innovations in post-socialist countries. This is an issue which is directly linked to the relationships between R&D organizations and the business sector. Similarly, the links between R&D organizations and other public bodies are likely to be of key importance. The overall challenge is to integrate the inherited R&D complex into the difficult societal context of transformation and reorientation.

The Challenge of Exploiting Inherited Competencies

Does the collapse of many important R&D organizations and production enterprises from the late 1980s onwards mean that the socialist historical heritage has been irrelevant in the post-communist context? Some authors have argued that inherited socialist strengths in science and engineering were largely obsolescent, and that Central and East European firms have therefore been compelled to start from scratch in their accumulation of relevant capabilities. For example, Pavitt argued that:

> the competencies in R&D generated under central planning .. turned out to be obsolete when brought face to face with the standards of the rest of the world (Pavitt 1997, p. 52).

Hirschhausen and Bitzer (2000, p. 13) went even further and suggested that:

> the socialist knowledge-base and the socialist technological trajectories did not significantly influence the development of post-socialist enterprises and sectors.

Other authors, however, have convincingly pointed to a number of cases where Soviet-era competencies have been successfully exploited in the post-Soviet period (e.g., Dyker, 1996, 2001; Shaw, 1996).

A better understanding of this issue can be arrived at by investigating what has happened with respect not only to *firms* and other organizations, but also to *individuals*. While many organizations – in particular production enterprises and applications-oriented R&D organizations – underwent a dramatic collapse in the post-communist world in the years around 1990, individuals who have accumulated far-reaching competencies within Soviet-era organizations have very often come to play important roles in the post-socialist system of innovation – though typically in other organizations than those in which they were working under socialism. A major source of such important individuals, who possess important competencies accumulated under communism, appear to be R&D organizations of various kinds – institutes focused on deep fundamental research as well as more applications-oriented design bureaus. Even more important, however, is the availability of socialist-era graduates from technical and other universities; these people show up nearly everywhere where creative innovation occurs. Inherited competencies are in that case not necessarily associated with the inherited R&D system, but rather with the Soviet educational infrastructure (Högselius, 2005).

At the level of organizations, the power of inherited competencies is not at all as obvious in the post-socialist context as at the individual level. Through the collapse of old production enterprises and applications-oriented R&D organizations, in particular, a great deal of competencies were lost at the organizational level. These lost competencies may in many cases have been obsolete, while in other cases they may have been potentially useful in the post-socialist era. It may also be seen that the formal or informal *reintegration* of inherited socialist networks following their legal split-up may in fact play important roles in stimulating innovation. These networks have in some cases been seen to play a constructive role in the transformation and reorientation of the inherited systems of innovation, for example, by creating a critical threshold demand for R&D or by creating subcontracting networks (Radosevic, 1997b).

With respect to inherited universities, post-socialist universities have, as mentioned above, suffered from a loss of teachers and researchers, mainly as a consequence of under-financing and deteriorated opportunities within Soviet and East European educational networks. Nevertheless, they undoubtedly provide a highly valuable asset for post-socialist dynamics of innovation due to their extremely important role as competence-creating organizations. The value of inherited universities becomes particularly obvious when looking at their organizational histories, with the gradual emergence of complex structures in terms of their various departments and curricula. It takes time to establish such structures and build educational strengths, and if they had to be created out of nothing starting from the years around 1990, post-communist systems of innovation would have faced an immensely more difficult situation. Although the inherited universities came to face extremely important processes of adaptation to the radically altered systems of innovation of which they are part, the departments and curricula that exist today have often been able to successfully exploit their past in the new capitalist context. This is so at least in fields where the underlying principles of science and engineering that were taught under socialism did not differ radically from what was taught in the capitalist world (in contrast to, for example, social sciences and the humanities, where this was much more difficult).

This line of reasoning can be generalized to include the entire educational infrastructure, not least with respect to primary and secondary schools. In particular secondary schools are probably an underestimated source of competencies and absorptive capacities in East European systems of innovation. Compared to Western EU countries, Central and East European countries are placed much more favorably with respect to the number of graduates from secondary schools. Thus the share of adult population with at least secondary education was 64.6 percent for the Western part of the EU, while the corresponding figure for Estonia was 87.5 percent, for Latvia 82.6 percent, for Lithuania 84.8 percent, for Poland 80.8 percent, for Slovakia 85.8 percent, for Slovenia 76.8 percent, for the Czech Republic 87.8 percent and for Hungary 71.4 percent (see, e.g., *Ny Teknik*, 28 April 2004).

Moreover, the strong educational traditions in Eastern Europe, as inherited from the socialist past, can arguably be seen as part of a broader picture, in which one discerns the importance of being part of European culture, with its general interest in science, engineering, education and business. Central and Eastern Europe inherited from their socialist pasts a European tradition of seeing science and technology as integral parts of society at large, and the post-socialist era has added new dimensions to this: nowadays new technologies are not only found all around in everyday life, but they are also under constant scrutiny in the media, giving rise to intense debates and criticisms, etc. Such an omnipresence of science and technology in today's post-communist world can hardly be overlooked.

An interesting question is also which inherited competencies stem from the socialist period and which from the period before that. Here, it is important to remember the fact that most Central and East European countries experienced a period of independence between the world wars, in which organizations and individuals learned to act in the environment of Western-style capitalism. The orientation towards the West in that era was particularly strong due to the difficult circumstances in the young Soviet Union during that period. It was also in the interwar period that many of Central and Eastern Europe's most important businesses were founded.

In summary, even though the far-reaching changes in Central and Eastern Europe in the years around 1990 belong to the most radical political and economic disruptions of our time, their systems of innovation in the post-socialist period continue to show strong traces of their previous history. Understanding this – more or less strong – power of the past, is absolutely key when seeking to grasp the dynamics of innovation in post-communist countries.

Restructuring Innovation Networks

From the perspective of socialist production enterprises, the sudden introduction of a capitalist economic system with totally decentralized decision-making implied that innovation was suddenly not something that was enforced from outside anymore. Companies were suddenly free to choose their suppliers and partners. The most dramatic change in inter-organizational linkages probably occurred in connection with privatization, especially when the buyers were foreign investors, since the strategy of the latter was typically precisely to integrate the Eastern enterprises into their existing networks. This view is supported by the observation that privatized firms are in general more strongly networked internationally than the remaining state-owned firms (Radosevic, 1999). Domestically, on the other hand, it is typically large state-owned and domestically privatized firms which are the strongest in inter-organizational networks that involve innovation. This is hardly surprising, as it is usually a question of linkages that have survived from the old system, though perhaps in new disguise (notably informal networks among individuals). Even in cases where, as was common in the early phase of transition, large enterprises were split up into a number of smaller units, these have often been seen to reintegrate in various ways under post-socialism. In some cases this has involved the reintegration also of R&D institutes into the 'new' conglomerates (Dyker and Radosevic, 1999; Radosevic, 1997b).

With respect to small firms, most of these were in the first half of the 1990s hardly involved in innovative activities at all (Radosevic, 1999). Several analysts have suspected that small and medium-sized firms in Eastern Europe have a much too low level of technological competency and are too static technologically for contributing in any significant way to building innovative strength in Eastern Europe (Gabor, 1997; Dyker and Radosevic, 1999). More recent research, however, has shown that small firms in reality often play key roles in many innovative projects. For example, nearly all innovative successes in the Estonian ICT sector have been dependent upon one or more small domestic firms in one way or the other. This is also so when innovation takes place in collaboration with foreign actors, who would be much more reluctant to engaging in innovation in the post-socialist context in the absence of local firms and other partners with advanced and relevant competencies for the creation of new products and processes (Högselius, 2005).

At the individual level, it is interesting to note the style of emerging networks between business, government and academia. On the other hand, as I have shown elsewhere (Högselius, 2005), it is obvious that post-socialist academic-industrial links have to be understood in somewhat different terms than in Western countries. For example, through the extremely low salaries typically paid to East European researchers at their university or academy positions, nearly all academic researchers are forced to work part-time in business or government organizations. The positive effect of this seems to be a myriad of both formal and informal links between academia, business and government at the level of individuals, to an extent that is hardly imaginable in Western countries.

Building Linkages to Foreign Systems of Innovation

Great hopes have been raised in the post-communist world since 1989 with regard to the potential roles that firms and other actors from more advanced countries can play in the rebuilding of the economy. In theory, foreign direct investment has thereby been seen as a powerful vehicle also for rebuilding innovative capabilities under post-socialism. Foreign investors are expected to bring with them modern technologies that increase productivity and inspire further innovation. Through the pressure of competition, domestic firms are also expected to be forced to invest into new technology and innovative activities, thereby enforcing a pattern of Schumpeterian competition and growth in the former socialist countries.

In reality, this is a distorted picture. Empirical research based on case studies of specific firms mostly indicate that foreign investment is as a rule *not* associated with any rebuilding of technological and innovative capabilities in Eastern Europe (e.g., Farkas, 1997; van Geenhuizen, 2001). The only obvious exceptions are the new R&D centers and software development departments that have been established directly by multinational firms in some of the post-communist countries (notably Hungary). Also the pattern with respect to *collaborative ventures* between East and West resembles that of foreign direct investment. Collaborative ventures have been seen to be almost exclusively based on *manufacturing*-related agreements, typically related to subcontracting in mostly non-innovative ways. Eastern firms are predominantly incorporated into the networks of Western firms at the *lower* stages of the industry value-added chain. When cooperative agreements have been related to technology, they have not been concerned with the development of new products or processes, but rather with adjustments such as adaptations to local conditions (Sadowski, 2001). These results are broadly in line with other research indicating that with transition, a trend towards labor- and resource-intensive industries has become dominant in the Eastern countries.

In addition, foreign firms appear to have further *reinforced* the already problematic decoupling of R&D from production typical for socialist systems of innovation. The reason is that cooperation in R&D typically takes place between the R&D complex of multinational firms and post-communist research institutes, while business enterprises are integrated separately into the multinationals in the form of manufacturing units. There has thus been almost no technological cooperation involving innovative activities between Western investors and Eastern production enterprises (Sadowski, 2001).

Hopes have also been raised for the potential of *foreign funding* to save the inherited research capabilities. Available data indicate that foreign funding has increased during the past few years. However, the actual foreign contributions are still very marginal in most countries. To the most encouraging examples in this respect belong Hungary and Russia, where around one-tenth of total R&D expenditures comes from foreign sources (OECD, 2004).

In general, it can thus be seen that the massive presence of foreign firms and the inflow of FDI has been quite disappointing in terms of effects on innovation. From a somewhat different perspective, however, it is clear that in those cases where important innovative projects do result in success, linkages to foreign firms and foreign systems of innovation play very important roles. As I have pointed out elsewhere (Högselius, 2005), innovative projects in post-communism can thereby be seen to draw actively on a surprisingly wide array of different cross-border relationships, such as:

- international trade;
- foreign ownership and investment;
- cross-border user-producer relationships (in particular subcontracting);
- financial support from abroad (for various activities);
- consulting as a way of transferring skills and knowledge from abroad (in business as well as in academia and government);
- international student and research exchange;
- foreign systems of innovation as inspiring models;
- cross-border joint innovation projects.

Some of these channels intersect with and influence each other. For example, foreign investment may be associated with consulting and user-producer relationships, which in turn may be linked to cross-border joint innovation. The above list is likely to be expanded through further empirical research, but the point is that the channels mentioned are not merely small details; rather, communication through these channels provide absolutely crucial pushes and pulls for the transformation and evolution of post-communist systems of innovation.

Hence, there is no doubt that interaction with foreign actors and foreign systems of innovation has the potential to contribute to innovation in the post-communist context. However, it is also clear that this potential is not at all utilized to the extent that it could be. Most promising in cross-border relationships are clearly the relations with culturally and/or geographically close countries. Central and East European countries can in this sense be argued to have an advantage over other catch-up countries in more remote parts of the world, to the extent that most of the Central and East European countries have a multitude of historical, linguistic, demographic, cultural and other linkages to advanced West and North European countries.

Where are Post-communist Styles of Innovation Heading?

The dynamics of innovation in post-communist countries must not be thought of primarily as a 'transfer' of Western technologies, practices and structures to the East. Instead, one has to point at the opportunity – or necessity – for Central and East European countries to use inspirations from and interactions with culturally and geographically close neighbors in the West to boost domestic innovation in accordance with local conditions and inherited competencies, i.e., by taking into account the logic and specificities of the domestic system of innovation. However, this conclusion leads to radically different scenarios with respect to the future. Let me here briefly discuss two extremes.

First, post-communist systems of innovation may very well choose to continue building on the availability of low-cost environments, using largely non-innovative activities in order to boost economic growth and exports. Eastern Europe would thus continue to be a conveniently located reservoir of relatively simple manufacturing services for large Western multinationals. This corresponds to the present paths of many post-communist countries, with close inter-organizational East–West integration in terms of user-producer networks, but reinforcing a non-creative style of innovation that considerably differs from Western systems of innovation.

When wages rise, this style risks being eroded through relocation of production to other low-cost countries, and this is likely to result in increasing unemployment and dramatic declines in exports. The only thing which could rescue this development path on the long term would be to imitate the East Asian experience of climbing the ladder towards increasing involvement in innovation (Hobday, 1995).

But there is considerable uncertainty with respect to the viability of such a strategy in the longer term: when the East Asian 'tiger' economies achieved their remarkable success, the world looked different. Their success built on exploiting technological discontinuities with a potential that may be of a different character today as compared to earlier. Much tougher global competition and vastly increasing technological complexity also reduce the prospects for small East European countries to become world leaders on their own, without integrating closely into global networks. Even enormous political efforts of the kind that have been commonplace in East Asia can hardly compensate for this in Central and Eastern Europe. Under these circumstances, it is difficult to know to what extent it will be possible for East European producers to move towards 'own-brand manufacture' (OBM) and frontier R&D.

A radically different scenario is one in which post-communist countries gradually leave their traditional style of economy behind in a politically conscious way. Eastern Europe would carefully use its geographical and cultural proximity to advanced West European countries in combination with its long tradition of higher education and other potential advantages in brave and clever ways, backed by broad local and national beliefs in the actual possibility to proudly fight its way into the global innovation economy. Post-communist Central and Eastern Europe would become a region famous for its courageous new developments, which would often surpass Western countries, the latter eagerly following the first-movers in the East. This could be made possible through the still much more loosely defined institutional landscapes in the Eastern countries, their lack of path-dependence-inducing inherited technical systems and their far-reaching experience of managing radical systems change.

The Eastern countries then become the ones that show the West how institutional bottlenecks can be resolved. They become the sites where new technologies of powerful Western firms are tried out in highly dynamic and rapidly evolving post-socialist markets (which lack the conservatism and inertias that become more and more characteristic of Western Europe). Eastern Europe, in this scenario, follows a completely different path of development compared to large Asian and Latin American countries such as China or Brazil, as they understand how to use their small size to move rapidly and cleverly and to retain a continuous dynamism, perhaps with a specialization in service sectors.

Global competition would then also encourage the formation of East–West joint corporations and conglomerates which would gradually learn to use the continuous flows of knowledge between East and West and their still vastly differing systems of innovation in order to boost the whole process of innovative development. The very gap between East and West thus becomes an engine of progress. While it remains difficult to create large independent hi-tech firms in the mostly small post-communist countries, many large Western brands soon become closely associated with the East European dynamism. Western EU support helps Eastern countries revive their advanced but heavily under-financed educational sectors, and the huge unemployment in countries such as Poland is reduced in connection to the appearance of new technological trajectories, with the formation of new industries that pull the Eastern countries fearlessly into the gales of radical innovation. While Western EU countries tend to stagnate in their conservatism and overly careful political arenas,

Eastern Europe, where a younger generation already rules in politics as well as business, moves ahead and becomes the new symbol of European progress.

How unrealistic is the latter scenario? One might argue that the most unrealistic aspect is the envisaged continuing division line between post-communist countries and the more advanced economies in the world. The general trend, after all, is that the differences in development levels *among* Western and *among* Eastern countries are becoming more pronounced than the differences between 'East' and 'West'. But again, when it comes to 'style' rather than 'level', the Eastern countries will for decades be heavily influenced by their socialist histories. Turning these difficult and traumatic pasts into new and flourishing systems of innovation continues to be an extremely difficult task.

Success has often followed when the key process of building linkages to geographically and culturally close countries has been combined with well-focused interactive learning between a wide range of actors – foreign and domestic, public and private –while both collaboration and competition have been allowed to function as driving forces. What lies behind this, however, is not merely the establishment of formal institutions; rather, the ability to uphold smoothly functioning relationships between components in a system is heavily dependent upon a genuine will to change and a belief in the power of their nations' capacities. The available evidence also points to the key role of the education system, a circumstance that is illustrated by the fact that educational activities have become both a crucial enabler of and an obstacle to further progress.

References

Amann, R. (1986), 'Technical Progress and Soviet Economic Development: Setting the Scene', in R. Amann and J. Cooper (eds), *Technical Progress and Soviet Economic Development*, Oxford, UK: Basil Blackwell.

Dyker, D. (1996), 'The Computer and Software Industries in the East European Economies – A Bridgehead to the Global Economy?', *Europe-Asia Studies*, Vol. 48, no. 6, pp. 915–930.

Dyker, D. (2001), 'Technology Exchange and the Foreign Businiess Sectopr in Russia', *Research Policy*, vol. 30, pp. 851–68.

Dyker, D. and S. Radosevic (1999), *Building the Knowledge-Based Economy in Countries in Transition – From Concepts to Policies*, SPRU Electronic Working Paper No. 36. Brighton, UK: University of Sussex.

Eurostat (2004), *European Business: Facts and Figures*. Luxembourg: Office for Official Publications of the European Communities.

Farkas, P. (1997), *The Effect of Foreign Direct Investment on Research, Development and Innovation in Hungary*. Working Paper no. 81, Institute of World Economics of the Hungarian Academy of Sciences, Budapest.

Freeman, C. and L. Soete (1997), *The Economics of Industrial Innovation*, Third edition, London, UK: Pinter.

Gabor, I. (1997), 'Too Many, Too Small: Small Entrepreneurship in Hungary – Ailing or Prospering?', in Grabher and Stark (eds), *Resturcturing Networks in Post-Socialism: Legacies, Linkages and Localities*, Oxford: Oxford University Press.

Geenhuizen, M. van (2001), 'Which Role for Foreign Direct Investment? Active Space Development in Central and Eastern Europe', in M. Geenuizen and R. Ratti (eds), *Gaining Advantage from Open Borders. An active space approach to regional development*, Aldershot, UK: Ashgate.

Hanson, P. and K. Pavitt (1987), *The Comparative Economics of Research Development and Innovation in East and West: A Survey*, Chur: Harwood Academic Publishers.

Hippel, E. von (1988), *The Sources of Innovation*, New York, NY: Oxford University Press.

Hirschhausen, C. von and Bitzer, J. (2002) (eds), *The Globalization of Industry and Innovation in Eastern Europe: From Post-Socialist Restructuring to International Competitiveness*, Cheltenham: Edward Elgar.

Hobday, M. (1995), *Innovation in East Asia: The Challenge to Japan*, Cheltenham, UK: Edward Elgar.

Högselius, P. (2005), *The Dynamics of Innovation in Eastern Europe: Lessons from Estonia*, Cheltenham, UK: Edward Elgar.

Kornai, J. (1980), *Economics of Shortage*, Amsterdam: North-Holland.

Malerba, F. (2002), 'Sectoral Systems of Innovation and Production', *Research Policy*, Vol. 31, pp. 247–264.

Ny Teknik, 28 April 2004.

OECD (2004), *Main Science and Technology Indicators*, Vol. 2004/2, Paris: OECD.

Pavitt, K. (1984), 'Sectoral Patterns of Technical Change: Towards a Taxonomy and a Theory', *Research Policy*, Vol. 13, pp. 343–373.

Pavitt, K. (1997), 'Transforming Centrally-planned Systems of Science and Technology: The Problem of Obsolete Competencies', in D. Dyker (ed.), *The Technology of Transition* (pp. 43–60), Budapest: Central European University Press.

Radosevic, S. (1997a), 'Systems of Innovation in Transformation. From Socialism to Post-Socialism', in C. Edquist (ed.), *Systems of Innovation: Technologies, Institutions, and Organizations* (pp. 371–394), London, UK: Pinter.

Radosevic, S. (1997b), 'Strategic Policies for Growth in Post-Socialism: Theory and Evidence Based on the Case of the Baltic States', *Economic Systems*, Vol. 21, No. 2, pp. 165–196.

Radosevic, S. (1999), *Patterns of Innovative Activities in Countries of Central and Eastern Europe: An Analysis Based on Comparison of Innovation Surveys*, SPRU Electronic Working Paper No. 34.

Radosevic, S. and D. Kutlaca (1999), 'Technological 'Catching-up' Potential of Central and Eastern Europe: An Analysis Based on US Foreign Patenting Data', *Technology Analysis & Strategic Management*, Vol. 11, No. 1, pp. 95–111.

Rosenberg, N. (1994), 'Telecommunications: Complex, Uncertain, and Path-dependent', in *Exploring the Black Box. Technology, Economics and History*, Cambridge, UK: Cambridge University Press.

Sadowski, B. (2001), 'Towards Market Repositioning in Central and Eastern Europe: International Cooperative Ventures in Hungary, Poland and the Czech Republic', *Research Policy*, Vol. 30, pp. 711–724.

Sandberg, M. (1989), *Learning from Capitalists. A Study of Soviet Assimilation of Western Technology,* Stockholm: Almqvist & Wiksell International.

Shaw, B. (1996), 'Networking in the Russian Aerospace Industry', *R&D Management*, Vol. 26, No. 3, pp. 255–265.

Chapter 6

Alternative International Trade Policies and the Role of Foreign Aid for Transition Economies

John Marangos

Introduction

The collapse of the centrally administered economies gave rise to economies based on market relations. The introduction of market relations transformed the decision-making process from a vertical one, between central authorities and enterprises, to a horizontal process, between enterprises. This automatically resulted in substantially reducing the relative value of vertical relationships. The term 'marketization' had the meaning of making enterprises interact with each other and with consumers through purchases and sales at equilibrium prices. Consequently, the hegemony of market process among economists as a means of stimulating growth implied a transformation in all dimensions of the economic system. While most economists agree on the introduction of market relations in Central and Eastern Europe and the Former Soviet Union (CEEFSU) economies, the market as such is not a homogeneous entity. As experience shows, different market economies have developed market relations in a different manner. Consequently, 'the question is not to what degree markets have emerged, but what kind of market economy is emerging in different regions' (Walder, 1996, p. 1068).

The aim of this chapter is to consider alternative international trade policies and the role of foreign aid as a result of alternative models of transition. Alternative models of transition are the result of different methods of economic analysis, different political structures and different speeds of implementing the transition policies. As a result five alternative models of transition are considered: *The Shock Therapy* model of transition (neoclassical economic analysis, pluralistic political structure and immediate transition), the *Neoclassical Gradualist* model of transition (neoclassical economic analysis, pluralistic political structure and gradual transition), the *Post Keynesian* model of transition (Post Keynesian economic analysis, pluralistic political structure, and gradual transition), and the Non-Pluralistic Market Socialist model of transition – *The Chinese* model of transition (Marxist-Maoist economic analysis, non-pluralistic political structure and gradual transition). As such, alternative models of transition result in alternative international trade policies and different roles associated with the provision of foreign aid. The chapter is restricted to the international trade policies and the role of foreign aid in alternative models of transition. In the following pages an analysis of the recommended international trade policies by alternative models of transition takes place, together with the role of foreign aid in assisting the transition process.

The Shock Therapy Approach to International Trade and Foreign Aid

The shock therapy supporters argued that mature market economies had an opportunity to consolidate capitalism as a global economic system, creating a law-bound and affluent international system by integrating the transition economies into the global market system. After a long period of self-imposed isolation the transition economies had the opportunity to be part of a highly integrated and interdependent global economy. The breakdown of COMECON resulted in a substantial decline or, even worse, a total collapse of trade, but it also forced enterprises to restructure. From the shock therapy perspective on transition, 'the collapse of the old intra-FSU trade flows was both inevitable and desirable' (Aslund, 1995, p. 112). The establishment of national currencies and free trade with free prices were essential to achieve stabilization. With the introduction of market relations the artificial nature of the old trade pattern was revealed. There was no incentive for firms to pursue international trade, as it was not profitable. Nevertheless, the rapid removal of trade barriers and implementation of policies, which encouraged direct integration of the transition economies with the international economy, would have brought large and immediate benefits and unleashed previously oppressed entrepreneurial activities, as the shock therapy supporters argued. International trade was considered a means for encouraging efficiency, introducing competition into domestic markets and increasing the availability of goods. In fact, the transition process was a combination of the marketization and the internationalization of economic affairs.

The shock therapy supporters advocated complete liberalization of the international trade sector by currency devaluation to the black market level and the removal of trade barriers. Radical trade liberalization was an essential component of the successful trade performance of transition economies. It also seemed likely that free trade was the way to initiate competition. Trade liberalization would have created positive externalities by stimulating privatization, even though privatization was taking place slowly due to political pressures and sectoral interests. Transition economies would have been able to import a rational price system and benefit from the transfer of technology, which would have stimulated increases in productivity growth. Due to international integration, a substantial increase in exports would have taken place, with the CEEFSU market economies removing their previous dependence on the Soviet Union.

The liberalization of international trade and the establishment of a convertible currency were among the most important prerequisites for a successful transition to capitalism (Aslund, 1995, p. 174). Essentially, 'convertibility and external liberalization are natural bedfellows' (Sutela, 1992, p. 89). The exchange rate should have been liberalized at the same time as domestic prices, which would have reaffirmed both the complementary nature of economic policies and the need for a shock therapy approach. The traditional arguments that devaluation would not have stimulated exports but only increased the price of imports, trade liberalization resulted in unemployment and protectionism had to remain, had no empirical basis. 'These arguments were false for Latin America, and they are false for Eastern Europe' (Sachs, 1991, p. 67). Limitations on international trade, such as tariffs, trade licenses and quotas should be eliminated.

The arguments that CEEFSU countries should not have opened their borders to free international trade, nor introduced a convertible currency, because enterprises were inefficient and could not have survived fierce international competition, were false. As Ricardo pointed out international trade was the product of comparative – not absolute – advantage. Any country could have engaged in free trade, and, similarly, any country could have had a convertible currency. Current account convertibility could have been introduced in one shot, as the experience of Poland indicated, which was in contrast to the experience of Western Europe in the 1950s. In any case, restrictions on capital account convertibility were ineffective due to modern market technology (Sutela, 1992, p. 92). It was fruitless to attempt to identify the firms or industries which had comparative advantage, because nobody, not even the government, had the knowledge to predict market outcomes. Hence a convertible currency was essential to achieve a reliable price system, competition, monetary discipline, make the comparative advantage principle workable, foster privatization and finally create property rights. The policies recommended by the shock therapy supporters ensured that the liberalization of foreign trade was irreversible.

A freely floating exchange rate would have adjusted to reduce inflation and stimulate competition. The achievement of a stable foreign exchange market was only possible by maintaining a restrictive monetary policy. The government might have wished to maintain a fixed exchange rate. I believe that both fixed and floating exchange rates are consistent with the shock therapy approach, since neither involves government intervention. Nevertheless, a fixed exchange rate eliminates the instability caused by a fluctuating exchange rate. Sachs (1996, p. 149; 1997, p. 249), Aslund (1995, p. 183) and Sutela (1992, p. 92) were in favor of a pegged exchange rate at the start of the stabilization programs, and then a more flexible rate after one or two years. The international experience revealed that the most successful stabilization programs were based on a pegged exchange rate, such as Bolivia in 1985, Israel in 1985 and Mexico in 1987 (Sachs, 1997, p. 251). In the transition economies, the early peggers –Czech Republic, Estonia, Hungary, Poland, and Slovakia – performed much better than the floaters in reducing inflation. The peggers achieved inflation below 100 percent per year by 1994 (Sachs, 1996, p. 149).

Foreign direct investment should be encouraged as long as the traditional conditions existed: political stability, free markets, an appropriate legal environment and a stable and convertible currency (Aslund, 1992, p. 58). These conditions could only have been achieved by using the market mechanism. The development of an institutional structure would have been able to attract foreign investment. Protectionism was inconsistent with the shock therapy model. Moreover, protectionism by mature market economies 'could undermine the economic logic of reform and eat away the political and social consensus of the reform program' (Sachs, 1993, p. 102). However, there might have been some justification for a low tariff in the initial stages of transition, of about 10 to 15 percent, to protect domestic industries for a very short time and to raise state revenues (Aslund, 1992, p. 48).

The shock therapy model presupposed debt cancellations, international transfers, balance of payments and budgetary support as a means of overcoming stagnation and maintaining political support for the reform program. 'No country this century has undertaken radical market reforms without sizeable foreign aid' (Sachs, 1995a, p. 22). Without relief from the large debt problem, the much-needed capital inflow would have been restricted, removing a major source of economic growth. All external debt should have been frozen and rescheduled to ease the burden and allow the transition economies to start afresh. It was the responsibility of the mature economies to assist the transition economies as much as possible because 'the world has much to gain from the emerging system and much to lose if we fail to act decisively to put it in place' (Sachs, 1995b, p. 50). If this assistance was not forthcoming it was possible that there might have been a rise in xenophobia, jeopardizing the vast opportunities associated with the opening of the CEEFSU market to international trade. Importantly, foreign aid and borrowing would have reduced the need for the monetary financing of the budget deficit. The budget deficit and the necessary social programs could have been financed by foreign aid and borrowing from international organizations without increasing the domestic money supply. Consequently, 'this money could help to make a democratic and economic transformation feasible which otherwise would not be feasible' (Sachs, 1992, p. 210).

The Neoclassical Gradualist Approach to International Trade and Foreign Aid

A sustained movement towards free trade was crucial for the successful transition to a market economy, to promote the growth of exports, curb the rise in imports and improve the trade balance and the balance of payments, as the neoclassical gradualist economists argued. However, since the economies in transition had inherited obsolete production methods, participation in international competition was very difficult. The collapse of COMECON trade had a serious impact, thus it was expected that transition economies would have had current account deficits, which were temporarily tolerable (Kornai, 1993, p. 218). There was an argument for maintaining a moderate level of tariffs and transforming quantitative restrictions into tariffs. This would have provided protection and given time for the firms to adjust, while also providing the government with an income. Temporary protection for some domestic industries had to be determined on the basis of economic rationality, not pressure from lobby groups, and to be in line with the prescriptions of WTO so that it did not lead to protectionist retaliation by foreign trading partners. International trade would have also contributed to the process of creative destruction.

It might have been in the interests of transition economies, especially the former republics of the Soviet Union, to have co-ordinated price liberalization, budgetary and credit reforms. Williamson (1991, pp. 11–14; 1992, pp. 29–31), Van Brabant (1991b, pp. 63–95), Kregel et al. (1992, pp. 102–103) and Dornbusch (1993, pp. 107–108) recommended the establishment of a 'Payments Union' between transition economies. An organization similar to the European Payments Union (EPU), which operated from mid-1950 to 1958, was suggested, because the convertibility of the currency would not otherwise have been sustainable, due to the inelasticity of import and export demand. Permanent current account deficits would have encouraged depreciation and detracted from the gains in international competitiveness due to the inflexibility of wages. Most European countries suffered repressed inflation. International financial markets were controlled heavily and capital account currency exchanges were only allowed in exceptional circumstances. If convertibility had been initiated immediately, rather than the EPU, European incomes would have been reduced by 1–2 percent, which was the same as the contribution made by the USA under the Marshall plan. This was an all-too-familiar scenario among the transition economies. Through the Payments Union, transition economies would have been able to establish current account convertibility more rapidly between member states and the rest of the world and avoid large depreciation (Williamson, 1992, p. 30). The Union would have achieved currency convertibility, intra-regional economic collaboration, exploitation of comparative advantage, structural adjustment, reduction in the social costs of transition, the development of rational trade and prices, and have prepared transition economies for participation in international trade. The Payments Union was a stage in the gradual transition process to reduce the social costs and create the pre-conditions for full membership in the European Union. The Payments Union did not require the removal of financial or fiscal policies by the sovereign state. Van Brabant (1991a, p. 64) argued that 'I see such a facility as an indispensable instrument of the reform process'.

However, the idea was rejected. The international organizations did not permit this idea to flourish, probably because the newly-formed ex-Soviet republics and Eastern Europe had to depend on trade with Russia for a substantial number of years. Such a union might have provided a mechanism to impose centralization of trade and restrictions on the free movement of capital. In addition, the EPU was associated with extended institutions and agreements which had the short-term goal of economic union. The long-term goal was political union. CEEFSU, encouraged by mature market economies and international organizations, were moving against these links and the degree of economic and political commonality was rather shallow.

The role of foreign aid was considerable for the transition economies, since it was intended to speed and increase the likelihood of the success of the transition reforms. 'I do not know if there has been a case of a country accomplishing this shift entirely out of its own resources' (Kornai, 1995, pp. 30–31). This, of course, was in the interest of mature market economies. Partial debt forgiveness was necessary, which was anathema to the IMF and World Bank (Nuti, 1991, p. 171). The World Bank's technical assistance and long-term project support would have remained invaluable, as well as the IMF's role as a short-term international crisis manager. However, they should not:

> bribe a country into opening its trade accounts since capital injected at the time makes liberalization much harder to sustain (McKinnon, 1993, pp. 116–119).

Unfortunately, however, Western aid did not have positive effects and there was excessive optimism and naïve hope placed in the scale of Western economic aid and its helpful stimulating impact on production. Had the transition economies followed the optimum order of liberalization recommended by neoclassical gradualists economists, their need for external finance would have been limited (McKinnon, 1993, pp. 16–19).

The Post Keynesian Approach to International Trade and Foreign Aid

Post Keynesians recognized the positive benefits associated with international trade. Meanwhile, because open economies are more complex than closed economies, the market outcome would have been even less likely to be a socially desirable outcome (Davidson, 1994). Active government intervention was essential from the start to restructure external trade and payments appropriate to what Post Keynesians define a civilized market economy.

Contrary to the neoclassical view, Post Keynesians argued that an appropriate level of protection would have been essential for enterprises to survive on an uneven playing field. The experience of mature market economies revealed that their development and industrialization was strongly linked with protectionist measures. Consequently, globalization did not automatically result in trade liberalization; rather, there seemed to be powerful forces which supported the construction of trade barriers. Post Keynesians argued that a flexible exchange rate system encouraged only financial currency speculation and not production, discouraged forward contracts, and encouraged stagnation in the domestic and world economy (Davidson, 1994, pp. 238–239). It prompted countries to solve the problems of unemployment and inflation by shifting them onto their trading partners, in an uncivilized way (Davidson, 1994, p. 262).

The comparative advantage theory of international trade was developed in a specific historical period where natural resource endowments and capital-labor ratios determined economic location. Today, this has been replaced by an era of knowledge-intensive industries where comparative advantage is man-made rather than created by Mother Nature and history (Thurow, 1996, p. 214). Natural resources have ceased to dominate economic activity. Long-run economic growth is the result not only of the country's resource endowments but also, most importantly, of its capacity to satisfy both domestic and foreign knowledge-intensive production processes. Differences in production opportunity costs are due to what each society believes to be civilized working conditions (Davidson, 1994, p. 242). The presence of high and persistent unemployment and of very large transaction costs contradicts the assumptions of comparative advantage. Hence that Post Keynesians argue comparative advantage is irrelevant. Industry policy should facilitate strategic economic advantage.

For the Post Keynesians, co-ordination of international trade was essential, especially for the republics of the ex-Soviet Union. Even though the break up of the Soviet Union and COMECON resulted in a variety of transition processes, which increased the complexity and the dimensions of the process, there still should have been co-ordination between the ex-COMECON countries.

> The economies of these states are still so greatly entangled that it is much less costly to gradually change the existing system of the division of labor than to abolish it at once (Yavlinsky and Braguinsky, 1994, p. 103).

For example, intra-trade between the ex-Soviet Union republics comprised 80 percent of their total trade. Trade diversion would have been extremely costly and these products would not have been able to gain access in the international markets. Additionally, trade restrictions between transition economies would have reduced output, magnifying the social cost of transition. As a result, economic links between enterprises in the ex-COMECON countries were necessary.

Post Keynesians viewed the recommendation for the establishment of a payments union by neoclassical gradualist economists as a positive element in the transition process. However, they were very critical of the temporary nature of the payments union in establishing only convertibility, after which it would have ceased to exist since no other goal justified its existence. A Post Keynesian approach would have favored a permanent mechanism for international trade between transition economies, which offered stability and the development of a civilized society. The Payments Union would have evolved, if it was established, into an Eastern European Clearing Union similar to the International Clearing Union suggested by Keynes for the international financial system. Through the clearing union, a fixed exchange system would have eliminated the instability and negative outcomes caused by the flexible exchange rate system. There would have been no advantage in engaging in export-led growth and importing inflation. In this international system, fiscal and monetary policies would still remain the responsibility of the sovereign state. Through the clearing union 'as in all civilized games, all participants are winners who reap benefits' (Davidson and Davidson, 1996, p. 206).

The free trade initiated by the shock therapy approach was 'overshooting in the sense that it is causing deindustrialisation' (Yavlinsky and Braguinsky, 1994, p. 103). The challenge for transition economies was:

> to savor the taste of trade without allowing trade to become an all-consuming force that threatens the development of social and economic life within a community (McClintock, 1996, p. 225).

The Post Keynesian model recommended an adaptive strategy that combined open but managed trade with government expenditure adjustment programs:

> A fixed exchange rate regime operating in tandem with intelligent internal demand and incomes management policies will create an environment where all nations simultaneously can be winners and economic growth increases globally without any nation necessarily running into a balance of payments constraint (Davidson, 1994, p. 256).

Economic policy co-ordination has, therefore, become a necessary condition for achieving sustained economic prosperity in the new globalized economic environment. A concurrent generalized expansion of income across countries, through a co-ordinated approach, might have helped to mitigate the problems of trade deficits and capital flight driven by international differences in inflation and interest rates. This would have enabled countries to stay on an expansionary course. In the absence of such co-ordination, the adverse policy incentives that promoted the macroeconomics of austerity and the lowering of the wage floor would have inevitably asserted themselves.

The financial assistance provided by the mature market economies has been disappointing. The transition economies had to depend on their own resources. In addition, due to the relative scarcity of foreign capital and international aid, transition economies competed only in providing concessions to foreign investment. This may have enabled them to acquire the necessary financial resources, Post Keynesians conceded, but it has had irreversible consequences for the future. It has created a heavy reliance on the voluntary movement of capital and handouts from international organizations, reducing national sovereignty and jeopardizing the development of a civilized society. The transition economies would have been able to stand on both feet only after an extensive debt cancellation program, together with substantial foreign aid, not only to assist the transition program, but also to maintain political support and the development of a civilized society. Foreign aid benefited the donor economy as well as the recipient transition economy because it helped to stimulate increased international trade and strengthened relationships in the international community. A prime example is the Marshall Plan's large military and economic aid programs after World War II. The European countries received financial aid to buy American products. This facilitated restructuring in both Europe and the United States (Davidson 1994, p. 246). The development of a civilized society, as Post Keynesians argued, requires an international financial system that prohibits the movement of financial capital for speculative reasons. Indeed, Keynes argued that capital controls, both inward and outward, should be permanent. Thus, the Post Keynesians concluded that the transition economies, due to the freely floating exchange rate and the free international market, were contributing to the international debt problem, which threatened the viability of the international financial system.

The Chinese Approach to International Trade and Foreign Aid

In 1979 in China, trade liberalization policies were introduced to facilitate exports and, for the first time, to allow for foreign investment. In essence, these efforts involved the break-up of the monopoly of foreign trade held by the central government, transferring this authority to local governments. Special economic zones were set up to free foreign investors and domestic exporters from red tape. Real devaluation, comparative advantage and the entrepreneurial energies of a receptive expatriate community also contributed to China's trade performance. Nevertheless, it is doubtful that trade would have grown in the way that it did if restrictive national regulations had not been substantially mitigated by local authorities taking advantage of the possibilities offered by extensive decentralization.

Nolan (1995, pp. 59–60) argued that reform of the Chinese industrial structure presented an extreme form of the 'infant industry' argument. Almost the whole of the Chinese industrial sector could be considered an infant industry. An 'infant industry' is not just one, which did not exist in any form and required protection to start up. An 'old' industry, which is out-of-date and uncompetitive on international markets, but which, is in the process of being modernized and restructured, can be considered to have the same characteristics as an infant industry. It is rational to argue that an industry, which at present is uncompetitive and would be bankrupted in open international competition, but which is thought likely to become competitive, should be given protection.

Extensive state action, through protection, was required to construct a competitive industrial sector, so that China could shift from a traditional anti-comparative advantage and heavy industry oriented development to a strategy that relied on comparative advantage. In this process, one of the key functions of planning was to identify sectors that were likely to become internationally competitive and to take measures to assist them. The East Asian experience demonstrated that government discretionary policy was exercized prior to and during the opening up of the economy to the world markets. In contrast, the typical advice of the IMF and World Bank to transition economies was to liberalize foreign trade immediately, which has driven them out into the world competition before their economies were able to withstand the pressure. The Chinese did not make this mistake.

China went to great lengths to attract foreign capital and foreign technology. Both rapid economic growth and higher incomes increasingly depended upon the input of ever-larger amounts of capital from abroad, and expatriate investors were a potentially important source of linkage with the world economy. In contrast to China, transition economies had relied too much, and to some extent even passively, on foreign aid and foreign advice in carrying out economic reform. In the Chinese case, foreign advice was accepted only selectively. 'China's reform program was largely shaped despite, not because, of foreign advice' (Nolan, 1995, p. 23).

However, 'opening to the world' can only be accomplished by increasing conformity to capitalist norms, which raises fundamental issues for the Chinese domestic society and its re-subordination to outside powers. The Chinese themselves are caught between their desire to hold on to an historic independence, which is seen as inseparable from the protection of national sovereignty, and their need for foreign investment and trade. In the first place, whether largely foreign-funded capitalist development, intentionally introduced by the government, can be controlled, or whether the most powerful figures in the current leadership even want to control it, is a fundamental issue today. From this perspective, the only question is whether there will be conversion to a totally private form of capitalism. No doubt a complete reversion to a capitalist system is the goal of many within the burgeoning privatized sector, while some elements within the government, especially those most closely tied into foreign ventures and joint enterprises, must share these ultimate aims. In reality, local governments competing to attract overseas capital typically bend to investors' demands. Moreover, many local cadres cultivate good relations with foreign owners for their own personal interest. Even though they know perfectly well what the working and living conditions in foreign owned factories are, they would never intervene to do anything about them (Qinglian, 2000, p. 85). In addition, illegal outflow of private funds, amounting to US $20 billion annually, even before the Asian financial crisis of 1997–1998, which has induced further illegal capital flight (Lau, 1999, p. 70). In this way, the internal 'socialist' market and the external 'capitalist' market have been employed to stimulate and accelerate economic growth, and have become inextricably linked, to the point that they are not distinguishable.

Conclusion

Distinct methods of economic analysis, political structures and speeds of implementing the transition policies gives rise to alternative models of transition. As such, alternative models of transition result in alternative international trade policies and different roles associated with the provision of foreign aid.

The shock therapy supporters favored the immediate establishment of free trade and a fully convertible exchange rate. They argued that a fully convertible currency would restore faith in the currency, reduce inflationary expectations, and stimulate foreign trade. A fully convertible exchange rate would make it possible to attract foreign investment, which was essential to overcome stagnation, since foreign investment provided resources, technology and expertise. Some allowance needed to be made to protect infant industries; consequently the state would be able to raise a certain amount of revenue from tariffs. The neoclassical gradualist economists were in favor of a gradual process of achieving full convertibility through a payments union. The Post Keynesians were in favor of maintaining tariffs through a permanent clearing union. They argued that the principle of comparative advantage was valid only in the ideal world of full employment. Thus tariffs and a discretionary exchange rate policy were essential. The non-pluralistic socialists in China, on the other hand, maintained tariffs and non-tariff barriers, implemented a discretionary exchange rate policy and the establishment of special economic zones.

Neoclassical and Post Keynesian economists highlighted the need for conditional foreign aid to assist with the transition process. They argued that the international community should only provide foreign aid to governments that initiate comprehensive and well-designed reforms. Meanwhile Chinese market socialists were suspicious of the terms and conditions associated with the provision of foreign aid. For the Chinese market socialists, only unconditional foreign aid could be accepted. However, capitalist market economies, and international organizations dominated by a capitalist free market approach, were not willing to assist in the development of a market socialist system. Consequently, the policies with regard to international trade and the role of foreign aid cannot be analysed independently of the transition model in question. It is the transition model, which determines what is desirable, acceptable, and feasible, which also determines the international trade policies and the role of foreign aid during the transition and not the reverse.

References

Aslund, A. (1992), *Post–Communist Economic Revolutions. How Big a Bang?*, Washington, DC: The Brookings Institution.

Aslund, A. (1995), *How Russia Became a Market Economy*, Washington, DC: The Brookings Institution.

Davidson, G. and Davidson, P. (1996), *Economics For A Civilised Society*, Second (Revised) Edition, London, UK: Macmillan.

Davidson, P. (1994), *Post Keynesian Macroeconomic Theory*, Hants, UK: Edward Elgar.

Dornbusch, R. (1993), 'Payments Arrangements among the Republics', in O. Blanchard, M. Boycko, R. Dabrowski, R. Dornbusch, R. Layard and A. Shleifer (eds), *A. Post–Communist Reform. Pain and Progress* (pp. 81–108), Cambridge, MA: The MIT Press.

Kornai, J. (1993), 'Transformational Recession A General Phenomenon Examined through the Example of Hungary's Development', *Economie Appliquee*, Vol. 46, No. 2, pp. 181–227.

Kornai, J. (1995), 'Lasting Growth as the Top Priority: Macroeconomic Tensions and Government Economic Policy in Hungary', *Acta Oeconomica*, Vol. 47, No. 1–2, pp. 1–38.

Kregel, J., Matzner, E. and Grabher, G. (1992), *The Market Shock*, Vienna: GENDA Group.

Lau, R.W.K. (1999), 'The 15th Congress of the Chinese Communist Party: Milestone in China's Privatization', *Capital & Class*, No. 68, Summer, pp. 51–87.

McClintock, B. (1996), 'International Trade and the Governance of Global Markets', in C.J. Whalen (ed.), *Political Economy for the 21st Century* (pp. 225–244), New York, NY: M.E. Sharpe.

McKinnon, R.I. (1993), *The Order of Economic Liberalization: Financial Control in the Transition to a Market Economy*, Baltimore, MD: The John Hopkins University Press.

Nolan, P. (1995), *China's Rise, Russia's Fall*, New York, NY: St. Martin's Press.

Nuti, D.M. (1991), 'Stabilization and Sequencing in the Reform of Socialist Economies', in S. Commander (ed.), *Managing Inflation in Socialist Economies in Transition* (pp. 155–173), Washington, DC: The World Bank.

Qinglian, H. (2000), 'China's Listing Social Structure', *New Left Review*, Second Series, No. 5, September–October, pp. 69–99.

Sachs J. (1991), 'Sachs on Poland', *The Economist*, January 19, p. 67.

Sachs, J. (1992), 'The Grand Bargain', in A. Aslund (ed.), *The Post–Soviet Economy. Soviet and Western Perspectives* (pp. 207–216), New York, NY: St. Martin's Press.

Sachs, J. (1993), *Poland's Jump to the Market Economy*, Cambridge, MA: The MIT Press.

Sachs, J. (1995a), 'Why Corruption Rules Russia', *The New York Times*, November 29, p. 22.

Sachs, J. (1995b), 'Consolidating Capitalism', *Foreign Policy*, Vol. 98, Spring, pp. 50–64.

Sachs, J. (1996), 'Economic Transition and the Exchange-Rate Regime', *American Economic Review Papers and Proceedings*, Vol. 86, No. 2, May, pp. 147–152.

Sachs, J. (1997), 'An Overview of Stabilization Issues Facing Economies in Transition', in W.T. Woo, S. Parker and J.D. Sachs (eds), *Economies in Transition. Comparing Asia and Europe* (pp. 243–256), Cambridge, MA: MIT Press.

Sutela, P. (1992), 'The Role of the External Sector during the Transition', in A. Aslund (ed.), *The Post-Soviet Economy. Soviet and Western Perspectives* (pp. 85–101), New York, NY: St. Martin's Press.

Thurow, L.C. (1996), 'Comparative Advantage, Factor–Price Equalisation, Industrial Strategies, and Trade Tactics', in C.J. Whalen (ed.), *Political Economy for the 21st Century* (pp. 213–224), New York, NY: M.E. Sharpe.

Van Brabant, J.M. (1991a), 'Property Rights Reform, Macroeconomic Performance and Welfare', In H. Blommenstein and M. Marrese (eds), *Transformation of Planned Economies: Property Rights and Macroeconomic Stability*, Paris: OECD.

Van Brabant, J.M. (1991b), 'Convertibility in Eastern Europe Through a Payments Union', in J. Williamson (ed.), *Currency Convertibility in Eastern Europe* (pp. 63–95), Washington, DC: Institute for International Economics.

Walder, A.G. (1996), 'Markets and Inequality in Transitional Economies: Toward Testable Theories', *American Journal of Sociology*, Vol. 101, No. 4, pp. 1060–73.

Williamson, J. (1991), 'The Case for a Payments Union', *International Economic Insights*, September/October, pp. 11–14.

Williamson, J. (1992), *Trade and Payments After Soviet Disintegration*, Washington, DC: Institute of International Economics.

Yavlinsky, G. and S. Braguinsky (1994), 'The Inefficiency of Laissez–Fair in Russia: Hysteresis Effects and the Need for Policy-Led Transformation', *Journal of Comparative Economics*, Vol. 19, No. 1, pp. 88–116.

Chapter 7

Agriculture Reforms and Development in East-Central Europe

Pavel Ciaian and Ján Pokrivčák

In 1989 the Berlin wall, a symbol of Communism, fell – leading to the collapse of Communist regimes in Central and East European Countries (CEECs) and in the former republics of the Soviet Union (FSU). During the subsequent transition period, the CEECs and FSU turned their socialist, centrally planned economies based on state ownership into a market-driven system with private ownership of production resources. This occurred on the backdrop of the transformation of their societies from dictatorship to democracy.

All economic activity in socialist economies of the CEECs and FSU was directly regulated by the government and the whole economy was treated as a single firm. Central planners set production quantities at each unit of production (factory, cooperative farm, office) and the pattern of trade between individual units of production. Allocation of production resources (labor, land, and capital) among production units was also decided centrally.

In a socialist economy prices do not transmit the right signals to producers and consumers on which resource is scarce and which is abundant. Prices do not adjust up when there is a lack of some production resource and/or a good and neither do they go down in the case of a surplus. The allocation of production resources is therefore the sole responsibility of the central planners. The ability and motivation of central planners therefore, affects the performance of the economy. Prices in a centrally planned economy are only used to reduce the cost of exchange (transaction costs) rather than to provide incentives for economic agents.

State ownership of all production factors is another salient feature of the socialist economy. Decisions regarding the use of production resources are made by the state and all income from their use also accrues to the state. State ownership has a pronounced influence on the incentives of private agents. In socialist economies there is a weak motivation of individuals to engage in innovative and production increasing activities because the reward from it is reaped by all.

The road from socialism to market economy can be characterized as a process of institutional change. Socialist institutions are being replaced by those of market economy and democracy. The term institution refers to 'rules of the game', that is constraints on human behavior. These constraints include constitution, written laws, but also unwritten codes of conduct. Individuals maximize their utility constrained by these rules. Any alteration of rules leads to change in individuals' behavior and thus affects economic performance. Institutions in market economy support (in most cases) private incentives unlike socialist institutions that encourage collective behavior and free riding. The most important market institutions are private property rights and market mechanism.

Agriculture was an integral part of the socialist centrally-planned economy in the CEECs and FSU. The State regulated all agricultural production in the same way as it regulated industrial production. Resources used in agricultural production, including land, were also *de facto* owned by the state, though legally most of land was owned privately. Farms had to execute the central plan. Production was delivered to the state selling companies and could not be sold freely on the market.

The structure of socialist agriculture was strongly biased towards extremely large farms. As table 7.1 shows the average farm size ranged from 1,157 hectares in Poland

Table 7.1 Socialist Agriculture in the 1980s

	Average farm size	Workers per 1000 ha	Tractors per 1000 ha	Workers/Tractors per 1000 ha (B/C)
	(A)	(B)	(C)	(D)
Albania	1 907	628	20	32
Bulgaria	19 464	156	10	15
Czechoslovakia	2 988	156	24	6
Hungary	3 559	158	10	16
Poland	1 157	259	29	9
Romania	2 696	209	15	14
Estonia	4 490	92	16	6
Latvia	4 041	102	15	7
Lithuania	3 094	109	15	7
Armenia	1 621	167	10	16
Azerbaijan	2 765	164	10	17
Belarus	3 417	125	14	9
Georgia	2 148	209	10	21
Kazakhstan	75 555	9	1	7
Kyrgyzstan	21 626	41	3	14
Moldova	2 519	279	25	11
Russia	8 473	50	7	7
Tajikistan	8 352	114	9	12
Turkmenistan	124 770	7	1	10
Ukraine	3 930	145	11	13
Uzbekistan	13 637	77	7	11

Source: Lerman, Csaki, and Feder (2002).

to around 124,770 hectares in Turkmenistan. This size is very large compared to average farm size in market economies such as the European Union, USA or Japan (Table 7.2).

Table 7.2 Farm Size in Market Economies

	Average farm size (ha)
Japan	1.24
EU-15	18
USA	197

Sources: Ministry of Agriculture, Forestry and Fisheries of Japan; European Commission, USDA.

Agriculture in the CEECs and FSU was strongly subsidized during the socialist period. Figure 7.1. shows that state support of agriculture, as measured by the Producer Support Estimate (PSE)[1] calculated by the Organization for Economic Co-operation and Development (OECD), was high. In many CEEC and FSU countries agricultural support exceeded the EU protection level and in Russia and Estonia it also exceeded the protection level of the most protectionist countries such as Japan. Poland was an exception to the rule. Land in Poland was never fully collectivized and the majority of land was cultivated by family farms. For this reason there was no political will to strongly support agriculture.

Agricultural Reforms

Transition process in agriculture involved four different tasks: 1) privatization, 2) farm restructuring, 3) price liberalization, and 4) institution building.

Privatization

Land is a specific agricultural resource and it was cultivated collectively during socialist times. Land privatization was therefore a significant step towards a market economy. Through privatization process private property rights were restored. In Baltic States and in most CEECs, except for Albania, land was restituted to former owners. FSU and Albania distributed land to farm workers. Hungary and Romania combined the distribution of land to workers with the restitution to former owners (Lerman, Csaki, and Feder, 2002; Lerman, 2001; Swinnen, 1999).

1 PSE (producer support estimate) is an indicator of the annual monetary value of gross transfers from consumers and taxpayers to support agricultural producers, measured at the farm-gate level, arising from policy measures that support agriculture, regardless of their nature, objectives or impacts on farm production or income (OECD).

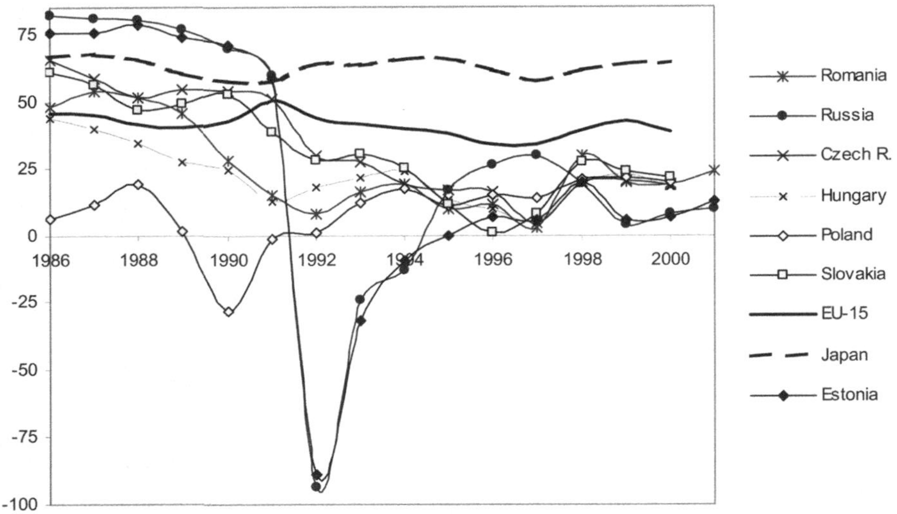

Figure 7.1 PSE in Selected Transition Countries

There are also countries where privatization of land was very limited, such as Belarus, Kazakhstan and Turkmenistan. In these countries usually only small household plots may be privately owned (Table 7.3).

Similarly, as in the case of land privatization, non-land assets were returned to original owners or distributed to workers and/or landowners.

Farm Restructuring

Farm restructuring followed after the privatization process. New private owners of farm assets and land were allowed to break away from cooperative farms and to start individual farming. This led to the creation of many family farms that were significantly smaller in size than cooperatives, but comparable to their Western European, Japanese or American counterparts (Tables 7.2 and 7.4). But not all cooperative farms broke up into family farms. Many cooperatives (those not entirely replaced by family farms) were transformed. That is, old socialist cooperatives were turned into cooperatives of owners of agricultural assets (including land), joint-stock companies, limited-liability companies or partnerships. During this process the size structure of farms changed towards smaller units for the sake of efficiency of management.

Depending upon the methods of privatization and government policies on restructuring different farm structures emerged in different transition countries. While in Slovakia, the Czech Republic and most FSU agriculture is still dominated by large transformed enterprises, Albania, Baltic States and Romania have created many small size family farms. There is a whole spectrum of farm structures in between these two extreme cases (Table 7.4).

Table 7.3 Land Privatization Strategy by Country

	Distribution to workers	Restitution to former owners	Distribution and Restitution
Albania	✔		
Bulgaria		✔	
Czech R.		✔	
Hungary			✔
Slovakia		✔	
Romania			✔
Estonia		✔	
Latvia		✔	
Lithuania		✔	
Armenia	✔		
Azerbaijan	✔		
Georgia	✔		
Moldova	✔		
Russia	✔		
Ukraine	✔		
Belarus		Limited land privatization	
Kazakhstan		Limited land privatization	
Turkmenistan		Limited land privatization	

Source: Lerman, Csaki, and Feder (2002).

Market Liberalization

In socialism production and trade was regulated centrally and reflected mostly the political preferences of the communist government. The role of prices was limited and relegated to the position of providing accounting information that could be used for the monitoring and control of enterprises by central authorities. Liberalization of markets re-established the crucial role of prices for allocation of resources. Because of inherent problems with central planning, socialist economies were characterized by chronic shortages of some goods and surpluses of the others. Imposition of liberalization in such circumstances led to significant adjustments of real prices.

Because of liberalization the majority of prices increased. The most significant increase occurred for prices of agricultural inputs that farms purchase on the market while prices of agricultural products stagnated or increased only slightly. That is, real prices of agricultural products (agricultural terms of trade) declined during transition. This was the reflection of supply-demand conditions prior to liberalization. There was a surplus of agricultural products and a lack of input. Figures 7.2 and 7.3 show the development of prices after liberalization in two selected countries, Hungary and Russia, respectively. The rates at which prices increased differed between countries.

Table 7.4 Farm Structures in Transition Countries

	Family farms		Transformed cooperative farms		Year
	Share in TAA (%)	Average size (ha)	Share in TAA (%)	Average size (ha)	
Albania*	96		4		1998
Bulgaria	44	1	55	861	1997
Czech R.	28	20	72	937	2003
Hungary	59	4	41	312	2000
Poland	87	8	13		2003
Romania	55	2	45	274	2002
Slovakia	12	42	88	1185	2003
Slovenia	94		6		2000
CEECs	**56**		**44**		
Estonia	63	2	37	327	2001
Latvia	90	12	10	297	2001
Lithuania	89	4	11	483	2003
Baltic States	**81**		**19**		
Armenia	32		68		1997
Azerbaijan	9		91		1997
Belarus	16		84		1997
Georgia	24		76		1997
Kazakhstan	20		80		1997
Kyrgyzstan	23		77		1997
Moldavia	27		73	1 400	1997
Russia	11		89	6 100	1997
Tajikistan	7		93		1997
Turkmenistan	0.3		99.7		1997
Uzbekistan	4		96		1997
Ukraine	17		83	2 100	1997
CIS	**16**		**84**		

Sources: Bulgaria: Bulgarian Ministry of Agriculture and Forestry; Czech Republic: Czech Statistical Office; Estonia: Statistical Office of Estonia; Hungary: European Commission; Poland: Central Statistical Office; Latvia: Statistical Office of Latvia; Lithuania: Statistical Office of Lithuania; Slovenia: Statistical Office of the Republic of Slovenia, Armenia, Azerbaijan, Belarus, Georgia, Kazakhstan, Kyrgyzstan, Moldova, Russia, Tajikistan, Turkmenistan, Ukraine, Uzbekistan: Lerman, Csaki, and Feder (2002); Albania: Albanian Ministry of Agriculture; Slovakia: Ministry of Agriculture; Romania: Romanian National Institute of Statistics.

Notes: TAA – Total Agricultural Area; * for arable land only

The highest price rise occurred in Russia. A much smaller price increase was reported in Hungary. However, in all transition countries retail and input prices increased at higher rate than farm prices.

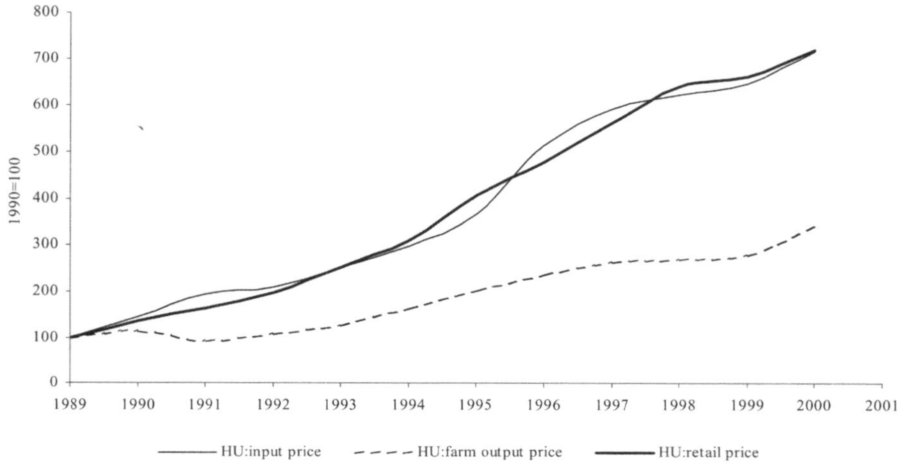

Figure 7.2 Development of Agricultural Prices in Hungary

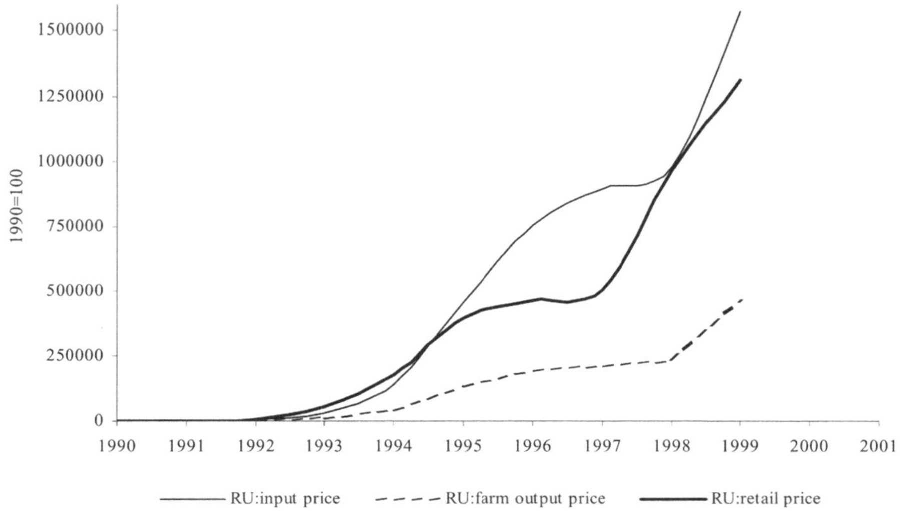

Figure 7.3 Development of Agricultural Prices in Russia

Institutional Environment

Transition also involved institutional changes, in addition to privatization and liberalization. The quality of the institutional environment determines economic performance, therefore the institutional change from socialism to democracy and market economy was of utmost importance.

Generally the CEECs and Baltic States introduced higher protection of private property rights than CIS. That is, there are more legal restrictions for land transaction and weaker enforcement of property rights in CIS. For example in some CIS countries (Belarus, Uzbekistan, Kyrgyzstan and Turkmenistan) legislation did not allow transferability of land through sale or purchase. Some countries did not even allow land lease. An important restriction is also related to weak enforcement of property rights. The cooperative managers and local politicians in CIS but also in CEECs are able to prevent land and asset owners to restructure the cooperative farm, most often by increasing their costs of withdrawing their assets from the farm. (Ciaian and Swinnen, 2006; Dale and Baldwin, 1999; Lerman, Csaki and Feder, 2002; Swain, 1999).

Agricultural Output in CEECs and FSU: Initial Fall then Recovery

Transition led to substantial adjustments in agricultural output. Figure 7.4 shows agricultural output developments for three geopolitical regions (CIS, Baltic states and CEECs) and also individually for several selected transition countries. All transition countries experienced output decline in the first years of transition. Four years after the beginning of the transition agricultural output fell more than 40 percent in the Baltic States, around 30 percent the CIS and around 20 percent in the CEECs.

After this initial strong decline, agricultural production picked up. The output recovery, however, differed among countries. The strongest recovery occurred in Albania, Slovenia and Romania. Output in Albania and Slovenia exceeded the 1989 level after four years of transition. In other CEECs output recovery was much weaker. A lot of countries experienced stagnation or only slight increases. In the Baltic States and CIS output recovery came much later. Agricultural output stopped declining only after 7–8 years of transition.

Output declines were caused by a reduction of use of the inputs. Variable inputs (fertilizer, labor) declined more than fixed inputs (tractors, land). Variable inputs are easer to adjust when prices or other things change. On the other hand capital inputs are more specific to agriculture and immobile in the short-run. The use of tractors and especially of land remained quite stable over the transition period.

Fertilizer use went down substantially in the first years of transition. For example, relative to the 1989 level, fertilizer use declined in 1992 by 83 percent in Hungary, by 78 percent in Albania, by 60 percent in Romania, and by 54 percent in FSU. After this initial decline, fertilizer use increased later in the transition, but it never reached the level of 1989 (Figure 7.5).

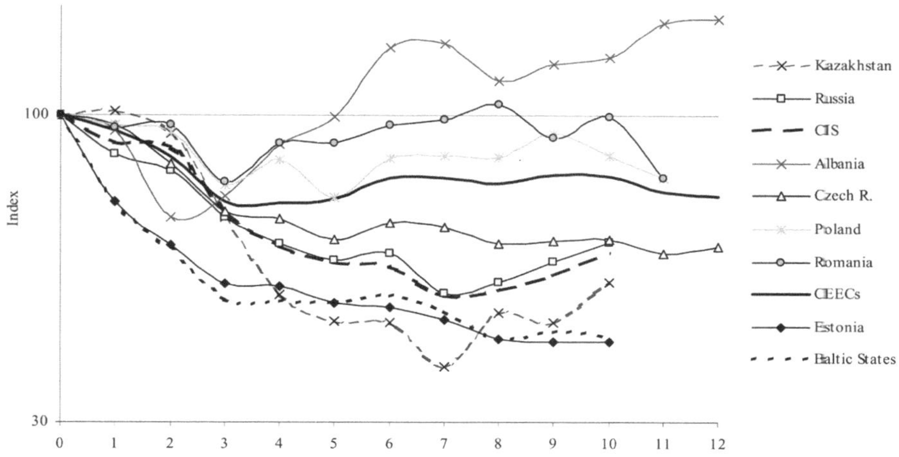

Figure 7.4 Agricultural Output Developments During Transition

The development of labor was different. Its adjustment largely depended upon the growth of the overall economy and the economy's potential to absorb surplus labor from the agricultural sector. In a number of countries labor employment in agriculture remained relatively stable during transition (Albania, Lithuania, Poland, Kazakhstan, Russia). In some countries (Romania, Bulgaria and Ukraine) there was an inflow of labor into agricultural sector, which provided a safety net for workers laid off from the industry. In countries where general economic performance was better and the state provided for substantial social security (Czech Republic, Estonia, Hungary, Slovakia) there was a substantial outflow of labor from agriculture (Table 7.5).

What Factors Caused Decline of Agricultural Output in CEECs and FSU?

The initial deep decline of agricultural output occurred due to the disruption of the socialist exchange system (Blanchard, 1997; Roland and Verdier, 1999). Downstream industries (those delivering inputs to farms) as well as upstream industries (those purchasing outputs from farmers) were in temporary disarray because of privatization and subsequent restructuring. This process disrupted the traditional channels of product transfer between farms and down and upstream industries while new channels based on market relations were still nonexistent. It took time and resources to establish new channels and to halt production decline.

Agricultural production in the CEECs and FSU has never reached the pre-transition level. Albania is an exception to this rule. Macours and Swinnen (2000) consider trade and price liberalization, as well as subsidy cuts, as the main reasons behind this development. Liberalization significantly worsened agricultural terms

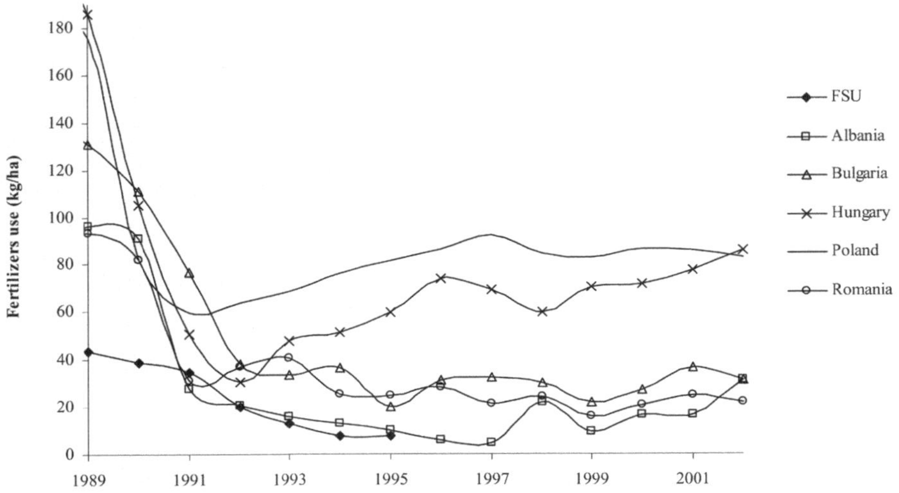

Figure 7.5 Fertilizer use in Selected Transition Countries

Table 7.5 Share of Agriculture in Total Employment (%)

	1990	1993	1995	1998	2000
Albania		71	65	64	
Bulgaria	18	22	24	25	26
Czech Republic	12	7.8	6.6	5.5	5
Hungary	18	9.3	8.1	7.7	6.5
Poland	27	25	26	26	28
Romania	28	35	34	37	41
Slovak R.	12	12	9.4	8.3	6.7
Estonia	12	15	8.5	6.8	6.9
Latvia	16	18	17	16	13
Lithuania	18	22	23	21	19
Belarus	19	20	19	17	14
Kazakhstan	23	20	21	24	23
Russia	13	14	15	14	13
Ukraine	20	20	22	22	24

Source: OECD

of trade as input prices grew faster than the output prices of farms. This is shown in figures 7.2 and 7.3 for Hungary and Russia, respectively. Profit maximizing farmers reacted to this negative development of their prices by cutting production.

Subsidy cuts exacerbated the situation of farmers. During the transition process government support to farmers declined from above the average of EU at the end of socialism to about half of the EU level after few years of transition (Figure 7.1). After 1997 agricultural support started to rise again. This induced farms to increase production and reversed negative output developments in some countries. In the Baltic States subsidy cuts were more pronounced than in the CEECs. The effect was that in CEECs output fall was smaller than in the Baltic States (Figure 7.4).

Transfer of property rights on agricultural assets from state to private individuals also had an impact on production. First of all private owners have more motivation to improve efficiency than state farms because the resultant higher profits would accrue to them rather than to the state. Second, private farms face hard budget constraints and cannot rely on selective assistance from the state if they make losses. Hard budget constraints and better motivation led to more efficient input use and higher production.

Property rights in the CEECs are better defined and protected than in the CIS, which implies that farms in the CEECs face harder budget constraints than farms in the CIS and additionally owners of agricultural assets are better motivated to increase efficiency than owners of agricultural assets in the CIS. As a consequence agricultural production in the CEECs grew faster in the CEECs than in the CIS (Figure 7.4). The output fall in the CIS was higher and lasted longer. It continuously declined for 7 years from the start of transition. The CEECs output decline was smaller and it stopped after the third year of transition.

Restructuring of the farm sector reduced the size of farms, which had an impact on efficiency of production and thus affected agricultural output. Size of farms affects production through two channels: 1) labor supervision and 2) economy of scale.

The problem of labor shirking in teams is well documented in the literature (Alchian and Demsetz, 1972; Calvo and Wellisz, 1978; and others). The nature of production makes the problem of shirking more pronounced in the agricultural sector than in industry. Agricultural production is spatially spread and significantly affected by weather, which makes it difficult for managers to supervise hired labor and to measure effort based on output (Pollak, 1985; Schmitt, 1991). In large socialist farms there was therefore a natural propensity to shirk. Additionally large farms must rely on hired labor which has less incentive to work than owner of the farm. Emergence of family farms naturally led to a reduction in shirking and to a higher productivity of labor that subsequently caused the growth of production.

The emergence of many small family farms therefore had a positive effect on production. This was the case in Albania, Moldova, Romania, and Georgia. Figure 7.4 shows that output development in Romania, and especially in Albania, was much different to other countries. In Albania output exceeded the 1989 level by around 20 percent in 2003. In other comparable countries this was not the case. The growth of agricultural production has not been realized in Latvia, Lithuania, and Estonia despite the fact that family farms also provide a significant share of agricultural production in these countries. Other factors like the reduction of agricultural subsidies offset the positive effect of the creation of family farms in the Baltic States. In the CIS development of family farms was slow which negatively affects the agricultural output. The situation is worsened by the fact that the size of cooperatives and transformed cooperatives is larger in the CIS than in the CEECs.

On the other hand, dividing large cooperatives into many small family farms reduces the gains from economy of scale. As a result, countries with capital intensive agriculture are more likely experienced output decline due to break up of cooperative farms. This was the case of Baltic States, and to some extent the Czech Republic and Slovakia because cooperative farms were broken in smaller units (Table 7.1 column A and C).

Taking into account both the impact of incentives and economy of scale there are both gainers and losers as measured by the development output. In countries with labor intensive agriculture, which broke up large cooperatives and re-introduced family farms (Albania, Romania), gains from incentives realignment offset losses from decreased economy of scale. These countries experienced growth in agricultural production. Agricultural production also fared relatively well in countries with capital intensive agriculture which transformed and scaled down socialist cooperatives without switching entirely to family farming (Slovakia, the Czech Republic, Hungary). In these countries the losses from economy of scale were compensated by the gains from improving incentives. On the other side of the spectrum are countries that have labor intensive agriculture and did not dismantle large cooperatives (CIS). In these countries agricultural output declined because gains from economy of scale did not compensate enough losses from bad incentives (see Table 7.1 and Figure 7.4).

Conclusions

Since the fall of communism substantial changes were introduced in agricultural sectors in former communist countries. They include privatization, market liberalization, farm restructuring and institution building. A parallel development occurred in other sectors of the economy, but there are some agricultural specifics related to the nature of agricultural production which is significantly dependent on land and nature.

The predominant form of privatization of agricultural land and other assets in CEECs was restitution to former owners while in the CIS it was distribution to farm workers. Privatization led to the break up of large cooperative farms into small family farms. Creation of family farms varied among countries being the strongest in Albania and Baltic States and weaker in CIS, the Czech Republic and Slovakia.

Transformation of cooperatives into family farms affected production through economy of scale and supervision of labor. In countries with labor intensive agriculture which broke up large cooperatives and re-introduced family farms (Albania, Romania) gains from incentives realignment offset losses from decreased economy of scale. These countries experienced growth of agricultural production. Agricultural production also fared relatively well in countries with capital intensive agriculture which transformed and scaled down socialist cooperative without switching entirely to family farming (Slovakia, the Czech Republic, Hungary). In these countries the losses from economy of scale were compensated by gains from improving incentives. On the other side of the spectrum are countries that have labor intensive agriculture and did not dismantle large cooperatives (CIS). In these countries agricultural output declined because gains from economy of scale did not compensate enough losses from bad incentives.

In all CEECs and FSU agricultural terms of trade declined and agricultural support from the state was lowered. As a reaction, agricultural production declined. The decline was stronger in countries where cut of subsidies and negative development of terms of trade was more pronounced (Baltic States). Later in transition some countries reacted to negative development of agricultural incomes by increasing agricultural support.

Security of property rights also affected agricultural production. In the CIS, where private rights to land were less secure than in the CEECs, decline of agricultural production was deeper and lasted longer. In contrast, in theCEECs after the initial drop, output has stabilized.

References

Albanian Ministry of Agriculture (2000), *Review of Albanian Agriculture, 2000*, Tirana: Albanian Ministry of Agriculture.

Alchian, A.A. and H. Demsetz (1972), 'Production, Information Costs, and Economic Organization', *American Economic Review*, Vol. 62, No. 5, pp. 777–795.

Blanchard, O. (1997), *The Economics of Post-Communist Transition*, Oxford: Clarendon Press.

Bulgarian Ministry of Agriculture and Forestry (1998), *National Agriculture and Rural Development Plan over the 2000–2006 Period under the EU Special Accession Program for Agriculture and Rural Development (SAPARD)*, Soifia: Bulgarian Ministry of Agriculture and Forestry.

Calvo, G.A. and S. Wellisz (1978), 'Supervision, Loss of Control, and Optimum Size of Firm', *Journal of Political Economy*, Vol 86, No. 5, pp. 943–952.

Central Statistical Office (2004), *Maly Roczink Statystyczny 2004*, Warsaw: Central Statistical Office Poland.

Ciaian, P. and J.F.M. Swinnen (2006), 'Land Market Imperfections and Agricultural Policy Impacts in the New EU Member States: A Partial Equilibrium Analysis', *American Journal of Agricultural Economics*, 88 (4), pp. 799–815.

Czech Statistical Office (2003), *Strukturální Výsledky za Zemìdìlství ÈR v. Roce 2003*, Prague: Czech Statistical Office.

Dale, P. and Baldwin, R. (1999), 'Emerging Land Markets in Central and Eastern Europe', in *Structural Change in the Farming Sectors in Central and Eastern Europe: Lessons for EU Accession,* Second World Bank/FAO Workshop, Warsaw, Poland, June pp. 27–29.

European Commission (2002), *Agricultural Situation and Prospects in the Candidate Countries*, Country Report on Hungary, Brussels.

European Commission (2003), *Agriculture in the European Union Statistical and Economic Information 2002*, Brussels.

FAO, FAOSTAT Internet Database, faostat.fao.org. Food and Agricluture Organization of the United Nations.

Lerman, Z. (2001), 'Agriculture in Transition Economies: From Common Heritage to Divergence', *Agricultural Economics* Vol 26, pp. 95–114.

Lerman, Z., Csaki, C. and Feder, G. (2002), 'Land Policies and Evolving Farm Structures in Transition Countries', Policy Research Working Paper No. 2794, World Bank.

Macours, K. and Swinnen, J. (2000), 'Causes of Output Decline in Economic Transition: The Case of Central and Eastern European Agriculture', *Journal of Comparative Economics* Vol. 28, No. 1, pp. 172–206.

Ministry of Agriculture, Forestry and Fisheries of Japan (2005), *Abstract of Statistics on Agriculture Forestry and Fisheries in Japan*, Ministry of Agriculture, Forestry and Fisheries of Japan.

OECD, *Agricultural Policies in OECD Countries, Monitoring and Evaluation*, Paris, OECD, various years.

OECD (2002), *Agricultural Policies in Transition Economies*, Paris: Paris OECD.

Pollak, R.A. (1985), 'A Transaction Costs approach to Families and Households', *Journal of Economic Literature*, Vol. 23, pp. 581–608.

Roland, G. and Verdier, T. (1999), 'Transition and the Output Fall', *Economics of Transition*, Vol. 7, No. 1, pp. 1–28.

Romania National Insititute of Statistics (2002), *Agrocensus 2002*, Bucharest: Romania National Institute of Statisitics.

Schmitt, G. (1991), 'Why is the Agriculture of Advanced Western Countries still Organized by Family Farms? Will this continue to be so in the Future?', *European Review of Agricultural Economics*, 18, pp. 443–458.

Slovak Ministry of Agriculture (2004), *Green Report for 2004*, Bratslavia: Slovak Minisry of Agriculture.

Statistical Office of Estonia (2001), *Agricultural Census 2001*, Tallinn: Statistical Office of Estonia.

Statisticla Office of Latvia (2001), *Agricultural Census 2003*, Riga: Statistical Office of Latvia.

Statistical Office of Lithuania (2003), *Agricutlural Census 2003*, Vilnius: Statistical Office of Lituania.

Statistical office of the Republic of Slovenia (2001), *Statistical Yearbook of the Republic of Slovenia 2001*, Ljubljana: Statistical Offic of the REbublic of Slovenia.

Swain, N. (1999), 'Agricultural Restitution and Co-operative Transformation in the Czech Republic, Hungary and Slovakia', *Europe-Asia Studies*, 51, pp. 1199–1219.

Swinnen, J.F.M. (1999), 'The Political Economy of Land Reform Choices in Central and Eastern Europe', *Economics of Transition*, 7, pp. 637–664.

USDA (2005), *Agricultural Statistics 2005*, Washington: United States Government Printing Office.

Chapter 8

Practices and Policies in Building Relationships with Stakeholders

Dovilė Juršytė and Gediminas Ramanauskas

Introduction

> I have found no greater satisfaction than achieving success through honest dealing and strict adherence to the view that, for you to gain, those you deal with should gain as well.
>
> Alan Greenspan,
> Federal Reserve Chairman of America

Together with a rapid expansion of the global economy, a substantial number of social and environmental problems concerning organizations have emerged. As a consequence, many business leaders and managers put considerable emphasis, not only on shareholder profitability from the company, but also more and more attention is given to relationship building with various groups of stakeholders – employees, customers, suppliers, communities, governmental bodies, and the media. If in the past the company was seen predominantly as an instrument for its owners and as a tool of economic value creation for people who risk capital in the corporation, it is now agreed that companies have some role to play in society as well (Greenwood, 2001, pp. 29–49). Though this attitude varies among countries, some researchers claim that 'management has undergone a shift in world view from "stockholder" to "stakeholder"', which resulted in building long term relationships through improved employee treatment, development of innovative products and services for customers changing from manufacturing, packaging and distribution processes, to having a lower impact on the environment, engage in important philanthropic activities, etc. (Freeman and Reed, 1983, p. 88). To meet the needs of all stakeholders:

> a company must harness the energy, ideas and commitment of diverse groups of interested actors inside and outside its boundaries to create value from intangible, network-related assets that clearly exist in the 'space' between the company and its key stakeholders (Svendsen and Wheeler, 2003, p. 33).

The stakeholder model according to which 'sustainable success rests, to a great extent, with a systematic consideration of the needs and goals of all key stakeholders'

(Fraser and Zarkada-Frazer, 2003) and which 'provides means for uncovering the relevant participants in the process' (Bronn and Bronn, 2003), is an important contributor to the great change in management thinking. It is highly believed that the adoption of a stakeholder approach to management will help a good deal with the long-term-survival and success of a firm. Positive and mutually supportive stakeholder relationships encourage trust, and stimulate collaborative efforts that lead to relational wealth (*Business Ethics Quarterly*, 2002, p. 257). It can be assumed that companies will do well and can do good at the same time. Considering the results of previous research carried out in a number of different countries, it is worthwhile noting that similar issues are topical all around the world. Therefore Lithuania, with its fairly recently introduced market economy and private ownership of firms, appears to be particularly interesting to investigate. New conditions such as increased local and international competition, development of new technologies, and growing customer requirements force a change in terms of how companies work and management system performance.

The aim of this chapter is to find out who the stakeholders are, according to management within Lithuanian companies, and how the latter perceive their relationship with different stakeholder groups. It is also an attempt to investigate what management does and how they interact with various stakeholder groups. Moreover, bearing in mind that during recent years Lithuania has undergone a number of economic changes, including transition from state-ownership and central planning to private ownership and a market economy, this chapter seeks to find to what extent these factors influenced the work of management and its relationship towards different stakeholder groups.

Taking into account the fact that not much exploration has been done in the field of stakeholder relationship building in Lithuanian companies, this study could be helpful in revealing the existing quality of overall stakeholder relationships within Lithuanian companies. Consequently, business leaders and managers could make further improvements in different areas of stakeholder relationship if necessary. In addition, they could benefit themselves from the present research, as it mainly analyses the positive side of a particular company. Moreover, future employees could also make use of this research as it could guide them in choosing the right company to work for. This increases the strength of companies engaged in these positive practices, and provides a market incentive to continue to improve the building of long-term stakeholder relations.

This chapter will be constructed in the following manner. First, theoretical material discussing the concept of stakeholders as well as various stakeholder groups is considered. Secondly, existing quantitative and qualitative research in the field dealing with different stakeholder groups is examined. Then the section describing methods and materials used in the chapter will be presented. Subsequently, results concerning the investigation will be reported and discussed. Finally, conclusions as well as additional observations *vis-à-vis* the relationship between the different stakeholder groups (i.e., shareholders, employees, community, customers, suppliers, governmental bodies, media, etc.) and management will be made.

Theoretical Background

The Stakeholder Concept

During recent decades stakeholder related issues have been a topic of investigation for a number of researchers all over the world, which have explored the phenomenon from different angles.

Many scholars have primarily attempted to specify the very concept of stakeholder, which turned out to be rather vague and ambiguous. A substantial number of stakeholder typologies exist, primarily consisting of shareholders, investors, employees, customers, suppliers, governments and communities, and secondarily including the media and a wide range of special interest groups, such as owners and non-owners of the firm. Also, owners of capital or owners of less tangible assets, being actors and those acted upon, rights holders, contractors or moral claimants, as risk takers and influencers, etc., have been found in the stakeholder literature.

Later, the distinction between the broad and narrow types of definitions are observed. First attempts to define the concept of stakeholder are found in Stanford Memo, defining stakeholders in a rather narrow sense as those groups 'without whose support the organization would cease to exist' (1963 quoted in Mitchell, Agle, and Wood, 1997, p. 18). Freeman, a main supporter and developer of the stakeholder theory, proposes a much broader view in respect of stakeholders in an organization, referring to them as 'any group or individual who can affect or are affected by the achievement of an organization's objectives' (1984, p. 46, quoted in Mitchell, Agle, and Wood, 1997, p. 4). Clarkson (1994, p. 5, quoted in Mitchell, Agle, and Wood 1997, p. 19) offers a narrower definition of the term and claims that stakeholders:

> bear some form of risk as a result of having invested some form of capital, human or financial, something of value, in a firm or are placed at risk as a result of the firm's activities.

Moreover, Clarkson (1995) in her further research claims that a corporation's survival and continuing success depend upon the ability of its managers to create sufficient wealth, value or satisfaction for those who belong to each stakeholder group, so that each group continues as a part of the corporation's stakeholder system. The author admits that failure to retain the participation of a primary stakeholder group will result in the failure of that corporate system.

It has to be noted though that the distinction between both of the definitions is made mainly for practical reasons. Broad views are based on the reality that companies can be vitally affected by or can vitally affect almost anyone, whereas narrower views are based on the actuality of limited resources, limited time and attention, and limited patience of managers for dealing with external constraints (Greenwood, 2001, pp. 29–49). If proponents of the former view emphasize 'the stakeholder's power to influence the firm's behaviour, whether or not there are legitimate claims', thus supporters of the latter view, to the contrary, emphasize:

the claim's legitimacy based upon contract, exchange, legal title, legal right, moral right, at-risk status, or moral interest in the harms and benefits generated by company actions (Mitchell, Agle, and Wood, 1997, p. 6).

Stakeholder Relationships and Company Strategy

While most business leaders today accept the idea that companies have 'stakeholders' that both affect and are affected by the company, the dynamism of the relationship and the degree of interdependence between companies and their stakeholders is less widely understood (Svendsen 1998, p. 49). Scholars interested in the stakeholder-related issues devote their time and efforts to investigate different groups of stakeholders as well as relationships existing among them. Even though opinions of the scholars as regards stakeholder relationships diverge considerably, the commonly held belief is that there is a certain degree of prioritizing among different stakeholder groups, which can be found in a number of studies.

Goodpaster (1991) views stakeholder relationship from the ethical perspective and claims that despite the fact that ethically responsible management pays attention to all stakeholders in the decision-making process, the relationship between management and stockholders is different. However, the author does not include the method according to which managers distinguish some stakeholder groups over the others. Mitchell, Agle, and Wood (1997) try to evaluate stakeholder-manager relationships in terms of certain stakeholder attributes they share. After in-depth examinations of the existing stakeholder definitions, along with differences between broad and narrow concepts of stakeholders as well as various attributes related to them, the authors propose that stakeholder groups can be identified depending on three attributes, namely the power, legitimacy, and urgency they possess in respect to the firm (see Table 8.1).

Based on the stakeholder identification typology presented in the table below, the authors offer a theory of stakeholder salience, which aims to explain to whom and to what managers actually pay attention. Thus, they make a proposition that it is the possession of one of the three attributes that determines certain groups as stakeholders and that conditions stakeholder salience and the kind of attention given to different stakeholders. Considering the fact that previous research was predominantly constructed on the basis of legitimacy in stakeholder-manager relationships (e.g., contract, legal rights, moral rights, property-based rights, legal title, etc.), Mitchell, Agle and Wood strongly believe that power and urgency must be attended to as well if managers are to serve the legal and moral interests of legitimate stakeholders. Moreover, in the subsequent study, Mitchell and Agle (1999) provide empirical results obtained from the CEOs of 80 large US firms with respect to the relationship among the stakeholder attributes of power, urgency and salience as well as CEO values and corporate performance based upon Mitchell and colleagues' theoretical model of stakeholder identification and salience. The research confirms validity of the model and thus, suggests that companies' leaders give different priorities to different stakeholder groups regarding the three attributes they posses. However, the

Table 8.1 Stakeholder Identification Typology

Stakeholder Types		Possession of the Attributes			Description and Examples
		Power	Legitimacy	Urgency	
Latent	Dormant	+			Have no or little interaction with the firm: fired employees filing for wrongful dismissal or calling the attention of the media, etc.
	Discretionary		+		Have no power to influence the firm and no urgent claims: non-profit organizations that receive donations and volunteer labor from companies, etc.
	Demanding			+	Have rather bothersome, but not dangerous claims on the firm: a picketer marching in front of the office with a sign blaming a particular company, etc.
Expectant	Dominant	+	+		Receive much of management attention due to their formal rights: corporate boards of directors often including shareowners, important creditors, community leaders; human resource departments or public affairs offices.
	Dependent		+	+	Gain attention with help of others: local citizens, animals, birds, etc. that are protected by state governments, courts, etc.
	Dangerous	+		+	Are coercive and possibly violent: wildcat strikes, employee sabotage, terrorism, etc.
Definitive		+	+	+	Get attention and are given priority from the management due to obligations: stockholders seeing that their legitimate interests were not properly acknowledged and necessary actions regarding decreased stock value were not employed from management's perspective, thus were able to remove them.

Source: Mitchell, Agle, and Wood (1997).

authors do not discuss organizational as well as managerial attributes that might be of great influence as regards stakeholder relationships.

Berman and Wicks (1999), in their empirical study investigate the connection of stakeholder relationship to company strategy and financial performance testing two theoretical models, namely, the strategic stakeholder management model approaching stakeholder claims solely with respect to improvement of firm financial performance; plus the intrinsic stakeholder commitment model, based on moral stakeholder treatment, which consequently influences firm strategy and financial performance. The authors choose five stakeholder areas including employees, the natural environment, workplace diversity, customers and issues of product safety, and community relations for their investigation. The results revealed that only the strategic stakeholder management model appeared to have influence on firm financial performance with a direct link to employees and product safety/quality, whereas community, diversity and natural environment seem to have no great influence on company financial performance. Thus it can be assumed that development of profit based relationships with key stakeholders, has direct impact on firm financial performance, however, moral commitments *vis-à-vis* stakeholders appear to be of little importance.

Bridges and Harrison's (2003) investigation on the relationship between company performance and employee perceptions of balance in stakeholder value creation, reveals that involvement of workers in high-performance work practices, such as new methods for worker-management collaboration or greater reliance on front-line workers, not only makes employees feel more valued but their performance regarding productivity levels is increased as well. Thus the authors assume that companies would better serve not only their employees, but also themselves, 'by doing more to create value for those who create values for others'. It has to be noted though that the paper is not without limitations as its main focus is merely on employee perceptions towards company performance, thus the perceptions of other stakeholder groups are not taken into consideration, which might be of equal weight while examining the relationship between company performance and stakeholder perceptions.

Taking into account the fact that corporations today operate in an increasingly boundaryless world in which information and relationships are both more important and more fluid, Svendsen (1998) claims the necessity of a theoretical framework that could be dynamic enough to meet the existing challenges. She offers a systems view of the corporation according to which the corporation is embedded in a network of interdependent stakeholder relationships that are evolving and mutually defined (Svendsen, 1998, pp. 49–50). Considering the manager's role from a systems-based perspective, they are seen not as separate from the stakeholder relationship, but as part of it. Within a systems-based theory, the term 'stewardship' is introduced following the principle by which 'employees define themselves as stewards of organization and beyond that, of the community' (Block quoted in Svendsen, 1998, p. 52). It is believed then that:

individuals who see themselves as stewards are naturally committed to ensuring the well-being of others and the sustainability of the enterprise and the broader society (Svendsen, 1998, p. 79).

Svendsen and Wheeler (2003) discuss how and to what extent the quality of the stakeholder relationship is interconnected with business value creation from intangible assets. Grounding their model on the resource-based view, the authors refer to the company's access to non-material resources predominantly emphasizing social capital or goodwill, namely, sharing information and other resources, adhering to group norms/solidarity and exerting influence on behalf of another. More interestingly, the model is tested within a context of three Canadian companies, which proves business value creation from social capital as having a direct link towards ongoing improvement of strategically relevant stakeholder relationship quality, as well as better access to information and other resources. This also includes influence and solidarity within a company's key stakeholder group, which in turn allows for further assessment of a company's future performance.

Donaldson and Preston (1995) in their thesis, discuss stakeholder theory from a normative perspective and claim that stakeholder theory is a managerial theory, which not only describes situations and predicts relationships, but also recommends attitudes, structures, and practices that, taken together, constitute stakeholder management. Moreover, they believe that managers following stakeholder management philosophy have to pay attention to the interests of all stakeholders, involving them in the development of organizational structures, general policies, and decision-making. According to the authors, it is not only the stakeholders' instrumental value to the company that matters, but also their claims based on fundamental moral principles that may not necessarily serve company strategic interests, which have to be considered as well. Bearing in mind that often managers themselves are stakeholders, and thus possibly exercise greater power than other stakeholder groups, it is very likely that their attitudes shape the nature of the relationship between the company and its stakeholders, whether it is right or not.

Greenwood (2001) in her paper, examines stakeholder relationships considering not only who a stakeholder is and how different stakeholder groups are identified, but rather the nature of the relationship between the organization and the stakeholder, namely, society from business leaders' perspectives. The investigation reveals that companies' leaders from different industries perceive community in different ways. Thus, service and retail sectors view community from a wider perspective 'concerned with broader societal issues', whereas manufacturing and primary industries consider it in highly local and regional terms, which may be accounted for through 'their heavy reliance on the local community for skilled employees' (Greenwood, 2001, p. 44). However, the author observes that together with greater growth of the company as well as the spread of complexity, diversity, and globalization in the business world, a broader view regarding community is emerging within Australian organizations. Even though this study provides an in-depth analysis in respect to manager-community relationships, it does not include views as regards to the relationship between managers and other stakeholder groups.

Considering previous stakeholder literature, a number of theoretical articles dealing with the stakeholder related issues could be found. However, at the same time, a substantial number of aspects are still debated and need further investigation. Besides disagreements regarding the stakeholder definition, the issue of prioritizing among different stakeholder groups is widely discussed. Even though the majority of the researchers agree that prioritizing among stakeholders exists, little investigation has been carried out to examine the qualitative nature of the matter. In that respect, explanatory patterns are of importance in identifying the reasons for different types of relationships between various stakeholder groups and companies. Furthermore, the existing research discusses the influence that different stakeholder groups have on the relationship between them and companies, but it is also the managers and their attitudes that are of immense importance while building and developing stakeholder relationships. Also cultural differences, though being singled out as important in stakeholder relationship building, are not fully revealed within some countries. From that perspective, Lithuania appears to be particularly interesting to investigate as recent historic events related to the transformation from communism to capitalism were important while shaping attitudes with respect to the stakeholder relationships within Lithuanian companies.

Bearing in mind that most of the research regarding stakeholder issues has been mostly focused upon the quantitative aspect; the current study is an attempt to consider the phenomenon from the qualitative perspective. This chapter also seeks to get a closer look at managers' perceptions regarding different stakeholder groups as well as measures employed to develop relationships with these stakeholders, rather than merely examining the connection between stakeholder relationships and company financial performance. Moreover, the chapter attempts to relate the effects of the recently introduced market economy on stakeholder relationship building within Lithuanian companies.

Materials and Methods

This chapter seeks to find out who the stakeholders are according to business leaders, and how the latter perceive their relationship with different stakeholder groups. Also, it is an attempt to find out what management does, if anything, and how they interact with various stakeholder groups. Moreover, the chapter attempts to investigate the influence of quite recent changes in the Lithuanian economic system, namely, the market economy and private ownership on the development of stakeholder relationships within the firms.

In order to evaluate the existing management relationship *vis-à-vis* different stakeholder groups, an investigation within the three Lithuanian companies that cooperate on the basis of the production and service network was carried out. The three companies differ with regard to industry type and history, organization size, and type of ownership (see Table 8.2). The managing directors from the companies were chosen on the basis of accessibility and availability.

The companies in Table 8.2 were selected with intent to examine the influence of different industry sector and ownership types on stakeholder management and relationships within the firm. It has to be noted that due to the relatively small sample, no definitive conclusions are expected to be made, however, some interesting tendencies are very likely to emerge.

To achieve the objective, five managing directors including the VP for Finance and the marketing manager from Company A, the project manager from Company B, and a CEO and a board member from Company C were interviewed. To get a better understanding of the respondents' perspectives and perceptions regarding stakeholder relationships, semi-structured interviews were employed (Daymon and Holloway, 2002, pp. 166–185). Questions in the interview guide are constructed under the typical corporate and stakeholder issues as proposed by Clarkson (1995, pp. 101–102; see Appendix 1). Thus the interview guide consists of a number of open-ended questions that are followed by customized questions regarding specific details attributed to particular stakeholder groups (see Appendix 2). Although the respondents represent different companies and interests, they were given the same set of questions, which may slightly vary in terms of sequence and wording depending upon the process of each interview, and the responses of each interviewee. The interviews were conducted in Lithuanian, which accounted for the fact that English is a foreign language, and thus the interviewees may feel uncomfortable in expressing themselves in English. The conversations were tape-recorded and then transcribed in the original language. With the relevant quotes translated into English.

To get an in-depth insight into the information provided, the transcripts of the interviews were analyzed using an editing approach applied to qualitative data analysis (King referred to this in Greenwood, 2001, p. 36). The editing analysis is based on the search for meaningful segments in the transcribed text, which are later reconstructed and assigned to particular categories, patterns and concepts relevant to the research question (Cassel and Biswas, 1996). The collected data was thoroughly examined to ensure that all issues topical to the present study are covered and identified.

Another set of data that emerges from company annual reports, internal letters and other available financial information indicating firm profitability and success, was revised to validate the information collected. This data was grouped into the same categories as the above and was constantly compared to crosscheck the findings of the research, looking for similarities and differences within and between the multiple sources collected.

In terms of validity and reliability of data measurement quality with respect to qualitative analysis, the former appears to be more powerful in providing important insights, observations and detailed illustrations while collecting and analysing the data (Eisenhardt, 1989). Also, it can be a valuable basis for further research, whereas the issue of reliability is rather controversial from that perspective, as it is believed that some of the measurements employed in the qualitative data analysis

Table 8.2 Description of Organizations

Company	Industry type	Organization history and activities	Ownership	Size
A	Manufacturing and Supplying Polyethylene Materials	In 1993 – started as a supplier of polyethylene raw materials. In 1997, together with the acquisition of modern German and Italian technology, the manufacturing branch was established. The joint stock company Ltd. produces shrink film and bags for packaging, LDPE film for construction and agricultural industry, etc.	Private	97
B	Projection and Construction of Water Supply and Sewage Pipelines, Electricity Supply Networks, Telecommunications	The company started its activities in 1950 with the installation of telecommunication networks. In 1994 it was reorganized into the joint stock company Ltd. In 2004 it changed its name due to the increased number of activities such as high quality projection, construction and renovation services.	Private	112
C	Delivering and Supplying Water	Established in 1973. The main activities of the company include underground water delivery, water works and supply; waste water collection, treatment and outlet to surface water. In 1999, wastewater biological treatment equipment was modernized. In 2003 the company was reorganized into the special-purpose joint stock company.	Public	176

Source: Based on Greenwood (2001).

might be quite unfair and subjective due to personal experiences and convictions (Babbie, 2000). To avoid a comparative evaluation between interview material and the company, financial information was constantly used and certain quantitative measures were incorporated.

Results and Discussion

After analysing the interviews with the five managers, including the VP for Finance and the marketing manager from Company A, the project manager from Company B, and the CEO and board member from Company C, the following issues emerged.

Stakeholder Identification

Generally, all managers named shareholders, employees, customers, suppliers, community, governmental institutions and the media as stakeholders of the companies. However, their relationship in respect to each stakeholder group varies to a certain extent starting with financial responsibility in terms of shareholders, moral and professional commitment in terms of employees, to social duties in terms of the community.

Stakeholder Attributes and Salience

Even though the management identifies seven stakeholder groups as being involved with the company to a greater or lesser extent, only three of them, namely, shareholders, employees and customers are emphasized over the others (see Table 8.3). However, priorities among the three stakeholder groups are distributed slightly differently depending upon each company. Traditional views that shareholders are the most important or at least very important stakeholder group predominate. It is particularly evident with one private company involved in manufacturing and supplying of polyethylene materials. The VP Finance of the company claims that:

> shareholders are actively involved in management of the company and they are particularly interested in profitability and the future success of the firm.

This might be related to the fact that there are only two shareholders of the company, who are the founders of the firm and who are tied by family relationships, namely, a father and a son. In addition to that, a majority of the strategic positions including the CEO, VP Finance, marketing manager, and personnel director are distributed among the family members, therefore, it can be referred to as a family run business.

As far as employees are concerned, all of the respondents gave considerable emphasis while discussing them. However, only the project manager from Company B identifies employees as number one among the other two groups. This might be due to the reorganization within the firm, which resulted in a considerably increased scope of services, consequently leading to a great need for skilled workers. Nevertheless, all of the respondents agree that companies could not do much without its employees.

In terms of customers, all companies included them among the three major stakeholder groups. Considering the case with the water company, the CEO sees customers as their priority stakeholder group and thus their opinion is highly respected. It is worthwhile noting that though this company is a monopolist in the field and customers do not have much choice, they still are thought to be the most important among the other stakeholders. Besides this, one technical aspect regarding use of different words such as purchasers, subscribers, and consumers while referring to customers, has emerged. This might be accounted for by the fact that all the companies are very specified, and thus particular terms are used within their specialty fields.

Table 8.3 The Importance of Stakeholders According to Managers of the Firms

Company	Shareholders	Employees	Customers	Suppliers	Community	Governmental Institutions	Media
A	+++	++	++	++	++	+	++
B	++	+++	++	+	+	+	+
C	++	++	+++	+	++	++	++

\+ Important
++ Very important
+++ Exceptionally important

Considering the results in Table 8.3, it has to be noted that the degree of importance as regards to different stakeholder groups was assigned after careful analysis of the interview transcripts. Emphatic words such as *very*, *particularly*, *first of all*, *most*, *less*, *etc.* used in combination with various adjectives including *important*, *significant*, *essential*, *etc.* which were employed by the management while ranking different stakeholder groups, were thought to be adequate and convincing evidence to support the conclusions.

When viewing stakeholder importance from a stakeholder salience perspective, as offered by Mitchell et al. (1997), attitudes towards different stakeholder groups vary due to the unequal salience distribution among stakeholders within the companies. The results of the current research suggest that the same three groups including shareholders, employees and customers, can be singled out as the key players who not only have legitimate and urgent claims over the firm, but in some of the cases, particularly in terms of the shareholders, also have power to launch these claims (see Table 8.4).

Table 8.4 Stakeholder Attributes as Reported by Managers of the Firms

Company	Power	Urgency	Legitimacy
A	Shareholders, governmental institutions	Shareholders, employees, customers, governmental institutions, media, natural environment	Shareholders, employees, customers, suppliers, governmental institutions
B	Shareholders, governmental institutions	Shareholders, employees, customers, governmental institutions, media, natural environment	Shareholders, employees, customers, suppliers, governmental institutions
C	Shareholders, governmental institutions	Shareholders, employees, customers, governmental institutions, media, natural environment	Shareholders, employees, customers, suppliers, governmental institutions

As far as governmental institutions are concerned, their purpose is recognized as legitimate, urgent, and important, and is referred to merely in formal terms. It is worthwhile noting that even though the influence remaining stakeholder groups exercise over the firms is of a lesser importance in terms of legitimacy and power, their voices are listened to and much respected, especially *vis-à-vis* the community and media.

Stakeholder Classes and Managers' Role

Shareholders

The results of the research reveal that shareholders predominate among other stakeholder groups within the companies; however, the attitudes towards them vary to a certain extent not only among the three firms but also between the representatives of the same company (see Table 8.5). Two of the respondents see the shareholders as the most influential stakeholder group of the firm. The VP for Finance from the polyethylene company claims that it is the:

> shareholders who set goals in terms of profit and results and it is for them to decide to sell out the business if these goals are achieved or not.

It has to be singled out that it is the private company set up by the two entrepreneurs, who successfully managed to comply with the conditions of an emerging market economy, and from that perspective it can be speculated the company is particularly important to them.

As can be seen from Table 8.5 for board members of company C, which is different when compared with the CEO's view, one can believe that shareholders represent company interests in terms of further development, competitiveness, profitability, etc. and thus are the most important group among other stakeholders. It should not be forgotten that the board member is delegated by the municipality, and we can speculate that it is not only the economic interests he stands for, but rather political aims that are actively pursued, particularly before the local elections.

Table 8.5 Shareholder Classification According to the Managers of the Firms

Company	Representative	Shareholder Evaluation	Attitudes of the Managers
A	VP Finance	Most important	Shareholders are the most important and it is them who set goals and make important decisions vis-à-vis company strategy
	Marketing director	Very important	Shareholders are very important and influential in the management of the company as they are particularly interested in the further development of it.
B	Project manager	Very important (in terms of decision-making)	Shareholders are very influential in the strategic planning of the development of the company; however, they are not most important.
C	CEO	Very important (in terms of legal roles assigned)	Shareholders can be placed after the employees. They are legally responsible for the company and they take part in decision-making procedures.
	Board member	Most important	Shareholders are the most influential stakeholder group as they are delegated by the municipality and represent the interests of local consumers.

Moreover, considering the fact that 100 percent shares of Company C belong to the municipality, it can be assumed that it is the shareholders who make final decisions even though these decisions sometimes turn out to be strategically and financially unprofitable for the company, though politically convenient and are officially accounted as improving the well-being of consumers. To be more precise, even though the company earns a profit it is not in their disposition to allocate financial resources and make decisions related with issues such as renovation of waste water systems, purchasing of new equipment, employee training, charity activities, etc. It can be assumed that arguments such as increasing water prices for the consumers due to 'unnecessary expenditures' by the company, are often unsound and lead to speculation it is merely a way for shareholders to achieve either political or personal goals. More interestingly, the fact that the board member, actually chairman of the board, not only represents the municipality interests in the water company, but also is the CEO of another large company, allows one to make further speculations that a conflict of interests might be involved.

Considering the option of privatization with respect to the water sector, it has to be pointed out that according to the Law on National Security, only 25 percent of shares can be acquired by private parties, which would not significantly change administration of the water companies. Therefore, it can be assumed that if no further restructuring is made regarding administration of the water companies, stakeholder relationships will merely be shaped by the interests and values of CEOs, who not only have to motivate and inspire the employees, keep good relations with suppliers and communities, but must also skillfully maneuver while negotiating with shareholders represented by municipalities.

The rest of the interviewees admit that the role of shareholders is very important, particularly emphasizing their legal rights and responsibilities regarding the company, however, their participation in company management is seen in terms of strategic decision taking. A project manager representing an underground construction and engineering company, even though agreeing that shareholders have considerable influence while making important decisions, also states that knowledge and opinions of employees are highly respected, and always taken into account. This might be due to the fact that together with introduction of the market economy, Company B has undergone a number of institutional changes, including restructuring of the company, resulting in considerably increased number of services, therefore, to withstand local and international competition, shareholders are currently more interested in investment and further development of the company, including particular emphasis on employee training rather than profit taking. It is also worthwhile noting that the restructuring process for some of the staff from Company B, due to favorable legislative conditions including concessionary shares for employees, took over the majority stake in a formerly state-owned company, and thus became shareholders and managers of the firm. Though employee ownership is sometimes associated with financial gain on the part of shareholders rather than prosperity for the company, it seems this cannot be applied to Company B as analysis of the interview and financial data reveals considerable improvements in company operations after the restructuring process.

Employees

Employees being among the three major stakeholder groups are viewed from several different perspectives. The project manager from Company B assuredly believed that employees are the greatest asset of the firm without whom the company would hardly be able to operate at all. The VP for Finance from Company A sees the relationship with employees in terms of being a means to achieve desired results and creating a positive image for the company. This might be accounted for by the fact that the company is relatively young and seeks further recognition by various means, including enhancing of the name as a good employer. The CEO from the water company places employees into third position after customers and shareholders however, he is absolutely convinced it is the workers who carry out the majority of operations, beginning with extraction to water supply for consumers, therefore, for the most part, because of them the company operates efficiently.

It has to be noted though, that managers of the firms do not take the issue of employees for granted, as all of them admit that substantial investment is needed regarding ongoing learning, such as university studies, seminars, trainings, etc. to improve skills and qualifications of the employees (see Figure 8.1).

Figure 8.1 presents financial data with annual expenditures for employee training in the three companies. It can be observed that Company B, as was declared by the project manager, makes relatively the least net profit, allocates the greatest amount of the money, which accounts for almost half of the company's profit going to labor training, if compared with Company A and C. Financial data for the years 2002–2003, show basically similar tendencies concerning investment in employees within

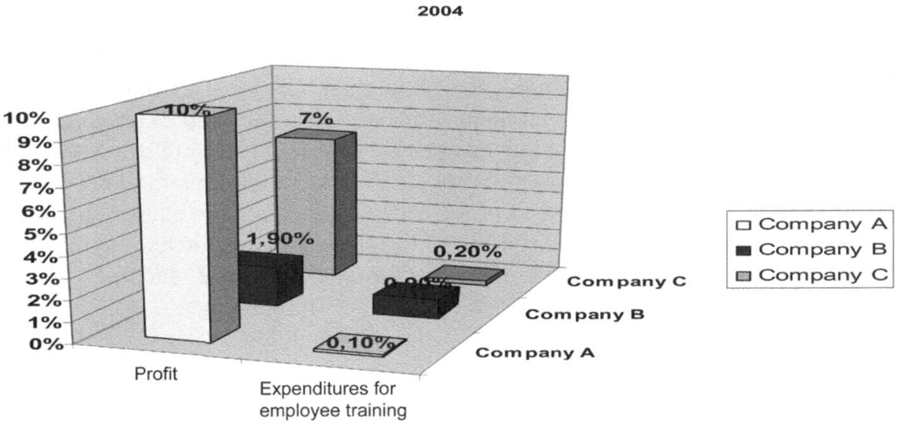

Figure 8.1 Annual Employee Training Expenditures (2004)

the three companies (see Appendix 4). It can only be speculated that Company B representing the service sector has more reason to be proactive with respect to its employees due to the very nature of its industry type, which mainly involves employees and customers. Company A sees the necessity in investing not only in employees, but also in local community, which is considered to be their major source of skilled labor. In terms of Company C, it has limited power in allocating its budget, and thus is heavily reliant on decisions of the board members, who represent the local municipality.

As regards employee involvement in the decision making procedures, all respondents assure that employees are highly encouraged to express their opinion and initiate work projects as well as in the two private companies. They are promoted to do this in terms of bonuses, fringe benefits, etc. Nevertheless, their offers as regards projects have to be approved by higher authorities that have power to control budget and other resources. In that respect the CEO of the water company admits that even though opinions of the employees are encouraged, in reality all of the decisions are taken by management personnel and shareholders. It might be speculated therefore, that employees are not strongly motivated to share their ideas. In addition, no company could identify formal evaluation criteria measuring employee performance, though the polyethylene company is in the process of implementation of such standards.

As far as employee rights are concerned, only the public company has trade unions to represent the interests of its workers. This might be accounted for by the fact that trade unions are legally defined as representatives of the employees in collective agreement with the company. The two private companies see no real necessity in either trade unions or company unions, as the companies are relatively small and thus all problems, which arise, can be solved individually. It can be assumed that arguments by managers appear to be quite reasonable; however, it might be that employee rights are violated in that respect as managers' opinions do not necessarily represent the attitudes of all employees, and thus formation of company unions could be one of the ways to foster employee representation within the company. It has to be noted that if current regulation of relations between employer and employee through either trade unions or company unions was not strictly defined by laws as regards the private sector, before long then it would become a prerequisite when employing people to sign contracts with them. Thus, it can be concluded that joining western markets would not only offer greater possibilities, but would also require certain changes to be made.

Considering social communication among the employees and management, it is becoming an inseparable part of the successful operation of the company. Among the ways to strengthen the relationship between then, the management mentions team building seminars, weekend trips with the families, canoeing trips, diners, bowling matches, etc. Nevertheless, the marketing manager from the polyethylene company admits that the gap between the administration and manufacturing sector can be observed. The reasons for that might be related with physical distance, as the two branches are located in separate buildings, including as well different educational backgrounds between the two and thus differing social interests.

As far as cooperation with universities is concerned, one regional company, namely, Company A is particularly interested in communication with the local college and technical universities as one of the ways to attract young specialists to the region (see Table 8.6). In that respect, the company actively participates in career days, prepares information guides about the company, as well as always is open for students to do their internships. The CEO from the water company claims that due to the necessary reduction of staff, there is not much change as regards the employees. Nevertheless, when choosing new specialists, which occurs once or twice every two years, the company gives priority to students from Vilnius Gediminas Technical University, which is particularly valued for engineering studies. In terms of related construction and the engineering company though, they realize that a program involving students in an internship in cooperation with the universities, is not yet developed.

Table 8.6 Cooperation with Educational Institutions

Company	Universities	Relationship	Internship Students in 2004
A	Vilnius Gediminas Technical University, local college	Continuous	3–5
B	–	Do not cooperate	2–3
C	Vilnius Gediminas Technical University	Sporadic	1–2

Customers

Besides the above stakeholder groups, customers were identified as being among the most important players affected by and affecting the firms. As far as formal treatment of the customer is concerned, no company could admit to having developed a policy for it. However, all of them have customer grievance procedures including a complaints book employed by the public water company and ISO 9000 family standards, clearly defining company responsibilities regarding customer use in two private firms. The differences between the companies are due to the fact that the latter two see the accomplishment of ISO standards as an integral part of a companies' strategy to be competitive in western markets. Even though implementation of the standard is sometimes referred to as mere formality or prestige, the marketing manager from Company A, claims it helped to improve the efficiency of production and services, as well as to attract more foreign customers and to strengthen the name of the firm.

The water company operates according to classical standards of the water sector, and representatives from the firm see no real necessity in changing that because these standards satisfy theirs as well as their customer needs. On one hand, their arguments might be questionable as only the opinions of the firm representatives are considered. On the other hand, they might be absolutely right because the services they provide are rather classical and thus the standards they apply seem to be relevant and effective. However, the CEO accepts the idea of implementing ISO standards in the future as it could improve the quality of customer service.

Besides that, the marketing director of the polyethylene materials company assures that they distribute customer surveys as a means to find out customer opinions about the quality of the services and products, manager performance, etc. (see Appendix 5). However, only the company's business clients are surveyed, which might be accounted for by the fact that business customers purchase the greater majority of their products, whereas individual clients comprise only a small part and company managers have the possibility of talking with them on other occasions such as exhibitions, product presentations, etc. From that perspective, it is worthwhile noting that only the latter company makes a firm distinction between business and individual customers (see Table 8.7).

Table 8.7 Customer Classification According to Managers of the Firms

Company	Business customers	Individual customers	Relationship	
			Business customers	Individual customers
A	91%	9%	Very important	Important
B	100%	–	Very important	Might become important
C	60% (50% private companies, 10% public institutions)	40%	Very important	Very important

Table 8.7 reveals that even though Company A recognizes that polyethylene products are used not only for industrial needs of the companies, but also in everyday life by ordinary people, for instance, to cover greenhouse construction, protect plants from bad weather conditions, pack food or cover furniture, etc. The company earns most of its profits from its business customers. The project manager representing the underground construction and engineering company, claims:

> the distinction as regards customers can only be made regarding the size and length of the order, but only for internal needs of the company for the purpose of knowing its schedule so that forthcoming orders can be planned efficiently.

This might be related to the fact that the very nature of the services provided by Company B is related with the large orders and large customers, namely, companies, but not individuals. However, the manager does not reject the idea that due to increasing global competition, the scope of their operations might broaden and include individual orders as well, thus from that perspective to claim that individual customers are not important would be wrong. As regards the water company, they give equal importance to both individual and business customers, though as can be seen from Table 8.8, the latter consume the majority of water and consequently are levied with slightly lower tariffs (see Appendix 6).

Considering company investment in keeping old clients and attracting new ones, the managers of the private companies name such aspects as product or service quality, price, and new technological innovations as being important factors to attract customers. Besides that, the VP for Finance from the polyethylene company sees social communication with customers as an inseparable part of long-lasting and mutually successful relationship building. The CEO, whereas, states the water company claims that due to the very nature of the ' product' they supply, i.e., water, which is vital for everyone as well as their natural monopolist position in the region, there is not much necessity for investing in clients as they themselves come to the company.

Suppliers

Considering suppliers, the three companies appear to have rather similar policies towards them due to branch peculiarities, particularly as regards Companies B and C as well as materials, which they supplied (see Table 8.8).

The analysis of the interviews revealed that the level of company dependence on the suppliers could be assessed in the range of independent to highly dependent. As can be seen from the table above, the representatives of the public company are absolutely independent of their suppliers because they have a choice of quite a number of foreign and local companies who offer almost the same quality and similar price combinations for equivalent products. Besides that, their operations regarding that field are very clearly defined by the general procurement laws and regulations, and thus they try to follow them.

The project manager from the underground construction and engineering company puts considerable emphasis on first-tier suppliers, which might be accounted for by the fact the company purchases very expensive and multi-functional equipment. Thus it has to make a careful choice which supplier to cooperate with, as the agreement conditions tend to be very individual and highly determined by the success of communication during negotiations.

On the contrary, the polyethylene manufacturing and supply company does not have many or sometimes any options regarding first-tier suppliers, as 'it is the suppliers who dictate the rules and the company either accepts these rules or not'. However, refusing the offer is rarely the case because of the constant shortages of polyethylene materials in the world market. Besides that, after joining the EU the company had to reduce its imports of raw materials from Russia, as current requirements do not allow exporting of such polyethylene production into western

Table 8.8 Supplier Classification According to Managers of the Firms

Company	Suppliers		Level of Dependence	
	First-tier Suppliers	Second-tier Suppliers	First-tier Suppliers	Second-tier Suppliers
A	Foreign suppliers of polyethylene raw materials and special equipment	Local suppliers of office materials, distribution and consultancy services, etc.	Highly dependent	Independent
B	Foreign suppliers of multi-functional trenchless technologies	Mainly local suppliers of construction materials including pipelines, cables, polyethylene; office supplies; logistics, consultancy, accounting services, etc.	Partially dependent	Independent
C	Foreign and local suppliers of special equipment and clothes, water pipes, meters, etc.	Local suppliers of office equipment, consultancy services, etc.	Independent	Independent

markets. This resulted in even greater dependency on first-tier suppliers because imports from Russia have decreased from 70 percent before joining the EU, to 30 percent after accession to the Union, thus the company had to look for new suppliers in western markets, where prices are relatively higher. To compensate for their losses related to polyethylene materials, the company tries to find the best quality and price combinations, while negotiating with the second-tier suppliers for other resources.

Community

While considering various stakeholder groups, managers recognize that the reputation of the company is to some extent dependent on the community. This might be related to the fact that some respondents view the community in terms of customers, as they see not much difference between these two interest groups, predominantly in the case of the water company, which is a monopolist in the field serving vitally important 'good' water, thus the majority of the community are their customers as well.

One more tendency can be observed in that the impact on the community seems to be greater in regional areas as the companies, namely, Company A and C there tend to link their interests to regional needs. It is particularly evident considering Company A and its close cooperation with the local college, while looking for future employees and offering them internship possibilities in the company. Bearing in mind that the three firms are involved in very specific areas, their interests as regards future specialists go beyond the scope of the regional to country levels as well.

Another commonly held attitude that community needs charitable action was emphasized by most of the respondents. The VP for finance claims that they never say 'no' to almost anyone. 'We support all regional festivals, children dancing clubs, church activities, etc.' Besides that, the two private companies support sporting activities, including the ice-hockey team and automobile sport club. The latter is worthwhile noting, as it has not only very good technical support, including garages and sport cars, but also has its own name, internet site and even attributes related to the club image. It has to be noted though, that the main driver of the team is the son of the company owner, formerly a rally driver. Thus these are all reasons to believe that their charity might be in direct connection with their personal needs. In the case of the public company, a certain sum of money is donated each year, but this is done through the local municipality, which distributes the money according to regional needs. Figure 8.2 below provides the financial data, which indicates the amount of money allocated to charitable activities.

As can be seen from Figure 8.2, Company A allocates the greatest sum of money towards charitable activities. It has to be noted though that this company sees community in terms of future employees, therefore this suggests some part of the charitable expenditures might be related to employee expenditures. Similar results with respect to philanthropic activities can be observed from the financial data for years 2002–2003 in the three companies (see Appendix 4).

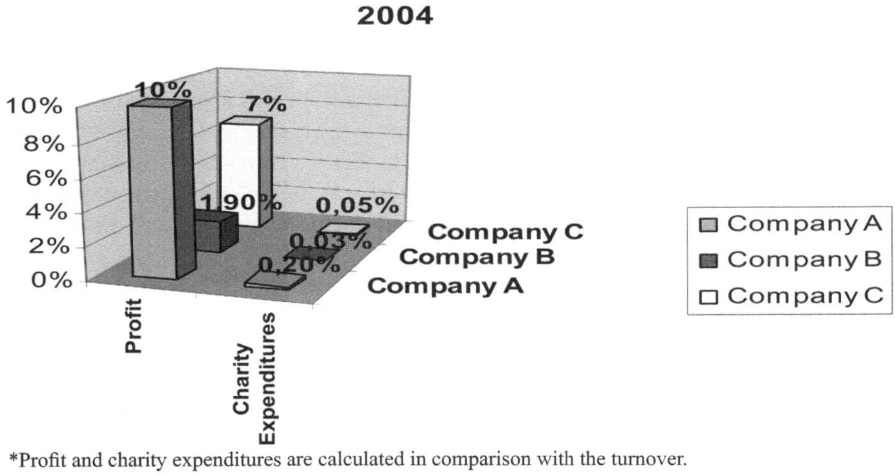

*Profit and charity expenditures are calculated in comparison with the turnover.

Figure 8.2 Annual Charity Expenditures (2004)

Asked to name the benefits of charitable activities, the VP for Finance representing the polyethylene company claims that sponsorship is mainly about image creation as a generous company and a way of attracting new employees. The marketing director of the same company relates community with their production, as she believes the latter must have positive influence on the community for the product to be strong and well-known. The CEO of the public company, on the other hand, says 'the only thing that he expects is to help those who really need that now, because for some people it might be a question of surviving'.

Different from the two companies above, the project manager from the underground construction and engineering company views the community in much broader terms, and thus does not consider it only in terms of geographical proximity. This might be accounted for by the fact the company does work, having less impact on the community where they are located, and consequently they are less focused on their immediate environment. Previous investigations of industry differences with respect to community reveal that companies, which define their community in global terms and are concerned with broader societal issues, are from retail and service sectors (Greenwood, 2001, pp. 43–45). Thus, it can be assumed the very nature of the industry that Company A is involved in determines its relationship towards the community.

Governmental Institutions

All respondents view their relationship with governmental institutions in terms of due collaboration, predominantly in the case of the two private firms. Governmental institutions are seen as 'tax collectors', 'law regulators and implementers' as well as 'customers'. The VP for Finance claims 'they deal with them as much as every other company has to deal with them'. It can be assumed that private companies participate in collaborative processes solely to protect their own interests, and to ensure their opinion is heard. Bearing in mind there is a substantial number of governmental institutions that companies are involved with, duties of the employees as regards cooperation with governmental institutions are distributed according to the area they are involved with. For example, accountants deal with the State Tax Inspectorate, whereas the personnel department is concerned with the Labor Exchange, etc. (see Table 8.9).

It is worthwhile noting that the CEO from the public company singles out the importance of mutual collaboration between companies and governmental institutions, because:

> the latter do not only implement the laws but also establish them and thus only practical consultations between both parties can result in successful enforcement of the law.

It is particularly topical to the present situation, as after accession to the EU, the legislation framework in the water sector must be transposed and enforced in a very short time. Besides that, Company C is in closer cooperation with governmental

Table 8.9 Governmental Institutions Named by the Managers

Company	Governmental Institutions	Relationship
A	State Tax Inspectorate, Labor Exchange, Ministry of Environment, Customs Services, Ministry of Transport and Communications, etc.	Formal
B	State Tax Inspectorate, Labor Exchange, Ministry of Environment, Ministry of Transport and Communications, Geological Service, etc.	Formal
C	Ministry of Environment, State Tax Inspectorate, Ministry of Health, State Food and Veterinary Service, Geological Service, Labor Exchange, etc.	Formal, based on mutual consultation and collaboration

institutions due to the company's clearly defined status of being a public company, and thus being more dependent on them.

Natural Environment

Many respondents maintain the activities of their companies do not cause harmful effects to the natural environment. However, board members from the water company believe that despite the fact that a number of standards and regulations are employed to ensure safe operations, there is always some environmental threat posed by the activities of the company, as in this case wastewater treatment.

When asked about the ISO standards concerned with environmental management, representatives from the private companies refer to the ISO 9000 family, which deals with quality management. Thus, none of the companies have implemented ISO 14000 environmental standards, however, operations of each company in that respect are strictly defined by national laws and regulations. It has to be noted that representatives from the polyethylene company seriously consider the possibility of implementing ISO 14000 standards, referred to as an environmental management standard. To do that they expect governmental support, because implementation and maintenance of the system requires substantial financial as well as technical investment for the company, 'as the customers are not going to pay more just because the waste materials of the company became "environment-friendly"'. From that perspective, the VP for Finance is quite right, because the majority of people still do not pay enough attention to environmental issues, which is due to the fact that their needs are still very basic and mainly deal with such issues as employment, food, etc. As a result, other needs such as recycling, 'environmental-friendly' products, etc. are not considered to be important enough to challenge the companies and require more innovative environmental solutions. The VP for Finance from the company admits that implementation of the standard not only would contribute to a sound environment, but also serve the company to enhance competitive advantage and good reputation among the locals, and particularly foreign partners, as the company's exports to western countries currently comprise about 70 percent of all sales, and amounts to almost 19 million litas in the recent year (see Appendix 3).

It is worthwhile mentioning that respondents from the water company relate the natural environment with various environmental projects. Currently, the company participates in a huge project funded by the EU, the objective of which is to build new wastewater networks for a safer environment, as well as laying new water lines to improve the quality of drinking water for people. It can be assumed the company is constantly involved with environmental issues, and puts in considerable effort to improve their surroundings with the help of new technologies.

Media

All respondents recognize that to succeed in the current business world, open communication is particularly important. Due to the increased power of the media for impacting public opinion and consequently affect corporate profits, a relationship with them is seen as an inevitable part of successful operations for the firm. To enhance this collaboration, the water company annually organizes open day events where everyone can participate including media representatives. Besides that, this company similarly with the other two, inform the media about ongoing procedures within the firm, including implementation of new technologies, tariff changes, services, etc. Bearing in mind that the water company mainly serves the local community, communication with the mass media commonly occurs at the local level. It has to be noted that only Company A hires a public relations firm, responsible for communication with the mass media. The other two companies, namely, B and C have people in their companies who deal with journalists, though it is considered to be their secondary duties. In addition, collaboration at the national level with business related newspapers, namely, *Verslo žinios* (*Business News*), is highly valued. It is particularly evident when referring to company A, as the articles referring to it not only can be most frequently found in newspapers, but it was also among the first companies to start participating in the annual Lithuanian Top Leader rankings organized by *Verslo žinios* (*Business News*). Because of this, the two other companies announced their financial results as well, however, not until recently. In terms of the underground construction and engineering company, it might not be accounted for because of the fact the company underwent a re-organizational period, and thus the company's turnover was not high enough to be included among the 500 best companies in Lithuania. This can be evidenced by the turnover rankings for the year 2004–2005, where the company stands in the last 100 among the 500 best firms, whereas the polyethylene manufacturing company, according to the same measure, can be found among the 100 best Lithuanian companies. It should be noted as well that Company C, which shows similar financial results to Company B, and once was included among the best 500 companies in Lithuania, no longer provides the journal with its financial data. This might be accounted for by the fact that publicity had a negative impact on company operations, as some of the municipality representatives used situations for their own benefits, i.e., good financial results appeared to be a fairly good reason to insist on the water tariff reduction for the community, even though it could have harmful effects on the company.

On the one hand, respondents believe that communication with the media is one of the ways to ensure transparency of the company, to inform society as well as make advertising for the firm. On the other hand, many respondents claim that journalists sometimes misinterpret their words, which consequently, according to one of the interviewees, says 'requires explanations from the company's side to their partners or customers'. Moreover, several respondents name unfair articles directed towards them as a threat to the image of the companies. Despite that, all respondents agree mutual collaboration not only helps to develop understanding, but also brings more objectivity and transparency to the public.

Customer–Supplier Cooperation

An interesting fact has emerged during the investigation, which is related with customer–supplier cooperation within the three companies. The phenomenon observed might be referred to as production networking. Discussing the issue of production networking as regards the three companies, it is useful to consider several aspects in respect to networks. Marceau (1999), in her article claims that while referring to networks, it is important to take into account 'the direction of the sectors where the networks are working'. In the case of this research, one particular sector cannot be clearly identified, however, due to the fact that the water supply company is provided with the services for the projection/company, while the construction company is involved with water supply and sewage pipeline building, with the latter buying secondary resources, namely, polyethylene materials from the polyethylene manufacturing and supplying company. It can therefore be assumed the three companies are interconnected on the product/service specificity basis (see Appendix 7).

Another aspect referred to while discussing production networks deals with the production relationships among the three companies, which are based on commercial transactions and contracts determining the form of productive activity, either traded goods or services. In terms of the period of linkage, the water supply company cooperates with the projection and construction company sporadically, depending on the necessity of their services, whereas the latter is linked to the polyethylene manufacturing and supply firm continuously. It has to be noted that cooperation between the water and construction companies, even though being discontinuous, is based on mutual trust, high quality services, and reasonable pricing.

Most importantly, it is worthwhile understanding the sociological and professional aspect as regards production networks, and the relationships among the companies and thus among its stakeholders. It is particularly evident while discussing employees, because people working in three firms, emphasizing Companies B and C, share particular technical education and professional experience in engineering, and thus it is very likely they will find similar interests while working together. Bearing in mind that all companies recognize the importance of employee training and involvement in the decision making process, it only strengthens the idea that employees working in the three companies manifest similar values and thus due to this, the inter-firm collaboration is successful and efficient.

Conclusions

This study was intended to find out who the stakeholders are, according to management within Lithuanian companies, and how the latter perceive their relationship with different stakeholder groups. Using the evidence from interviews with the managers from different firms, as well as additional company related data, this chapter suggests that the ways in which stakeholders are defined and treated by the managers vary to some extent due to various internal and external factors. Theoretical analysis based on the existing stakeholder theory reveals the stakeholder concept is deceptively simple. Its simplicity lies in the identification of those groups and individuals who can affect or are affected by the fulfillment of firm goals, whereas its deceptiveness is related to management of the relationship with these identified stakeholder groups.

Qualitative research suggests that overall, managers of the firms indicate shareholders, employees, customers, suppliers, community, governmental organizations and the media are stakeholders of the companies, and acknowledge that development of the relationship with them is an inseparable part of successful operations for the company. Nevertheless, stakeholders are categorized within the respective role-based stakeholder groups, consistent with the stakeholder theory in terms of power and salience, and thus they are given unequal priorities. It has to be noted that though the attitudes of managers towards stakeholder management, from both private and public sectors are quite similar, their decisive relationship/ capabilities as regards stakeholders are largely determined by ownership type of the company. The study also reveals that shareholders, employees and customers are considered to be the most important stakeholder groups, due to the attributes power, legitimacy and urgency they possess. It appears that the relationship between managers and stakeholders with private companies are largely shaped by the interests and values of the department managers, even though major strategic decisions are made by the shareholders. The manager relationship with stakeholders within the public sector tends to be highly dependent on the shareholders, who not only allocate financial resources but also influence organizational policy as regards different stakeholder groups. Moreover, the study discloses that due to increased national and international competition, customer targeted policies in terms of technological innovations, service, or product quality and price within the private sector, have greatly improved. Considering community, it might be surmized this view exists either in terms of charitable actions or the potential of employees, depending on geographical proximity.

Regarding governmental institutions, managers from the private sector indicate their collaboration is merely based on formal obligations rather than mutual collaboration, as is the case with the public sector. As far as the natural environment is concerned, it is noticed that though all managers declare environmental standards as being implemented and followed within the companies, their policies towards this issue are quite passive, which might be partly due to the fact that needs of the wider community are rather basic including employment, better salaries, food, whereas environmental issues need additional assets such as recycling, therefore, environmental friendly products are not considered to be important enough to challenge companies into promoting a safer environment. In terms of the media, managers from both private and public sectors agree that currently the media is particularly powerful in the formation of public opinion. Thus, mutual collaboration with them is seen as one of the ways to ensure transparency of the company while making company operations visible, as well as strengthening the name of the firm relative to the private sector overall.

It can be concluded that a rapid acceleration in the development of positive stakeholder relationships within Lithuanian companies is evidenced. Nevertheless, due to quite recent market reforms such as introduction of the market economy, transition from public to private ownership, some undesirable outcomes such as management inefficiency or lack of implemented standards concerning stakeholder management within some companies, can be observed. For this reason it is essential to understand different stakeholder groups following the ideas of De Jongh (2004):

> in today's world, everything we do as individuals and companies is exposed in seconds, and therefore it's so important to understand exactly who all the stakeholders are, that are affected by our business and how they again affect our business on a daily basis (De Jongh, 2004, p. 34).

It must be added that due to the fact the interview questions were based on the theory review, answers to them could to some extent be preconditioned by the interview design. Besides, though the interview questions were distributed before hand, some of the managers because of lack of time, might have responded without due consideration to the importance of the question. Moreover, though the sample is not large enough to make valid statistical conclusions, a number of trends are observed. Thus, it would be worthwhile to extend this work including data from a wider range of companies, and undertaking in-depth quantitative analysis of the results obtained.

References

Appendix: 'Principles of Stakeholder Management', *Business Ethics Quarterly* (2002), Vol. 12, No. 2, pp. 257–64.

Babbie, E. (2000), *The Practice of Social Research*, USA: Wadsworth Thompson Learning.

Berman, S.L. and Wicks, A.C. (1999), 'Does Stakeholder Orientation Matter? The Relationship Between Stakeholder Management Models and Firm Financial Performance', *Academy of Management Review*, Vol. 42, No. 5, pp. 488–504.

Bridges, S. and Harrison, W. (2003), 'The Relation Between Employee Perceptions of Stakeholder Balance and Corporate Financial Performance', *S.A.M. Advanced Management Journal*, Vol. 68, No. 2, p. 50.

Bronn, P.S. and Bronn, C. (2003), 'A Reflective Stakeholder Approach: Co-orientation as a Basis for Communication and Learning', *Journal of Communication Management*, Vol. 7, No. 4, p. 291.

Cassel, C. and Biswas, R. (1996), 'Strategic HRM and the Gendered Division of Labor in the Hotel Industry: A Case Study', *Personnel Review*, Vol. 25, No. 2, pp. 19–35.

Clarkson, M.E. (1995), 'A Stakeholder Framework for Analysing and Evaluating Corporate Social Performance', *Academy of Management Review*, Vol. 20, No. 1, pp. 92–117.

Daymon, C. and Holloway, I. (2002), *Qualitative Research Methods in Public Relations and Marketing Communications*, London, UK: Routledge.

De Jongh, D. (2004), 'Know Your Stakeholders', *Finance Week*, 30 June, p. 34.

Donaldson, Th. and Preston, L.E. (1995), 'The Stakeholder Theory of the Corporation: Concepts, Evidence, and Implications', *Academy of Management Review*, Vol. 20, No. 1, pp. 65–91.

Eisenhardt, K.M. (1989), 'Building Theories from Case Study Research', *Academy of Management Review*, Vol. 14, No. 4, pp. 532–550.

Frazer, C. and Zarkada-Frazer, A. (2003), 'Investigating the Effectiveness of Managers through an Analysis of Stakeholder Perceptions', *Journal of Management Development*, Vol. 22, No. 9, p. 762.

Freeman, R.E. and Reed, D.L. (1983), 'Stockholders and Stakeholders: A New Perspective on Corporate Governance', *California Management Review*, Vol. 25, No. 3, pp. 88–106.

Goodpaster, K.E. (1991), 'Business Ethics and Stakeholder Analysis', *Business Ethics Quarterly*, Vol. 1, No. 1, pp. 53–73.

Greenspan, A., Federal Reserve Chairman of America (2004), www.federalreserve.gov/BoardDocs/speeches/2004/20040513/default.htm.

Greenwood, M. (2001), 'The Importance of Stakeholders According to Business Leaders', *Business and Society Review*, Vol.106, No. 1, pp. 29–49.

Marceau, J. (1999), 'Networks of Innovation, Networks of Production, and Networks of Marketing', *Creativitiy and Innovation Management*, 8/1, pp. 20–27.

Mitchell, R.K., Agle, B.R. and Wood, D.J. (1997), 'Towards a Theory of Stakeholder Identification and Salience: Defining the Principle of Who and What Really Counts', *Academy of Management Review*, Vol. 22, No. 4, pp. 853–886.

Mitchell, R.K. and Agle, B.R. (1999), 'Who Matters to CEOs? An Investigation of Stakeholder Attributes and Salience, Corporate Performance, and CEO Values', *Academy of Management Review*, Vol. 42, No. 5.

Svendsen, A. (1998), *The Stakeholder Strategy*, USA: Berrett-Koehler Publishers, Inc.

Svendsen, A. and Wheeler, D. (2003), 'A Model Relationship', *CA Magazine*, Vol. 136, No. 6, pp. 33–34.

Wolfe, R.A. and Putler, D.S. (2002), 'How Tight are the Ties that Bind Stakeholder Groups?', *Organization Science*, Vol. 13, No. 1, pp. 64–80.

Appendices

Appendix 1

Table 8.10 Typical Corporate and Stakeholder Issues

Stakeholder	Related Issues
Employees	General policy
	Benefits
	Compensation and rewards
	Training and development
	Career planning
	Employee assistance program
	Health promotion
	Absenteeism and turnover
	Leaves of absence
	Relationships with unions
	Dismissal and appeal
	Termination, layoff, and redundancy
	Retirement and termination counseling
	Employment equity and discrimination
	Day-care and family accommodation
	Employee communication
	Occupational health and safety
	Part-time, temporary, or contract employees
Shareholder	General policy
	Shareholder communications and complaints
	Shareholder advocacy
	Shareholder communications and complaints
	Shareholder advocacy
	Shareholder rights
	Other shareholder issues
Customers	General policy
	Customer communication
	Product safety

Table 8.10 continued

Stakeholder	Related Issues
	Customer complaints
	Special customer services
	Other customer issues
Suppliers	General policy
	Relative power
	Other supplier issues
Public stakeholders	Public health
	Conservation of energy and materials
	Environmental assessment of capital projects
	Other environmental issues
	Public policy involvement
	Community relations
	Social investment and donations

Appendix 2: Interview Questions

1. General information:
   - Industry type
   - Short company history
   - Mission statement
   - Organization structure
   - Ownership (private/public/non-profit)
   - Economic Performance
2. Identify whom do you consider as stakeholders of your company?
3. Describe each of the stakeholder groups from your/company's perspective?
   - Shareholders
   - Employees
   - Customers
   - Suppliers
   - Community
   - Natural environment
   - Governmental bodies
   - Media
   - Others
4. Do you prioritize some stakeholder groups over the others? Why?
5. What do you/your company do towards different stakeholder groups? How do you interact with these stakeholder groups? In what ways do you try to build the relationships with a particular stakeholder group? What do you expect to gain from

the activities directed towards these stakeholder groups? Which stakeholder groups are represented in the board of directors? What is the role of the board in relation to various stakeholder groups?

1. *Shareholders*
   Do you find shareholders the most important stakeholder group? If yes, why? Do you meet with them in the shareholders meetings only? Are any of the shareholders involved in the management of the company? What is their role in the company? Are they involved in the decision-making processes? How much power do they have to influence company's activities? Are their interests always taken into consideration?
2. *Employees*
   Does your company encourage employees to form groups to represent or convey their interests to management? If yes, what are they? How do they function? If employees disagree with how they are being treated by their supervisors what options do they have to get those complaints addressed by another party? Is there a formal grievance procedure? Are any employees working on self-directed work groups or work teams? Do these teams have the authority to make decisions, control budgets and resources? Do employees have the power to initiate work projects they may be interested in pursuing? What kind of approval process is involved? How much money does your company invest in the training and development of its employees? Do you cooperate with colleges or universities in looking for potential employees? Do you take on student trainees in your company? Does your company promote those employees who have been loyal and productive? Does the company have a competitive salary and fringe benefit program? Are formal and informal communication and collaboration among staff encouraged? Does the company demonstrate some flexibility with regard to employee working hours and arrangements? Do you encourage your employees to be active in the community life? If yes, in what ways?
3. *Customers*
   Does your company have formal customer treatment policy? Are there any formal rules regarding them? If customers are happy or unhappy with the quality of your product or service, how do you know that? What steps have been taken to find out? Do you employ open-ended customer surveys? What options do they have? Is there a formal complaint procedure? How much do you invest in keeping good relations with the old customers and looking for potential ones? If yes, what forms do you use (information letters, telephone calls, discount programs, greetings, etc.)? Does the company demonstrate flexibility regarding specific request from individual customers?
4. *Suppliers*
   Do you treat all of your suppliers in the same way? Are there any priorities regarding them? If yes, why and in what ways does it differ? Do you try to make contracts with the local suppliers or look for the best financial offers? Do you have one or two major suppliers that provide you with the necessary

materials? What is the percentage of the part they supply? Does the level of involvement with your company matter? Are any of your suppliers involved in the management of the company? If yes, in what form?

5. *Community*
   Do you have any formal policies regarding community? Do you spend money in developing relationships with the community? If yes, how much and in what ways do you support the community? Do you support any sport team, music group or any other activity? If yes, what do you expect to gain from your philanthropic actions? Do you treat the community as present or potential customers? Do you view the community as your future employees?
6. *Governmental Bodies*
   How often do you deal with governmental officials? What's your company's policy regarding them? Are they reached largely through official proceedings or personal contacts? Do you have one or more people from your company who usually deal with them? Do you treat them as the representatives of legal procedures implementation? Do you base your relationship on mutual collaboration? Do you consult them on certain issues that relate to the community? Do you consider them as the guards of the community interests?
7. *Natural Environment*
   Have you implemented worldwide environmental standards regarding goods manufactured in your company? If not, are you going to do that? Do you face any problems in terms of environmental pollution? Does your company contaminate surrounding environment? If yes, what actions do you take to stop that? Do you take part in any projects related to environment protection?
8. *Media*
   Do you communicate with the media? Do you make constant press releases or write reports regarding activities within your company? Do you have a person who is responsible for communication with the media representatives? Do you have any bad experience with them?

Appendix 3

Table 8.11 Financial Data of Companies A, B and C for the Years 2002–2004

In Lithuanian Lt thousands	2002			2003			2004		
	Company			Company			Company		
	A	B	C	A	B	C	A	B	C
Revenue	26,694.0	9,724.0	9,408.0	27,734.0	10,275.0	9,333.0	32,725.0	12.343	9,224.0
Net profit (before taxation)	2, 849.0	124	1,535.0	2, 952.0	221	1,390.0	3, 142.0	230	660
Employee training expenditures	28.9	38.4	11.2	32.8	78.5	12.1	37.4	90.3	16.7
Charity expenditures	48.32	2.48	2.0	56.72	3.29	4.0	72.45	4.91	5.0

Table 8.12 Exports and Imports of Company A in 2003–2004

In Lithuanian Lt thousands	2003	2004
Exports of products	15,272.0	19,091.0
Imports of products	21,114.0	26,3925.0

Appendix 4

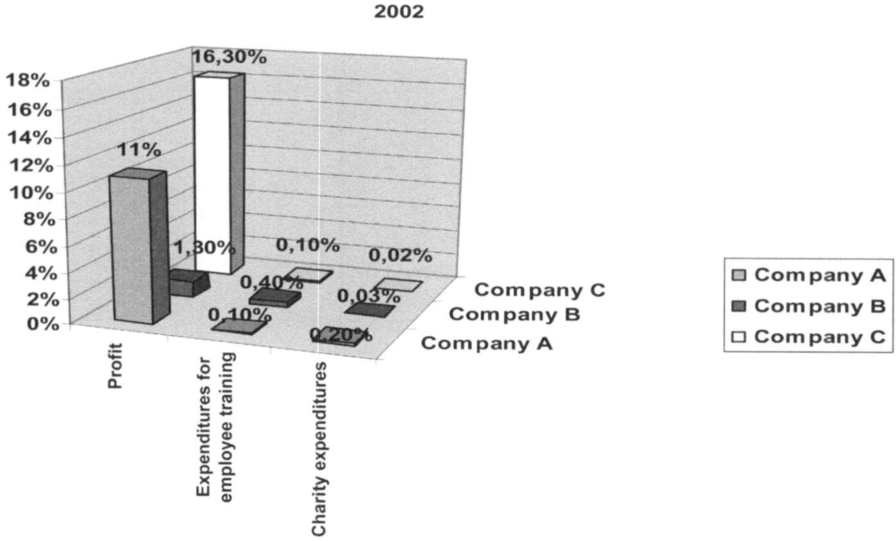

Figure 8.3 Annual Employee Training and Charity Expenditures

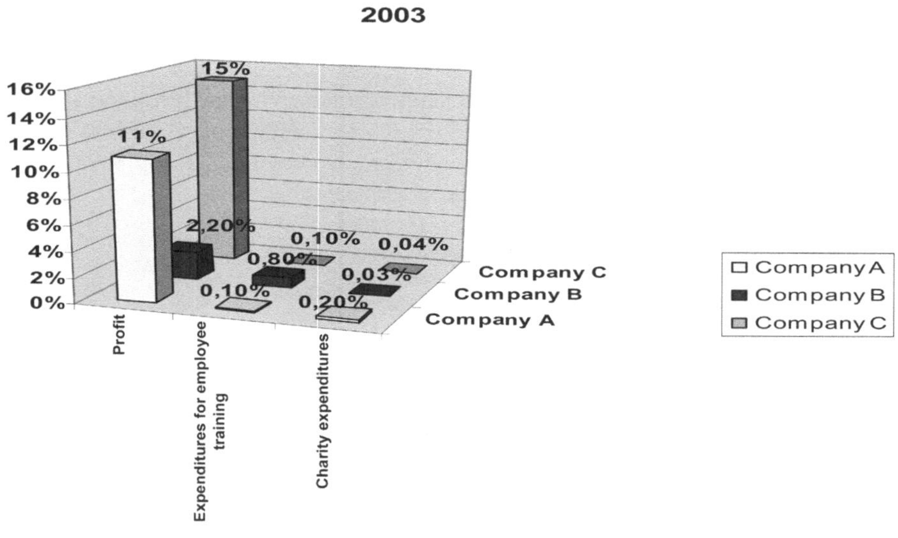

Figure 8.4 Annual Employee Training and Charity Expenditures

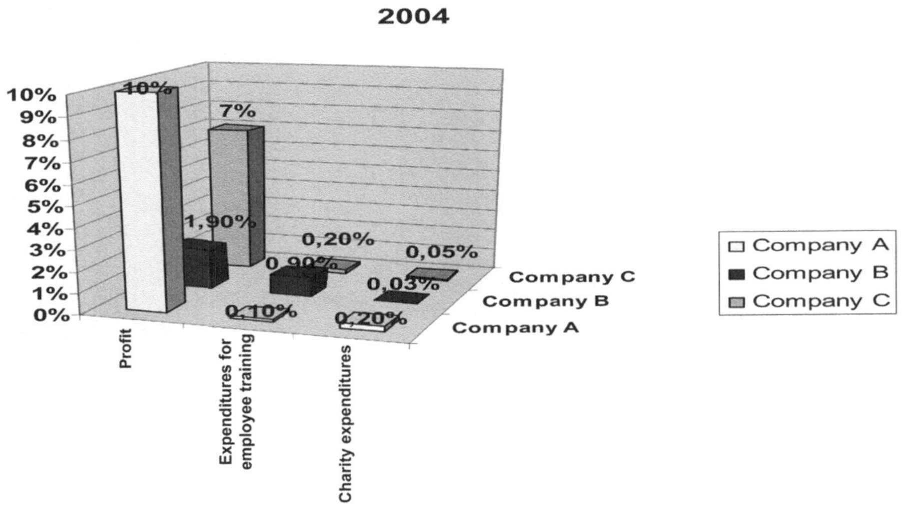

Figure 8.5 Annual Employee Training and Charity Expenditures

Appendix 5

Dear Customer,

As the manager of Company A, I want to thank you for giving us the opportunity to serve you. Please help us serve you better by taking a couple of minutes to tell us about the services and products that you have received so far. We appreciate your business and want to make sure we meet your expectations.

Sincerely,

Manager of Company A

Product/Service Satisfaction Survey

1. In thinking about your most recent experience with COMPANY A, was the quality of customer service you received:

- Very Poor
- Somewhat Unsatisfactory
- About Average
- Very Satisfactory
- Superior

2. If you indicated that the customer service was unsatisfactory, would you please describe what happened?

3. The process for getting your concerns resolved was:
   - Very Poor
   - Somewhat Unsatisfactory
   - About Average
   - Very Satisfactory
   - Superior

4. Would you please take a few minutes to describe what happened?

5. Now please think about the features and benefits of our production. How satisfied are you with the polyethylene production:
   - Very Poor
   - Somewhat Unsatisfactory
   - About Average
   - Very Satisfactory
   - Superior

6. Would you please take a few minutes to describe why you are not satisfied with the product?

7. The following questions pertain to the customer service representative you spoke with most recently. Please indicate whether you agree or disagree with the following statements

	Strongly Agree	Agree	Neutral	Disagree	Strongly Disagree
The customer service representative was very courteous	[]	[]	[]	[]	[]
The customer service representative handled my call quickly	[]	[]	[]	[]	[]
The customer service representative was very knowledgeable	[]	[]	[]	[]	[]

8. Are there any other comments about the customer service representative you would like to add?

9. The following questions pertain to the process by which your most recent service contract was handled. Please indicate whether you agree or disagree with the following statements.

	Strongly Agree	Agree	Neutral	Disagree	Strongly Disagree
The waiting time for having my questions addressed was satisfactory	[]	[]	[]	[]	[]
My phone call was quickly transferred to the person who could best answer my question	[]	[]	[]	[]	[]
The automated phone system made the customer service experience more satisfying	[]	[]	[]	[]	[]

	Very Satisfied	Somewhat Satisfied	Neutral	Somewhat Dis-satisfied	Very Dis-satisfied
Considering the total package offered by COMPANY A including customer service, production features and benefits, and cost; how satisfied are you with our company?	[]	[]	[]	[]	[]

Thank you for your feedback. We sincerely appreciate your honest opinion and will take your input into consideration while providing products and services in the future. If you have any comments or concerns about this survey please contact:

Company A
Vilnius Str. 22-22
Vilnius 2000
Lithuania
Tel.: +370 5 212 2222
Fax.: +370 5 212 1111

Appendix 6

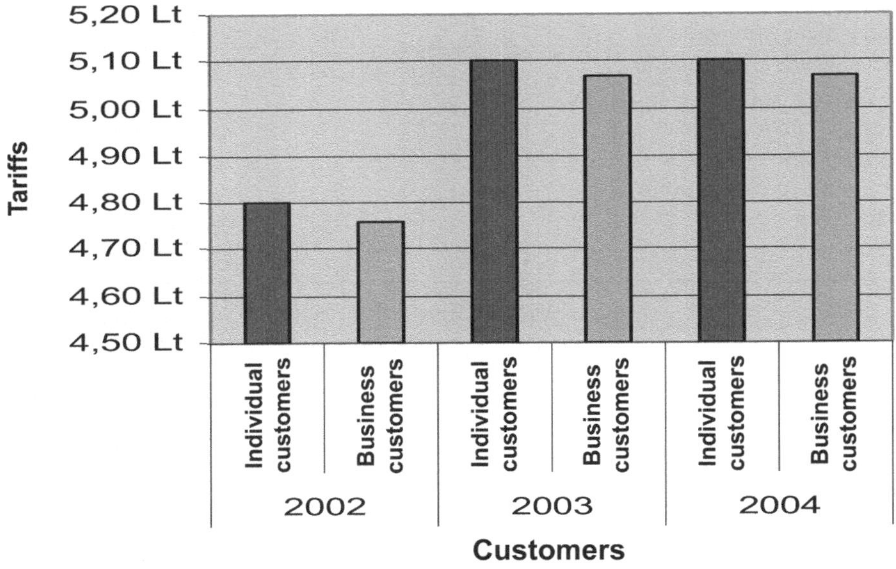

Figure 8.6 Water Tariffs for Individual and Business Customers (2002–2004)

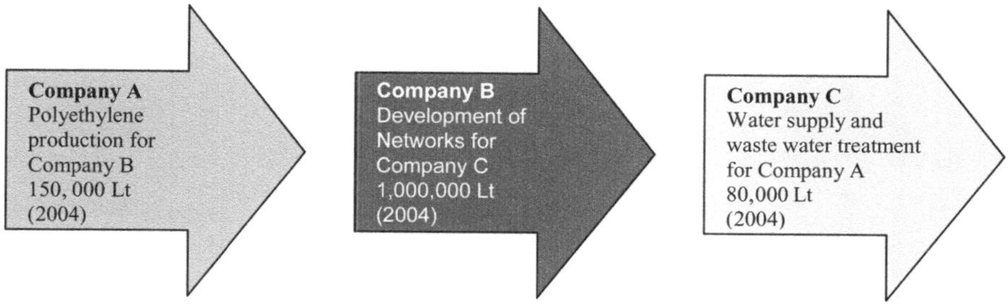

Figure 8.7 Production Networking Among Companies A, B and C (2004)

Chapter 9

The State of the Capitalist State in East-Central Europe: Towards the Porterian Workfare Post-National Regime

Jan Drahokoupil

Introduction

Recent emergence of the 'regional tiger under Tatras', as the financial press refer to radical neo-liberal reform in Slovakia, marks a shift in policy orientation for East-Central Europe (ECE).[1] This shift reflects in particular the way of recent transformations of global capitalism. The post-socialist states in the ECE have embarked upon developmental strategies based upon supply-side management and foreign-direct-investment attraction. In the ECE after 1989, the practice of capitalist governance were inculcated in the complex process of re-contextualization, within which the 'inflows' of such practices were not a matter of simple replications or homogenization, but processes whose outcomes depended upon the local history, its environment, and upon the strategies pursued by both local and ' external' agents.

This chapter provides a Regulationist, state-theoretical account of the transformation of state projects, intervention, and strategy in relation to their effects on the production and reproduction of capitalism in ECE (see Jessop, 2002; Boyer, 1990). Thus, it is concerned with the role of the state in the mutual constitution of economic and extra-economic realities. The underlying concern of this inquiry is how the reproduction of capital accumulation, which includes the reproduction of labor-power as a fictitious commodity, can be achieved. Given the fact that the ECE states have experienced the transformation from state socialism to capitalism only recently, I focus not only on the *re*production but also on the very *production* of capitalist relations and forms. Thus, first, I investigate a state project that enabled *generic* forms of capital relation to institutionalize in the ECE. My primary concern is,

1 East-Central Europe is used here to refer to post-socialist states in Eastern and Central Europe; in particular, I refer to the Czech Republic, Poland, Hungary, Slovakia, and to the Baltic States. This detailed analysis deals with the Visegrad Four countries only (i.e., the Czech Republic, Poland, Hungary, Slovakia).

second, to describe *particular* state forms that have co-constituted specific economic dynamics in the Visegrad Four (V4) states. Thus, I the describe emergence and transformations of dominant state projects, and accumulation strategies with respect to their functional adequacy in relation to the dynamic of capitalist accumulation.[2] There are two caveats I wish to raise in order to make clear what this chapter is *not* about. First, this is not an explanatory account and a history of events. Instead, it is a generalized characterization of descriptive nature. It is not possible to provide an explanation of the processes I describe in this chapter. Nevertheless, the description is theoretically rich as it helps to understand the economic dynamics that the state co-constitutes. Second, this is not an exhaustive description of state policies or of the 'actually existing states'. Rather, it is a stylized account of the dominant policy orientations or state projects.

The chapter proceeds as follows. First, I introduce methodology and analytical dimensions of this inquiry. Second, I focus on the role of the state in introducing generic forms of capitalist relations into the ECE. Then, I investigate the transformation of particular state projects and accumulation strategies according to theses dimensions. Finally, I try to bring these threads together and provide stylized models of dominant state projects and accumulation strategies with respect to their functional adequacy to socio-economic reproduction in ECE after the fall of state socialism. I claim that after a period of distinctive national projects, there has been a relative convergence towards an emerging dominant state project, which I call Porterian workfare post-national regime.

Analysing the (Capitalist) State in Post-Socialism

Given the incomplete, contradictory, conflictual, and crisis-prone nature of the capitalist economy, the state and other extra-economic institutions have a crucial role in reproducing capital relation, which comprises both economic and social reproduction. A comprehensive analysis of the state in these respects has to move along four dimensions (Jessop, 2002). The first dimension refers to the role of the state in securing conditions for the *continuation of private business* from the viewpoint of particular kinds of capital and capital in general (i.e., realm of economic policy). Market forces alone cannot secure the basic conditions for capital accumulation that are unprofitable from the viewpoint of individual forms of capital. The second dimension relates to the *reproduction of the labor-power* from the viewpoints of particular forms of capital, capital in general, and workers (i.e., the realm of social policy).[3]

Labor power is a fictitious commodity (Polanyi, 1944/1957) – even though it is bought and sold in markets, it is not itself directly (re)produced in and by capitalist

---

2 For a detailed discussion regarding the concepts of state project and accumulation strategy, see Jessop (1990).

3 Social policy is analysed here primarily in the context of reproduction of labor power, which implies that some aspects of welfare are ignored.

firms; therefore, its (re)production, complementary with the requirements of capitalist accumulation, is by no means guaranteed. The third dimension concerns the structured coherence in the *scalar organization* of economic and social policy. In order to achieve relatively stable conditions of reproduction of an accumulation regime, there has to be a relative degree of structural coherence or compatibility between the ways of securing social and economic reproduction so that different forms, institutions, and practices become mutually reinforcing or at least relatively non-contradictory. Finally, the fourth dimension refers to the primary *mechanism of coordination* (i.e., governance) of supplementing market forces in socio-economic reproduction and compensating their failure. There is no guarantee that any of these conditions for relatively stable economic reproduction will be performed functionally from the viewpoint of accumulation; instead, it is a matter of evolutionary search and trial-and-error with identifiable agents behind this process. These analytic dimensions cannot be analysed separately but in their mutual articulation. Thus, one tries to identify a dominant state form which may co-constitute an accumulation regime.

When analysing post-socialist regimes that introduced capitalist forms only recently, it is necessary to deal with the role of the state in relation to the capitalist accumulation on two levels. First, we have to focus on the *generic* features of capital relation.[4] Thus, one has to deal with the questions of whether and how the basic forms of capitalist relation were institutionalized and whether the capitalist state in the generic sense has emerged in post-socialist societies. Second, only after considering the problems on the generic level, can we deal with the *specific* forms of state and accumulation regimes.

A conventional Regulationist, state-theoretical analysis cannot be applied when studying post-socialist transformations.[5] One cannot expect to identify coherent organization of social forms in societies undergoing radical transformation. Moreover, we are dealing with social formations where the basic social forms are in the process of institutionalization and are thus possibly contested by different social actors and path-dependencies. There are two solutions to this problem. First, one may use the form analysis by following Robert Boyer's distinction between two ways of understanding of social form hierarchies. Accordingly, in the periods of transformation:

---

4 The generic features of the capitalist type of state comprise institutional separation of state and economy, monopoly on violence, tax state, specialized administrative body, rule of law, and formal sovereignty (see Jessop 2002, pp. 36–48).

5 A form analysis identifies dominant social forms (e.g., commodity form, exchange value, use value, money, capital, the wage form, the price form, legal form, and state form) and contradictions; investigates whether and how they correspond to each other (institutional separation of economic and political is advantageous but also problematic for capital accumulation and interest of capital); and it examines how the dominant forms shape possibilities of action – identify their strategic selectivities (Jessop, 1982, 1990, 2002).

> [a]n institutional form may be said to be hierarchically superior to another if *its development implies a transformation of this other form,* in its configuration and logic (Boyer 2000, p. 291, emphasis original).

That is, it may impose its developmental logic on other forms in the process of co-evolution (cf. Jessop, 2000a). The second solution is to give up the ambition of considering formal adequacy of state forms and conduct a path-dependent, path-shaping *functional* analysis of the state *projects* in respect to particular dynamics of capitalist accumulation and thus to focus on the trial-end-error search for an 'appropriate' state project that would co-constitute a relatively stable accumulation regime.[6] Since an object of regulation and its mode of regulation are mutually co-constituted; one cannot presuppose its functionality. Thus, a state project or form would be functional if it co-constitutes with its object of regulation a relative functional coherence that manages to reproduce itself. Therefore, functionality is a descriptive feature of a state project or form, not an explanation of its existence.

In the analysis that follows, I follow mainly the second solution. Thus, I assess primarily functional adequacy of the state projects with respect to the particular dynamics of accumulation that they co-constitute. Thus, I try to identify a dominant logic of state intervention (if any), which may co-constitute a growth dynamic. The analysis on the level of generic forms of capital relation and capitalist state form follows the functional logic as well. Thus, I do not provide an ideal type of a formally adequate state for the transition from state-socialism to capitalism; instead, I deal with the functionality of the state project that emerged in respect to introducing generic forms of capitalism.

Introducing Capitalism into East-Central Europe: The Neo-liberal Transformational State

The transition of post-communist regimes to capitalism started at the time when global hegemony of neoliberalism was at its height (cf. Bryant and Mokrzycki, 1994). Thus, the neoliberal premises and respective advisors shaped the policies aimed at radical systemic transformation from non-capitalist regimes to capitalist ones. The transition to capitalism was designed to be essentially market-led. The invisible hand of the market was expected to discipline social actors on their way to capitalism. The policies also included the IMF one-size-fits-all monetarist panacea of anti-inflationary policy based on fiscal and monetary restraint. Moreover, for various reasons, it was considered crucial to introduce the conditions for emergence of the market at once and as soon as possible. Thus, most of the policy packages implemented in the post-socialist state comprised the above-mentioned anti-inflationary measures

6 State projects are attempts to give a given contradictory complexity of state institutions relative internal unity to guide its action. They may give rise to state forms. Accumulation strategies are attempts to give a certain substantive unity and direction to the circuit of capital (Jessop, 1990, Chapters 11 and 12).

for budgetary and monetary restraint, shock price liberalization, privatization, and shock trade liberalization.

The similar policy configuration was implemented in all countries of ECE, and in many other post-communist states. Moreover, speaking about the V4 countries, the reformers' original neo-liberal enthusiasm for austerity measures was not fully materialized. Hence, some form of compensation and compromise to preserve social cohesion was an important element of the policy-mix on the way to capitalism. For instance, Poland experienced huge political backlash against the downturn caused be the textbook shock-therapy measures; thus, as early as 1991, Olszewski's government 'forfeited shock therapy', and attempted a social compromise by a more cohesion-oriented strategy (Orenstein, 2001, Chapter 2). Thus, on the level of introducing *generic* conditions of capitalist accumulation, we can witness a distinctive form of state, which I call *Neoliberal transformational state* (see Table 9.1).

Table 9.1 Neoliberal Transformational State in the ECE

Shock stabilization
Shock price liberalization
Shock trade liberalization (+ reorientation)
Privatization
Some form of compensation and compromise to preserve social cohesion

The neo-liberal transformational state was relatively successful in the ECE states. It institutionalized basic forms of capital relation such as money form, wage form, and commodification of labor power; moreover, it managed to create states that have basic generic features and fulfill basic functions of the capitalist state, such as institutional separation between state and economy, monopoly of coercion, tax capacity, and the rule of law. However, the neo-liberal transformational state failed in these respects in the post-Soviet states, leading to what Burawoy (1996) calls 'involution' to a non-capitalist social formation (cf. King, 2004).

The basic measures of property-rights provision, institutionalization of wage form, tax-raising capacity have been comparable or similar in the ECE states to the situation in the advanced capitalist countries already by the early 1990s; the figures also show that the turnover in barter, which indicates institutionalization of the market and social forms it presupposes has been very low in the ECE states too (WB, 2003, 2005; WB and EBRD, 2005). Moreover, World Bank indicators of governance basically measure the formal adequacy regarding capitalist state cluster of ECE states close to the advanced capitalist states – in contrast, the post-Soviet states are grouped at the bottom (Kaufmann, Kraay, and Mastruzzi, 2003). The relative success in ECE in contrast to the painful failure elsewhere is usually being explained by the initial level of development, by the inherited institutional framework, by ECE's favorable location, and by the presence of foreign direct investment in ECE (e.g., King, 2004; Myant, 2004; Boer-Ashworth, 2000).

The State and the Conditions for the Continuation of Private Business (Economic Policy)

After considering the successful introduction of basic forms of capital relation and basic features of the capitalist state in ECE, I move to the analysis of the *specific* features of state projects in relation to the specific economic dynamics in ECE, after the fall of state socialism. Starting with the realm of economic policy, I will depict transformations of states in the V4 along the analytic dimensions outlined above. As far as the early 1990s are concerned, these specific and distinctive features are seen as a part of the broader project of the neo-liberal transformational state. Therefore, all these state regimes aimed at institutionalizing capitalist forms and relations. The neo-liberal orientation explains that in aiming to create a capitalist economy and economic outcomes, these states lacked positive industrial policy: it was assumed that introducing basic and narrow economic preconditions of a market economy would be sufficient. The actors were assumed to 'know how' and, if they did not, they would be taught by the market. Thus we cannot speak about developmental states.

The economic policies in the Czech Republic (Czechoslovakia) in the early 1990s were based on a peculiar mix of monetarism, economic nationalism, minimal regulation, and bank socialism. I call this policy mix *Klausian*, as it very much reflects the way of thinking of the emblematic figure of Czech transformation, Václav Klaus. Klausian strategy included fiscal and monetary restraint, rapid privatization, intentionally weak regulation and control of finance, and absence of positive industrial policy. With a naïve view of the country's economic and industrial levels, internal solutions, including domestic ownership, were preferred (e.g., the privatization method was designed in order to prevent foreign capital from buying out the Czech economy). Finally, there was an implicit policy of various forms of ad-hoc interventions to help potential bankruptcy-threatened enterprises (e.g., Myant, 2003; Orenstein, 2001; Gould, 2001).

The Klausian project, however, has been dismantled following the economic crisis of the mid-1990s, which was largely caused by some of its own elements. What followed was a sea-change in thinking about economic policy for all key actors, indicating a broader shift in the hegemonic outlook of Czech policy makers. It was a shift from an internally-oriented economic nationalism towards externally-oriented competitive policies of supply-side intervention. Since 1998, Czech policies are clearly oriented to attract appropriate capital and thus manage insertion of locality to the global economy. I call these policies Porterian since the management of investment flows follows the place-competition logic of Michael Porter (Porter, 1990). Accordingly, the policies aim at attracting skill-intensive and technology-rich investment and network the investors to local institutions (clusters). The main policy instrument at the moment is the scheme of incentives subsidies for potential investors (offering tax breaks, job creation and training grants, low cost land) and an emerging project of cluster promotion (see CzechInvest, 2004, 2005).[7]

After the split of Czechoslovakia in 1993, the Slovak part slowed substantially the implementation of market reform. However, it maintained the orthodox macroeconomic policy stance pursued until 1993 under the Czechoslovak federation (Marcincin and Beblavý, 2000). Thus, for instance, the monetary policy was kept tight. Mečiar's government subordinated economic policy to its nationalistic project of Slovak resurrection:

> [It] justified its privatization policy in terms of the need to create a 'nationally conscious' entrepreneurial class capable of sustaining Slovak independence (EIU, 1998, p. 20).

Most state-owned enterprises have been privatized by direct sales while keeping the sale terms, ownership structure and identity of the new owners out of public control. The government stimulated domestic demand by huge debt-financed public investments in highway construction and other infrastructure. The specificity of this policy mix and enormous influence of then Prime Minister Vladimír Mečiar leads me to call this strategy *Mečiarian*. The 1998 general elections brought a rightist coalition led by Mikuláš Dzurinda to power, which radically changed policy orientation for Slovakia. The government introduced fiscal restraint and subordinated its policy to boosting competitiveness and attracting foreign capital. In order to do so, the government pursues radical neo-liberal reform of the state and provides investment subsidies (tax relief, training and employment generation grants, cheap loans). The Slovak government has proven to be extremely accommodating in dealing with individual investors, willing to circumvent its own laws and to give up democratic accountability.

The strategy of economic reform in Poland was the least distorted translation of the developmental panacea of the neo-liberal Washington consensus in ECE (cf. Williamson, 1993; Lipton and Sachs, 1990). Thus, its shock therapy was based on the monetarist reasoning of a credit squeeze, fiscal consolidation, limiting wage growth, trade and price liberalization, and absence of positive industrial policy. In contrast to the Czech Republic, the shock therapy did not include shock privatization. In Poland, we cannot observe such a sharp break in economic policy orientation as in the Czech Republic and Slovakia. The process of policy change has been much more gradual and continual there (Orenstein, 2001). However, we can witness an analogous process of policy reorientation from a relatively inward-looking strategy towards a more outward-looking one.

Poland was already offering different subsidies to foreign capital such as tax privileges and 'preferential regime' in its Special Economic Zones, with the emergence of *Solidarność* in the early 1990s. However, its privatization strategy preferred domestic solutions (managers, employees), though kept it relatively

7 As in all ECE states, the subsidies package is offered to both foreign and domestic investors. However, given the undercapitalized environment, it is provided mainly to foreign capital.

open to foreign capital. There was a shift towards preferring foreign capital in privatization around 1995, which was also reflected in the increase in, what was until then relatively sluggish, FDI inflow (Uminski, 2001; Ádám, 2004). The attraction of FDI has become a key developmental strategy on various state levels (Young and Kaczmarek, 2000). The attracting of FDI follows the Porterian logic as it puts emphasis on bringing in investment 'concerning technological innovation' (PAIiIZ, 2005).

Hungary's reform strategy has been gradualist and more cautiously designed. Generally adopting a case-by-case approach, an aggressive privatization policy has been pursued since 1995. Due to high-levels of foreign debt and its position in the global political economy, Hungary was 'forced to steer privatization in a direction that explicitly favoured TNCs' (Uminski, 2001, p. 63). Hungary's economic policy has been very much externally oriented from the very beginning as its policies have been the most accommodating towards foreign investors among the V4. Until recently, no other country has been prepared to sell major stakes in sensitive or strategic sectors such as banking or energy to foreign capital.

Hungary guarantees free repatriation of after-tax profit and capital. Many earlier investment incentives have been phased-out; those remaining include an investment tax preference of 50 percent (100 percent in priority areas), subject to the value and value added of exports produced, and a reduction based on a percentage of future taxes to be paid, subject to the share capital invested, environmental factors and export potential, deduction and depreciation allowances for plant and machinery, as well as tax preferences for offshore companies registered in Hungary. Companies operating in free-trade zones are exempt from customs and indirect taxes. Tax holidays are available for investments in the depressed east of the country. Hungary grants the most tax and import duty allowances for green-field projects in the region (EIU, 2004a).

State and the Reproduction of Labor-Power (Social Policy)

While significantly varying in their shapes, all four countries followed similar paths of social policy transformation after the fall of state socialism. In the first year of transformation, countries established various welfare minded social policy systems, putting much emphasis on wage regulation and on setting up unemployment systems. Industrial relations were quite specific during the early 1990s, since the interests of capital and labor were not necessarily antagonistic. On the contrary, managers of large enterprises often welcomed protest from employees over social issues as it was a convenient bargaining issue in their quest for help from the government (e.g., Myant, 2000). In the late 1990s, ECE states began to transform their social-policy systems, converging and moving in a workfarist direction in line with neo-liberal thinking and advice primarily from the World Bank.

The actual reform strategy of the early nineties in the Czech Republic could be characterized as 'social-liberal' (Orenstein, 2001; cf. Dangerfield, 1997). The social protection was an aim in itself. An elaborate and relatively generous system of welfare provision was introduced in order to guarantee social peace during the process of post-socialist transformation. Social policies also included a soft approach towards large enterprises to keep them from falling. The collective bargaining mechanism was established within tripartite structures. On this platform, the government negotiated a wage control system, which meant that prices could rise faster than wages, but it was guaranteed that the latter would not fall substantially. Here, the government also committed itself to various safeguards for the lowest paid, such as the minimum wage. The wage controls actually continued until 1995 (Myant and Smith, 1999). Despite the devaluation of the generosity of the system and its targeting in the mid-1990s, overall trends remained stable (Potůček, 2004).

Slovakia introduced an analogous welfare system and labor code. In order to prevent unemployment, it kept subsidizing large enterprises even after their privatization. Moreover, these enterprises were not entirely separated from the government as they were interconnected via dense clientilist networks. Mečiar's government also kept regulation of a substantial part of consumer prices (EIU, 1998). In Poland, a deep economic downturn of 1990-91 caused a social and political backlash, which made policy makers forfeit orthodox shock therapy by a more cohesion oriented strategy (Orenstein, 2001).

Poland introduced a relatively less extensive and more targeted welfare system, provided flat-rate unemployment benefits and minimum-wage regulation. The industrial relations were complicated by the fact that the main trade union actually functioned as a (ruling) political party, which resulted in a blurred system of collective bargaining. A focal point of this blurred industrial struggle was the institution of the so-called *popiwek* tax on wage increases above a centrally mandated level in state enterprises, which among others, was introduced to limit room for maneuver of workers' council. These bodies had power to dismiss managers without having to gain permission from the Ministry of Industry.

Hungary introduced originally what was probably the most generous welfare system in the former Soviet Bloc (Baxandall, 2002). It was exceptional in the coverage and generosity of its family benefit system, as it also provided relatively generous unemployment benefits, access to the health-care system, and guaranteed minimum wage. In order to shrink the pool of potentially unemployed, a number of policies including parental leave, sick-leave, disability and early retirement benefits, facilitated exit from the labor market. However, in conjunction with other transformation policies and problems, the Hungarian welfare state failed to translate social spending into general welfare for its citizens (OECD, 1997; Boer-Ashworth, 2000; Baxandall, 2002). Hungary has imported the German system of national wage bargaining (Frydman, Murphy, and Rapaczynski, 1998). The government sought to depress wages by indexing them below inflation, with the policies negotiated within this framework.

From the mid-1990s, ECE states began to retrench their social systems. The retrenchment was most visible and dramatic in Hungary in 1995, when a Socialist government initiated severe cuts in welfare under the so-called *Bokros* package of reforms. Social-policy reforms not only dismantle and target welfare provisions, but they also reorient social systems into a *workfarist* paradigm (cf. Peck, 2001). Thus, they are aimed at motivating welfare recipients to actively look for jobs and discourage them from passively consuming benefits. Social policy aims at promoting workforce flexibility. It makes workers employable by training them according to the needs of capital (for an example from Poland, see Young, 2004, p. 114).

Slovakia is a European leader in reorienting its social system and labor code in neo-liberal directions of work. As a result of a comprehensive flexibility overhaul of the Labor Code in 2003, employers have received enormous flexibility in hiring and firing employees. In addition, Slovakia introduced a highly regressive tax system, setting a uniform 19 percent flat rate for corporate and personal income, as well as for value-added tax (EIU, 2004c).

The current policy-making context (environment of strategic selectivity) overly determines the workfare direction of social-policy reform. First, the competitive orientation of economic policy is a challenge for welfarist and redistributive measures. Thus, the policy makers are concerned with the implications of social policies on a country's competitiveness. It is extremely important that the welfarist and redistributive orientation is *perceived* as at odds with the locational preferences of mobile capital. We can witness the competition of regulatory regimes in these respects. Accordingly, the radical neo-liberal reform in Slovakia by Dzurinda's government is an important reference point in this discussion about social policy in ECE and beyond. Second, current global political-economic configuration makes welfarist and redistributive strategy and demand-side solutions extremely difficult for the ECE countries. The global financial system puts severe constraints on social policies with its monetary and fiscal imperatives (e.g., Gamble and Payne, 1996).

The policy adjustment in Hungary and the Czech Republic in the mid-1990s was largely driven by adverse financial flows. The *Bokros* package experience in Hungary demonstrated enormous influence the IMF and WB may exercise to push social policies in the direction of residual welfare state and workfare strategies. Third, the enlargement and EMU conditionalities of the EU have been pushing ECE countries into neo-liberal restructuring rather than exporting the EU's solidaristic project (Böhle, 2004). Fourth, neo-liberal reasoning has achieved hegemonic status in the discourse regarding social policy in ECE. Its elements are both imported by international organizations and domestic in origin (cf. Bockman and Eyal, 2002). For instance, the ideational origins of Slovak reform can be easily traced to the ideational production of the IMF and WB; the underclass discourse of non-deserving clients of the welfare state has gained in importance.

Primary Scale

For most of the 1990s, the national scale was a primary scale of intervention in the ECE.[8] For instance, in the Czech case, Klausian monetarist reasoning of national aggregates combined with some elements of economic nationalism, made the national economy and national society take for granted the object of intervention. It was the national open economy with its family-silver enterprises that competed in the wider environment. Foreigners were generally not welcomed in the privatization. Industrial relations were negotiated on the national tripartite platform. Policy making was very centralized; for instance, during the large-scale privatization, there were few colleagues and friends in Prague who would sit days and nights to make enormous an amount of decisions about the destiny of a majority of medium and large enterprises in the country (Husák, 1997), the same was true in Hungary (Uminski, 2001).

The late 1990s have seen some degree of rescaling of the state in all four countries. The power of the national state has shifted and transformed upwards, downwards, and sideways.[9] The accession of the Czech Republic to the European Union in 2004 represents a decisive shift of state power upwards. For instance, in the sphere of economic policy, most of the ECE states had to back pedal their investment-incentives schemes in order to comply with respective EU regulations. Other international governmental and non-governmental organizations such as CEE Bankwatch network play an important role in the decision making and political struggles. Moreover, ECE states engage in supranational marketing of place such as Euro-regions (shift upwards and sideways) (e.g., Young, 2004). As far as the shift downwards is concerned, Poland established regional self-governing units in 1999, the Czech Republic in 2000.

Polish *voivodships* and *gminas* have an important autonomous role in the area of marketing, including investment attracting; they can reduce local taxes and provide other incentives such as training of the labor force (Hardy, 2004; Young, 2004). In the Czech Republic, regional units have rather limited power; however, there are some areas where their power is significant or about to grow. The workfarist social reform shifts some responsibilities to the municipal scale. These scaled transformations make the ability of social actors to 'jump scales', an important asset in the social struggle. Moreover, rescaling, along with the shift of power sideways (see below), has changed the role of corrupt personal networks; these networks

8 Scale is a means of organizing space; it refers to the 'vertical' differentiation of social practices across geographical space. Thus, social relations are embedded in a hierarchy of spaces, stretching from the global, the supranational, and the national to the regional, the urban, the local, and the body. Scales are not static or fixed, but socially produced and therefore malleable (e.g., Smith, 1995; Brenner, 2001).

9 In no way do I wish to claim that the nation states are necessarily losing power in rescaling. This is not a zero-sum game. Instead, the role of the state is being transformed; they are acquiring a different position in respect to the scalar dimension of politics (cf. Brenner, 1999).

thus can be utilized as a mechanism of interscalar and inter-systemic steering (e.g., Drahokoupil, 2005).

Primary Means to Compensate for Market Failure

The state has been the main means of supplementing market mechanisms in ECE. Even though the market had primary and superior roles in the discursive construction of desirable governance mechanisms in the early 1990s, both direct state intervention and indirect steering through personal networks had an important role in economic governance at that time. A compensatory state was actively taking care of both moderating and compensating for the social costs of economic transformation (Greskovits, 1998). Nevertheless, we can witness some variation in the governance of privatization that had profound implications on policy outcomes. The particularly striking contrast is between Poland and the Czech Republic: while the Czech Republic relied primarily on state-induced market organization of privatization and industrial restructuring resulting in frequent market failures, Poland constructed 'deliberative governance structures' that helped public and private actors learn from and monitor one another (McDermott, 2002).

Some recent trends and governmental plans indicate that the transformation will probably shift some of the state responsibilities sideways. The growing importance of the non-governmental agencies and forms of public-private partnership are most significant in the process of investment attraction in which economic, state, and non-state actors operating on different scales meet (e.g., Drahokoupil, 2004; Young, 2004; Hardy, 2004). For instance, in the Czech Republic, 2004 has witnessed development of the policy to promote public-private partnership (PPP), including launching of the Centre for Implementation of PPP. The future will show how significant this change is.

Towards the Porterian Welfare Post-national Regime?

I have described distinctive features/state projects in relation to capitalist accumulation in V4. The early 1990s have seen a crystallization of distinctive state projects (see Table 9.2). Later transformations of these state projects went along similar lines. The Czech Republic and Slovakia have experienced radical transformation of their state projects since 1998. We have witnessed the emergence of state projects that co-constituted accumulation dynamics that failed to reproduce itself. I construct their ideal-typical mezzo-level characterizations in order to depict their specific features. Thus, I do not describe a solution for the reproduction of an accumulation regime. The transformation in Poland and Hungary was much more continuous and gradual. It seems that the developments have resulted in a relative convergence of state projects in the V4. After assessing functional adequacy of respective state projects, I describe the point of convergence: a model of the state form that is emerging in ECE, which I call the Porterian workfare postnational regime.

Table 9.2 State Projects and Forms in their Economic (Capital Theoretical) Dimension in the Early 1990s

Distinctive set of economic policies	Distinctive set of social policies	Primary scale (if any)	Primary means to compensate market failure
	Czech Republic		
Nationalist monetarism; Minimal regulation; Bank socialism	Silent welfare provision; Tripartite collective bargaining; Low-wage low-unemployment policy	Monetarist reasoning of national aggregates; Centralized administration; Economic nationalism in an open economy	Compensating state
Klausian	*Welfare*	*National*	*State*
	Slovakia		
Nationalism with economic means; Debt-financed demand stimulation; Tight monetary policy	Employment-keeping subsidies to private sector; Welfare state; Consumer-price regulation	Project of national resurrection; Centralized administration; Monetarist reasoning of national aggregates	Compensating state
Mečiarian	*Welfare*	*National*	*State*
	Poland		
Shock therapy; Gradual privatization	Modest, targeted welfare; "Blurred" collective bargaining; Wage indexation; Workers councils	Monetarist reasoning of national aggregates; Centralized administration; Shock therapy in an open economy	Compensating state; Deliberative governance structures
	Hungary		
Externally oriented; Gradual reform; Aggressive, case-by-case privatization	Relatively generous welfare measures; Tripartite collective bargaining; Wage indexation	National open economy	Compensating state

The Czech republic of the early 1990s has witnessed an emergence of a specific state project, a *Klausian welfare national state* (KlWNS). It was presupposed and co-constituted by a specific economic dynamic, which Martin Myant named 'Czech capitalism' (Myant, 2003). Thus, the monetary shock overkill of 1990 did not prevent economic recovery. Instead, the years after 1993 saw accelerating, low-wage, low-inflation growth. This economic boom, which was often interpreted as a 'Czech economic miracle' proving neoliberal prescriptions right, was not a 'non-hyphenated capitalism' that Klaus had announced he would construct; instead, it was largely based on particular driving forces produced by KlWNS's policies that can hardly be interpreted as *laissez-faire* like. The KlWNS was, to a limited extent, functionally adequate to the growth logic of Czech capitalism. It compensated for limited adjustment in some enterprises by securing conditions of soft-credit. KlWNS investment projects (such as rebuilding of infrastructure) and social spending also played an important role in stimulating demand. Further, KlWNS secured a low-wage, low-currency value, and low-inflation environment.

Among other realities, this environment enabled quick adaptation of existing enterprises, which was one basis of recovery from the depression.[10] Moreover, KlWNS had a crucial role in securing social reproduction by socializing costs of transformation. However, Czech capitalism was not able to reproduce itself even in the short-term perspective.[11] The functional adequacy of KlWNS had its narrow limits. The factors that caused the downturn were largely the very driving forces of Czech capitalism. The specific sources of growth were either exhausted (e.g., some transformation policies), or contradicted expanded economic reproduction (e.g., bank socialism and loose regulation). The Czech Republic had already experienced an economic downturn in 1996. The government reacted by introducing two 'little packages' of restrictive economic measures. The packages were not able to weaken the crisis; instead, they undermined some of the economic driving forces (Myant, 2003).

The story in Slovakia was to some extent analogous to the Czech one. A specific state project that proved to be to a limited extent functional for the local growth dynamic, was introduced. Slovakia has experienced one of the highest growth rates among the post-socialist states in the mid-1990s. This growth was preconditioned on the specific policies of what can be called *Mečiarian welfare national state*. It was largely driven by domestic demand and by the exports of semiproducts and/or products with low levels of processing. This growth dynamic was highly imbalanced and unsustainable (especially in the context of tight monetary policy) (EIU, 2004c; Marcincin and Beblavý, 2000). I surmise that Slovakia did not manage to develop a functionally adequate state form reproducible in the mid-term perspective.

10 This often happened, however, by regressing to exporting products associated with lower levels of development (Myant, 2003, p. 42).

11 Thus, from a Regulationist point of view, it is clear that, even without considering its formal adequacy, the KLWNS was not a part of a mode of regulation.

Nevertheless, the radical policy reorientation of 1998 did not react directly like the crisis of the Mečiarian model; instead it was driven by a political change.

Poland and Hungary did not experience such a distinctive period of a particular economic dynamic co-constituted by a specific state project. Hungary has been very much externally oriented from the beginning. It established itself as a low-cost assembly area for EU based supply chains in the early 1990s; however, government spending and small-medium enterprises were important driving forces of its growth as well (EIU, 2004a; Boer-Ashworth, 2000). After the shock-therapy big bang, Poland has been developing and adjusting its policies very much gradually and continuously, despite the political turbulence (Orenstein, 2001). Its economic recovery has been driven by consumption originally, then by investment, and later on by exports (EIU, 2004b).

From the vantage point of 2005, we can witness relative convergence of the dominant state projects in the ECE states. I call the dominant state project that is emerging in ECE as *Porterian workfare postnational regime* (PWPR) (see Table 9.3). First, PWPR is a competition state that aims at managing insertion of local economies into the circuits of European capitalism. In doing so, it follows the *Porterian* logic of competitiveness that puts emphasis on attracting skill-intensive and technology rich investment and embedding it in the local economy.[12] One should be aware that it is the state *project* that is Porterian in its logic. The actual practice of investment attraction for ECE, however, very often 'takes everything if big' (e.g., Mallya, Kukulka, and Jensen, 2004). Very often the policy makers justify this by the assumption that the respective regions cannot afford to attract anything better. 'The quality' is expected to follow later. Nevertheless, the states ultimately aim at attracting the 'high-quality investment'. In addition to investment, the PWPR competes for funding and support coming from higher scales such as the EU.

Second, the social policy dimension of PWPR is *workfarist* in its orientation. It is subordinated to the project of investment attraction and economic competitiveness. As I have mentioned above, social policy aims at promoting workforce flexibility and employability according to the needs of capital. This does not mean that the social policy would be expected to be abolished entirely, as this is a rather unrealistic expectation (cf. Pierson, 1994); but the point is that the aim and orientation changes from entitlements and compensation towards meeting the demands of capital. In this context, it is important to reiterate here that the dominant perception of the locational preferences is crucial in this respect. It is the neo-liberal 'low road' to development and cost competitiveness that is considered as crucial concerning locational decision of capital, even though that much of the empirical evidence suggests that other forms of competitiveness are much more influential in Europe (cf. Cooke and Noble, 1998; Ryner, 2002). In addition, Porterian demand management has a redistributive spatio-social dimension in all four countries under consideration: PWPR aims at attracting

12 The term Porterian needs a qualification. Michael Porter is putting emphasis on the domestic capital that is key to regional competitiveness accordingly (Porter, 1990). The developmental strategy of ECE states is based on attracting foreign capital instead.

Table 9.3 Porterian Workfare Postnational Regime (Accentuation of Trends)

Distinctive set of economic policies	Distinctive set of social policies	Primary scale (if any)	Primary means to compensate market failure
Manages insertion of the locality to global economy; Supply-side intervention; Emphasis on skill-intensive, technology rich activities	Subordinates social policy to economic competitiveness; Emphasis on employability; Downward pressure on the "social wage" and attack on welfare rights	Shift of power both upwards, downwards, and sideways; New role of the national scale; Equalizing/ compensating spatial project	[Shift to governance]
Porterian	*Workfare*	*Postnational*	*Regime*

investment to the underdeveloped regions, being more generous in its supply side intervention there.[13]

Third, given the process of rescaling that I have illustrated above, PWPR is *postnational*. The national scale is no longer a taken-for-granted primary scale of social action and state power. However, this does not mean that the national state would lose importance and power. Instead, it is acquiring a new role as far as the scalar dimension of politics is concerned. Finally, with considerable hesitation, I call this the PWPR regime, as it seems to me that different non-state means of compensating market failure will grow in importance. However, there is no sufficient empirical evidence of this process in the ECE at the moment.

PWPR is distinct from the state form that is crystallizing in the advanced capitalist countries as a result of a search for a solution to the crisis of the Fordist economies in the West. Jessop characterizes this form as the *Schumpeterian Workfare Postnational Regime* (SWPR) (Jessop, 2002) (see Table 9.4). Indeed, many social forms and projects have been imported to ECE from advanced capitalism, including the elements associated with the SWPR. The appropriation of these forms was a process of selection and recontextualization. Moreover, ECE has been an integral

13 This is interesting in comparison to what Brenner (2004) observes in European state restructuring. According to him, states cease to tame uneven development as they did with Keynesian management; instead, they promote competitive regions, facilitating thus uneven development.

Table 9.4 Schumpeterian Workfare Postnational Regime

Distinctive set of economic policies	Distinctive set of social policies	Primary scale (if any)	Primary means to compensate market failure
Focuses on innovation and competitiveness in open economies, with increasing stress on supply-side to promote KBE	Subordinates social policy to an expanded notion of economic policy; downward pressure on the "social wage" and attack on welfare rights	Relativization of scale at expense of national scale. Competition to establish a new primary scale but continued role of national state(s).	Increased role of self-organizing governance to correct both for market and state failures. But state gains greater role in the exercise of meta governance.
Schumpeterian	*Workfare*	*Postnational*	*Regime*

Source: Jessop (2002, p. 252, Table 7.1).

part of European capitalism for quite some time and thus a part of these social forms. The distinctiveness of PWPR largely reflects the mode of insertion of ECE into the flows of European capitalism. It is a question, which cannot be answered here, whether, or in what time horizon, we can expect a process of convergence or rather a crystallization of a specific state *form*. In contrast to the SWPR which promotes innovation in the Knowledge based economy (KBE), the PWPR's aims at attracting appropriate investment in a global economy of flows.

The PWPR may be acquiring functional adequacy in V4 states as it is the 'foreign capitalism' that is an important driving factor of growth in ECE these days (Myant, 2003; EIU, 2004a, 2004b, 2004c). This is not surprising as all the local articulations of the neo-liberal transformation state in ECE lacked the developmental dimension (positive industrial policy). Instead, its comparatively underdeveloped industries were exposed to external competition from the beginning of transition.[14] The experience of the advanced capitalist countries has shown that the underdeveloped industrial sectors have to be nurtured before they are able to compete. Thus, while not having

14 Paradoxically, the exceptions were some sectors that were bought by foreign companies who were able to negotiate with the state for their protection (e.g., Pavlínek, 2004b).

developed domestic capital to be competitive, the ECE states have to rely on foreign investors. Not surprisingly, the foreigners have proven to outperform domestic firms substantially (e.g., Uminski, 2001; Zemplinerová, 2004; Rojec, 2001).

Concluding Remarks

I have described transformations of dominant state projects and accumulation strategies in the Czech Republic, Hungary, Slovakia, and Poland. There has been a relative convergence towards the Porterian workfare postnational regime. Let me raise a few concluding clarifications and caveats. First, I have investigated functional adequacy of the respective state projects. It is an interesting question for future research, whether the PWPR may give rise to a distinctive state form and acquire formal adequacy to the emergent accumulation regimes. A thorough assessment of the potential of the PWPR to be a part of a (formally adequate) mode of regulation would have to leave the national scale. The potential object of regulation of the PWPR would be the V4 economic space as inserted in the globalizing knowledge based economy. Following the logic of scalar transformation, Czech PWPR as a mode of regulation has to be conceived as a part of the European triadic governance regime (possibly a SWPR). This is the level on which the emergent principal contradiction and dilemma can be addressed.[15]

Second, the emergence of PWPR is not a matter of necessity or automatic steering towards an 'adequate' regulatory regime; on the contrary, it must be perceived as one of the possible and contingent outcomes of the search for a solution to the transformational dilemmas of the ECE states. PWPR is a political project with social forces behind it. It is a challenge for future research to illuminate the conditions of its existence.

Third, in the cases of relative discontinuity (i.e., the Czech Republic and Slovakia), I have emphasized breaks in the dominant state projects. However, the transformation of the dynamics of accumulation has been much more gradual. The break here refers to the shift in the primary object of economic intervention, which is a subset of the real economy.

Finally, in the course of the presentation, I have mentioned some adverse consequences of the Porterian developmental orientation on social policy; however, it is necessary to be aware that even from a narrow economic point of view, this strategy may be deeply problematic and thus should be the object of critical social research (e.g., Turnock, 2004; Pavlínek, 2004a; Smith and Pavlínek, 2000).

15 On the new contradictions and dilemma of the knowledge based economy, see Jessop (2000b; 2002, pp. 138–140 and pp. 271–275).

References

Ádám, Z. (2004), 'Autonomy and Capacity: A State-centred Approach to Post-communist Transition in Central Europe. School of Slavonic and East European Studies', University College London, Centre for the Study of Economic and Social Change in Europe Working Paper, 40.

Baxandall, P. (2002), 'Hungary: Retrenchment amidst Radical Restructuring', in G.S. Goldberg and M.G. Rosenthal (eds), *Diminishing welfare: A cross-national study of social provision* (pp. 271–294), Westport, CT: Greenwood Publishing.

Bockman, J. and Eyal, G. (2002), 'Eastern Europe as a Laboratory for Economic Knowledge: The Transnational Roots of Neoliberalism', *American Journal of Sociology*, Vol. 108, No. 2, pp. 310–352.

Boer-Ashworth, E.D. (2000), *The Global Political Economy and Post-1989 Change: The Place of the Central European Transition*, New York, NY: Palgrave Macmillan.

Böhle, D. (2004), 'The EU and Eastern Europe: Failing the Test as a Better Power', in C. Leys (ed.), *Socialist Register 2005: The Empire Reloaded*, London, UK: The Merlin Press.

Boyer, R. (1990), *The Regulation School: A Critical Introduction*, New York, NY: Columbia University Press.

Boyer, R. (2000), 'The Political in the Era of Globalisation and Finance: Focus on Some Regulation', *International Journal of Urban and Regional Research*, Vol. 24, No. 2, pp. 274–322.

Brenner, N. (1999), 'Globalisation as Re-territorialisation: The Re-scaling of Urban Governance in the EU', *Urban Studies*, Vol. 36, No. 3, pp. 431–451.

Brenner, N. (2001), 'The Limits to Scale? Methodological Reflections on Scalar Structuration', *Progress in Human Geography*, Vol. 15, No. 4, pp. 525–548.

Brenner, N. (2004), *New State Spaces: Urban Governance and the Rescaling of Statehood*, Oxford and New York: Oxford University Press.

Bryant, C.G.A. and Mokrzycki, E. (1994), 'Introduction. Theorizing the Changes in East-Central Europe', in C.G.A. Bryant and E. Mokrzycki (eds), *The New Great Transformation? Change and Continuity in East-Central Europe* (pp. 1–13), London, UK: Routledge.

Burawoy, M. (1996), 'The State and Economic Involution: Russia through a China Lens', *World Development*, Vol. 24, No. 6, pp. 1105–1117.

Cooke, W.N. and D.S. Noble (1998), 'Industrial Relations Systems and US Foreign Direct Investment Abroad', *British Journal of Industrial Relations*, Vol. 36, No. 4, pp. 581–609.

CzechInvest (2004), 'Clusters: Programme Approved by Government Resolution no. 414/2004 on 28 April, 2004', Prague: CzechInvest/Ministry of Industry and Trade.

CzechInvest (2005), 'Official Webpage of CzechInvest', Retrieved January 08, from www.czechinvest.org.

Dangerfield, M. (1997), 'Ideology and the Czech Transformation: Neoliberal Rhetoric or Neoliberal Reality?', *East European Politics and Societies*, Vol. 11, No. 3, pp. 436–469.

Drahokoupil, J. (2004), 'Post-Fordist Capitalism in the Czech Republic: The Investment of Flextronics in Brno', *Czech Sociological Review*, Vol. 40, No. 3, pp. 343–362.

Drahokoupil, J. (2005), 'From Collectivization to Globalization: Putting Populism in its Place', *Slovak Foreign Policy Affairs*, Spring, pp. 65–74.

EIU (1998), *Country Profile 1998-99: Slovakia*, London: The Economist Intelligence Unit.

EIU (2004a), *Country Profile 2004: Hungary*, London: The Economist Intelligence Unit.

EIU (2004b), *Country Profile 2004: Poland*, London: The Economist Intelligence Unit.

EIU (2004c), *Country Profile 2004: Slovakia*, London: The Economist Intelligence Unit.

Frydman, R., Murphy, K. and Rapaczynski, A. (1998), *Capitalism with a Comrade's Cace.*, Budapest: Central European University Press.

Gamble, A. and Payne, A. (eds) (1996), *Regionalism and World Order*, Basingstoke, UK: Palgrave Macmillan.

Gould, J. (2001), 'Beyond Creating Owners: Privatization and Democratization in the Slovak and Czech Republics, 1990–1998', Unpublished PhD, Colombia University.

Greskovits, B. (1998), *The Political Economy of Protest and Patience: East European and Latin American Transformations Compared*, Budapest: Central European University Press.

Hardy, J. (2004), 'Rebuilding Local Governance in Post-communist Economies: The case of Wrocław, Poland', *European Urban and Regional Studies*, Vol. 11, No. 4, pp. 303–320.

Husák, P. (1997), *Budování kapitalismu v Čechách: Rozhovory s Tomášem Ježkem [Building capitalism in Bohemia: Interviews with Tomáš Ježek]*, Prague: Volvox Globator.

Jessop, B. (1982), *The Capitalist State*, Oxford: Oxford University Press.

Jessop, B. (1990), *State Theory: Putting the Capitalist State in its Place*, University Park, PA: Pennsylvania State University Press.

Jessop, B. (2000a), 'The Crisis of the National Spatio-temporal Fix and the Tendential Ecological Dominance of Globalizing Capitalism', *International Journal of Urban and Regional Research*, Vol. 24, No. 2, pp. 323–360.

Jessop, B. (2000b), 'The State and the Contradictions of the Knowledge-driven Economy', in J.R. Bryson, Daniels, P.W., Henry, N.D. and Pollard, J. (eds), *Knowledge, space, economy* (pp. 63–78),London, UK: Routledge.

Jessop, B. (2002), *The Future of the Capitalist State*, Cambridge, UK: Polity Press.

Kaufmann, D., Kraay, A. and Mastruzzi, M. (2003), *Governance Matters III: Governance Indicators for 1996-2002*, Washington, DC: World Bank.

King, L.P. (2004), 'Does Neoliberalism Work? Comparing Economic and Sociological Explanations', *American Journal of Sociology, [under review]*.

Lipton, D. and Sachs, J. (1990), 'Creating a Market Economy in Eastern Europe: The Case of Poland', *Brookings Papers on Economic Activity*, 1, pp. 75–133.

Mallya, T.J.S., Kukulka, Z. and Jensen, C. (2004), 'Are Incentives a Good Investment for the Host Country? An Empirical Evaluation of the Czech National Incentive Scheme', *Transnational Corporations*, Vol. 13, No. 1, pp. 109–148.

Marcincin, A. and Beblavý, M. (eds) (2000), *Economic Policy in Slovakia 1990-1999*, Bratislava: Slovak Foreign Policy Association, Centre for Social and Media Analysis, and INEKO.

McDermott, G.A. (2002), *Embedded Politics: Industrial Networks and Institutional Change in Postcommunism*, Ann Arbor, MI: The University of Michigan Press.

Myant, M. (2000), 'Employers' Interest Representation in the Czech Republic', *Journal of Communist Studies and Transition Politics*, Vol. 16, No. 4, pp. 1-21.

Myant, M. (2003), *The Rise and Fall of Czech Capitalism: Economic Development in the Czech Republic since 1989*, Cheltenham, UK: Edward Elgar.

Myant, M. (2004), 'Czech Capitalism - Towards a European Model?', Paper presented at the Managing the Economic Transition, 13th Research Seminar 'What Type of Capitalism in the Post-Communist Economies?', Cambridge University, Cambridge.

Myant, M. and Smith, S. (1999), 'Czech Trade Unions in Comparative Perspective', *European Journal of Industrial Relations*, Vol. 5, No. 3, pp. 265–285.

OECD (1997), *OECD Economic Surveys: Hungary*, Paris: Organisation for Economic Co-operation and Development.

Orenstein, M.A. (2001), *Out of the Red: Building Capitalism and Democracy in Postcommunist Europe*, Ann Arbor, MI: The University of Michigan Press.

PAIiIZ (2005), *Official Homepage of Polish Information and Foreign Investment Agency*, retrieved February 18, from http://paiz.gov.pl/.

Pavlínek, P. (2004a), 'Regional Development Implications of Foreign Direct Investment in Central Europe', *European Urban and Regional Studies*, Vol. 11, No. 1, pp. 47–70.

Pavlínek, P. (200b), 'Transformation of the Central and East European Passenger Car Industry: Selective Peripheral Integration through Foreign Direct Investment', in D. Turnock (ed.), *Foreign Direct Investment and Regional Development in East Central Europe and the Former Soviet Union: A Collection of Essays in Memory of Professor Francis 'Frank' Carter* (pp. 71–102), Aldershot, UK: Ashgate.

Peck, J.A. (2001), *Workfare States*,New York, NY: Guilford Press.

Pierson, P. (1994), *Dismantling the Welfare State? Reagan, Thatcher, and the Politics of Retrenchment*, Cambridge, UK: Cambridge University Press.

Polanyi, K. (1944/1957), *The Great Transformation*, Beacon Hill: Beacon Press.

Porter, M.E. (1990), *The Competitive Advantage of Nations*, London, UK: Macmillan.

Potůček, M. (2004), 'Accession and Social Policy: The Case of the Czech Republic', *Journal of European Social Policy*, Vol. 14, No. 3, pp. 253–266.

Rojec, M. (2001), 'The Restructuring of Firms in Foreign Privatizations in Central and Eastern European Countries', *Transnational Corporations*, Vol. 10, No. 3, pp. 1–24.

Ryner, J.M. (2002), *Capitalist Restructuring, Globalisation and the Third Way: Lessons from the Swedish Model*, London, UK: Routledge.

Smith, A. and P. Pavlínek (2000), 'Inward Investment, Cohesion and the 'Wealth of regions' in East-Central Europe', in J. Bachtler, R. Downes, and G. Gorzelak (eds), *Transition, Cohesion and Regional Policy in Central and Eastern Europe* (pp. 227–242), Aldershot, UK: Ashgate.

Smith, N. (1995), 'Remaking Scale: Competition and Cooperation in Prenational and Postnational Europe', in H. Eskelinen and F. Snickars (eds), *Competitive European Peripheries* (pp. 59–74), Berlin: Springer.

Turnock, D. (ed.) (2004), *Foreign Direct Investment and Regional Development in East Central Europe and the former Soviet Union: A Collection of Essays in Memory of Professor Francis 'Frank' Carter*, Aldershot, UK: Ashgate.

Uminski, S. (2001), 'Foreign Capital in the Privatization Process of Poland', *Transnational Corporations*, Vol. 10, No. 3, pp. 75–94.

WB (2003), *Developmental Indicators [CD-Rom]*, Washington, DC: World Bank.

WB (2005), 'World Business Environment Survey 2000 Webtool Interactive', retrieved February 17, 2005, from http://info.worldbank.org/governance/wbes/.

WB and EBRD (2005), 'Business Environment and Enterprise Performance Survey Dataset', retrieved February 17, 2005, from http://info.worldbank.org/governance/beeps/.

Williamson, J. (1993), 'Democracy and the 'Washington consensus'', *World Development*, Vol. 21, No. 8, pp. 1329–1336.

Young, C. (2004), 'Place Marketing for Foreign Direct Investment in Central and Eastern Europe', in D. Turnock (ed.), *Foreign Direct Investment and Regional Development in East Central Europe and the Former Soviet Union: A Collection of Essays in Memory of Professor Francis 'Frank' Carter* (pp. 103–121), Aldershot, UK: Ashgate.

Young, C. and S. Kaczmarek (2000), 'Local Government, Local Economic Development and Quality of Life in Poland', *GeoJournal*, 50, pp. 225–234.

Zemplinerová, A. (2004), 'The Importance of Foreign-owned Enterprises in the Catching-up Process', in K. Liebscher, J. Christl, P. Mooslechner and D. Ritzberger-Grünwald (eds), *The Economic Potential of a larger Europe* (pp. 97–109), Cheltenham, UK and Northampton, MA: Edward Elgar.

Index